A BIOLOGIST IN PARADISE

A BIOLOGIST IN PARADISE

Musings on Nature & Science

Roger Gosden

Jamestowne Bookworks, Williamsburg, Virginia

Roger Gosden is a Visiting Scholar at the College of William & Mary and a writer, publisher, and Virginia Master Naturalist in Williamsburg. He was lately Professor and Research Director in Reproductive Biology at Weill Medical College of Cornell University, New York, NY, and previously the Howard and Georgeanna Jones Professor of Reproductive Medicine and Scientific Director of the Jones Institute at the Eastern Virginia Medical School.

Jamestowne Bookworks, Williamsburg, Virginia
© 2017 by Jamestowne Bookworks
All rights reserved. Published 2017

ISBN: 978-0-9975990-2-2 (print edition)
ISBN: 978-0-9897199-2-6 (digital edition)

A Biologist in Paradise—Musings on Nature and Science by Roger Gosden
Biophilia
Origins
Perceptions
Victuals
Seasons
In Memoriam

Jamestowne Bookworks LLC
107 Paddock Lane
Williamsburg, VA 23188

For Lucinda

with love and admiration

Love to wonder, the seed of science
Ralph Waldo Emerson

And this gray spirit yearning in desire
To follow knowledge like a sinking star,
Beyond the utmost bound of human thought.
From *Ulysses* by Alfred, Lord Tennyson

In no fix'd place the happy souls reside.
In groves we live, and lie on mossy beds,
by crystal streams that murmur through the meads:
but pass yon easy hill, and thence descend.
The path conducts you to your journey's end.
From Virgil's *Aeneid*

The Author

Roger Gosden is a biomedical scientist who made a literary left turn in the second half of life. His career began at Cambridge University under Sir Robert Edwards (Nobel Prize, 2010) and was awarded a Ph.D. for research on ovarian aging. He earned a D.Sc. for reproductive physiology at Edinburgh University Medical School where he was on the faculty for 18 years. As professor and research director, he also worked at Leeds, McGill, and EVMS, and his last full-time academic post was at Weill Medical College of Cornell University in NYC. Besides academic publishing and lecturing, he has experience as an editor, broadcaster, and newspaper/ magazine writing, and he wrote two trade books with foreign translations (*Cheating Time* and *Designing Babies*). With his wife Dr. Lucinda Veeck Gosden, the clinical embryologist for the first successful IVF program in America, he lives in Williamsburg, Virginia, and the Allegheny Mountains of West Virginia.

Table of Contents

Preface

This album is a celebration of science and nature by someone who loves them. The author turned to full time writing after a career in reproductive science and became a Master Naturalist in Virginia. He writes about things he knows and cares about in forty essays and memoirs, offering them to readers who share his curiosity and concerns.

This is not a science book for scientists nor a nature book for naturalists, although he hopes both parties will read it, and not so much for information as contemplation. The narratives are mostly in the first person to grasp the power of story-telling, express passion for subjects, tell anecdotes, and share humor wherever possible. The concise essays divided among six sections are sprinkled with quotations and extracts from favorite authors and poets.

The subjects are close to the author's heart and experience. He writes about the struggle for a sustainable environment and how shifting baselines affect perspectives. He appeals for a new appreciation of animals, not just sentimental feelings but a fresh respect for their welfare, sentience, and distinct intelligence. From deep involvement in the fertility revolution and IVF technology, he looks back at the history of discovery and turns a lens on what the future may portend. He expresses outrage at pervasive prejudice against 'others' in an extraordinary collection of topics, including Neanderthals, cannibals, scavengers, crustaceans, and feral pets. The story of evolution is never out of focus, and he pays another visit to the ghost of Down House close to where he grew up. For a foody culture, he draws on physiology credentials to poke a head inside the pantry, and elsewhere celebrates seasons of the year from oblique angles. The six memoirs of the last section have an elegiac tone, although they are never gloomy narratives of special places and people we have lost and must not forget.

The reader will follow a zealous search in these pages for antidotes to the pessimism of our age through curiosity for knowledge and, finally, to hope. It is endless toil starting with questions for which the author does not pretend to offer prescriptions for hard issues, and, in the end, admits he is a philosopher with no clothes.

He only professes to be a journeyman, because the writing craft is never finished and perfect, and in aiming for economy he understands words are like ammunition, the fewer bullets in the magazine the more accurately they must be aimed. Primarily oriented to America where he lives and the British Isles where he spent half a lifetime, his subjects stretch beyond those borders as far away as New Guinea and New Zealand.

The style is personal, even intimate, as he reaches back to history, memory, and experience, aiming to create something that is as much a literary as a scientific work. He has thrown off the straight-jacket of academia to leave behind the buzz of lecture halls and nitty-gritty of laboratory life for the freedom a writer enjoys. His career stretched from Cambridge to Cornell Universities, and it was during those decades he began to hone the craft and published two trade books as well as public media works.

***

This is the first of two volumes. A second collection of essays is stewing on my hard drive for publication later next year, and a list of provisional topics and titles is appended to this book.

The title 'Paradise' is neither a teaser nor preparation for posthumous publication! Paradise suggests a blessed location. The cover picture shows a butterfly flying out of a laboratory through an arbor to the shining fields and sparkling river we might imagine beyond time. But I did not choose the word for its ordinary sense in the lexicon, but for the feeling I get at special moments that are sometimes realized while musing in an armchair, sometimes at my writer desk, but mostly outdoors.

A Greek synonym that better conveys the sense is, 'Elysium,' which means to be deeply stirred by joy. If images are summoned in a reader's mind of a soul in a dreamy state resting from his labors, my heaven is not a state of idleness for I must practice my harp! I discovered writing is more than doing, it is the engine of thought and a map for endeavor. I am thankful for the privilege of writing for living, instead of for *a* living. But enough of life's philosophy, let me begin!

Roger Gosden
Williamsburg, VA & Allegheny Mountains, WV
Roger.Gosden@jamestownebookworks.com
December 2017

Acknowledgments

This book started as a miscellaneous collection of journal notes and manuscripts before they were distilled, edited, and formatted for publication. Most of the essays were inspired by research for a blog[1] about subjects I care about and wanted to explore more deeply. The product abides by the principles of the imprint, Jamestowne Bookworks[2], by donating profits to charity[3].

It seemed fitting to season essays with quotations for which I acknowledge original sources. The main reason for taking many from classic sources is simply that I love them, but they also avoid the trouble and expense of seeking permission for copyrighted works. As this book is the non-commercial work of a scholar, I am entitled to use brief quotations of other published work, as sanctioned by the Code of Best Practices for Fair Use in Scholarly Research[4], but I don't take the privilege lightly. A longer extract from *A Sand County Almanac* by Aldo Leopold was kindly approved by Oxford University Press, USA, for essay #2 (*Green Fire*); *Mystery of Mysteries* (#9) is adapted from an article in the public domain I originally published in *Biology of Reproduction* (2013; 88: 4-11); *The Bard of Beckenham* (#38) is adapted from a book published from my imprint (*Various Verses by Gordon Burness*).

The miniature illustrations under headings are the author's property except where contributors are acknowledged in the list of captions or if the image was captured from Openclipart[5]. I thank the donors and anonymous artists who give freely for unlicensed use. Many of the illustrations are different to the eBook edition because the interior for this print version had to be black and white throughout to avoid an inflated sales price.

I have endeavored to make production costs minimal for marketing the book at the lowest price permitted by the host platform. I acknowledge an enormous benefit when a writer has an independent pair of expert eyes cast over a manuscript, and have used professional editors for trade books and served as an academic editor in the past. But to keep my pricing goal I had to sacrifice editorial support, hoping that readers will find few errors or infelicities that might detract from the enjoyment of reading.

I thank my wife Lucinda for advising, encouraging, and reviewing this book over several years of its evolution. My friend Clyde kindly allowed me to tell his story. I owe thanks to many other people for encouraging my efforts to write for non-specialists, not least Bob Edwards who recruited me to research and Gordon Burness who cultivated the love of nature in the heart of a boy. I have chased their breadth of interests into these pages. Lastly, I thank Lilah and Ben for days when I could not summon enough craft for writing or reach deep in my memory for arcane facts because a run in the park with them would usually relieve the block.

Captions for Illustrations

(Numbers correspond to the order of essays)

1. Virginia Master Naturalists (photo: Hart Haynes)
2. Howling wolf
3. Bald eagle (photo: Inge Curtis)
4. Gorilla
5. Not Peter Rabbit
6. Chestnut tree
7. New Zealand kiwi
8. Pagan fertility symbol from the Slavic Radimich tribe
9. Musing at breakfast
10. Human oocyte (egg) (photo: Lucinda Veeck Gosden)
11. The 'Chimera of Arezzo (Etruscan)
12. Golden retriever
13. The 'Sandwalk' at Down House, Kent
14. A shallop under sail
15. 'Jane's' skull
16. Neanderthal versus modern human skull
17. Eurasian badger
18. Gaffer Hexam and Lizzie rowing on the River Thames
19. Cat and kittens
20. Lobster
21. A slice of bread
22. Hamburger
23. Olive oil
24. Salt cellar
25. A spoonful of sugar
26. Eve's apple
27. Love Marmite!
28. Groundhog (woodchuck)

PART I. BIOPHILIA

THE HEART OF A NATURALIST

Is any vocation as open and welcoming as natural history? To be a naturalist you do not need a high school diploma or a university degree; you don't have to be under a 'certain age,' or even pass a fitness test. There are lots of clubs and societies to foster an interest in nature, but membership is optional because it is OK if you are a club of one. It helps to have keen senses and a memory for animal and plant names, but a curiosity and passion for nature are the defining characters of a naturalist. No higher qualifications are required.

I heard a boy in a park chuckle to his friends: "There's a funny bunch of naturalists over there!" He was laughing at a couple of heads peering over a bush through binoculars at a bird that darted away. A companion sat on the grass flipping through a field guide, and two more crouched to photograph a plant. The passion of naturalists for creepy-crawlies, swamps, and other offbeat subjects can make them subjects of mockery, but we say, "Thanks for the compliment!"

Naturalists express their love of the earth and strive for a sustainable environment in countless ways and places. Some are conservation volunteers; some are educators; some are citizen scientists helping professional researchers; some record nature through art and photography; some celebrate with essays, poetry, and music. Most naturalists find country walks and field trips satisfying not only for the healthy outdoor exercise but for the chance of seeing something to stir their curiosity on a wayside that most people are deaf and blind to. They never retire this interest, and even when too old or infirm to hike they can still enjoy butterflies in the garden and watch birds through a window. Everyone has a place at nature's table.

Nature can cast a spell on the human psyche at every age, but childhood is the most receptive time. We are inquisitive from birth, and the panoply of living things offers a constant stream of enthralling subjects for kids to discover outdoors, in books, and on screen. That was the age nature's arrow struck me. Parents, teachers, and friends helped to nourish a budding pursuit by taking me to parks, museums, and camping; and my growing passion survived the countercurrent of college life and romantic distractions in adolescence. It went underground during the busy years of parenthood and a career, but eventually surfaced for light and fresh air. There are few jobs as conservation officers or rangers, so naturalists must resign their interest to a hobby for it to be sustained, and there's the rub.

In an age that prizes academic qualifications and technical know-how, natural history is often relegated to a casual pastime, a soft and innocent amusement. It deserves more honor. All the early naturalists were amateurs, and some plowed personal wealth into their endeavors, or even put themselves in peril as explorers. In the Victorian Age, Alfred Russel Wallace was one of those globe-trotters. He became the father of biogeography, and, as the junior author of the famous 1858 paper, he helped to launch the theory of evolution by natural selection. His co-author Charles Darwin was a naturalist who rarely ventured far from his home turf after the *Beagle* voyage, but laid the foundations of modern biology by poring over specimens in his study and greenhouse, experimented with plants and worms in his garden, and would stroll around the local countryside with eyes wide open. Since Aristotle, there is a history that denies the rumor that natural history is merely armchair science.

The word *naturalist* was coined around 1587, long before the Victorians invented *biologist* and *scientist* to label a new profession. Regrettably, this vintage word can be confused with *metaphysical naturalist,* for someone who holds a materialistic philosophy, and sounds too close for comfort to *naturist,* for people who brazenly show their skin.

More confusion is created by the broad dictionary definition of *naturalist* as someone who is 'a student of natural history; especially a field biologist' (*Merriam-Webster*). There is a thin distinction between naturalist and biologist because some people wear both labels, and when a word is vague it recruits unexpected company. Is the astronomer Carl Sagan listed among American naturalists because he speculated about little green men in exoplanets? We prefer more specific definitions, believing a diffusion of meaning undermines the service words provide, but before the age of high specialization that balkanized science it was natural for people whose interests lay somewhere between an atom and the cosmos to be called a naturalist.

Amateur contributions to ecology, geology, and astronomy are more important now than ever for gathering data where funding for professional research is lean or axed. Unlike scientific 'heroes' in fashionable fields like biomedicine with deep pockets and dreams of Nobel Prizes, naturalists mostly go uncelebrated.

Their reward is the personal satisfaction of working in nature and caring for it, which is even more fulfilling when shared with like-minded souls.

They are a growing army of volunteers. My local chapter of the Virginia Master Naturalist[6] program celebrates the graduation of a score of new members every year, and there are 28 other chapters in the state with sister programs across America. It is inspiring to watch women and men from all backgrounds and all ages quietly giving their time and sharing knowledge. Their unpaid services to conservation save untold millions of taxpayer dollars.

Amateur naturalists and professional biologists look like twins, but like twins in real families they occasionally disagree. Naturalists acknowledge the authority of science, but are critical when they perceive policies are harming habitats and the commonwealth of nature. This is nothing new. Long before storm clouds began rising in the early 19th Century over pollution, overfishing, and animal vivisection, and before industrial agribusiness and GM crops arrived on the scene, there were naturalists casting doubts about certain aspects of progress engineered by science and technology.

> Sweet is the lore which Nature brings;
> Our meddling intellect
> Mis-shapes the beauteous forms of things—
> We murder to dissect.
> From *The Tables Turned* by William Wordsworth

When naturalists become activists championing planetary health and turning scornful eyes on government and industry, they no longer seem the innocent gray-haired birders I saw in the park. They have launched hundreds of environmental organizations — from the Ocean Conservancy and Greenpeace to the Sierra Club and the RSPB, to name a few. Some of us find ourselves torn between biology as a profession and natural history as a vocation, like chimeras with two talking heads. This is not a conflict of sentimental naturalism versus hard-headed science, but a tension between values and attitudes. Care and respect — even love — characterize the naturalist, whereas honesty, patience, and caution are the watchwords of the professional scientist.

Wordsworth's poem faintly echoes a mystical reverence that pagans once paid on the fells of his native Lake District, and it also gives a nod to the New Age movement today. There have always been people who immersed themselves in nature for spiritual refreshment, and land that was always sacred to Native Americans also inspired Celtic Christians and, before them, heathen tribes. You don't have to visit Yosemite Valley or the Great Barrier Reef to be stirred: joy can be found looking out of a prison attic at a living tree, if you have the heart.

> The two of us looked out at the blue sky, the bare chestnut tree glistening with dew, the seagulls and other birds glinting with silver as they swooped through the air, and we were so moved and entranced that we couldn't speak.
> Ann Frank writing from a secret annex, February 23, 1944

Since mainstream Western religions have long claimed a monopoly on spirituality and moral teaching, I wonder why they held a careless attitude to the environment for so long, and offered so little guidance for conscience and polity. In the first revelation, the God of Genesis said the creation was 'very good,' but most attention over the centuries has been paid to verses that crown humans over the rest of nature and justify unfettered exploitation of natural resources, even the cruel treatment of fellow creatures.

> Thou madest him to have dominion over the works of thy hands; thou hast put all things under his feet: All sheep and oxen, yea, and the beasts of the field ...
> *Psalm* 8, verse 6

Two fathers of Christendom, Saint Paul and Saint Augustine, upheld a hard doctrine of Original Sin, implying the whole environment is caught up in 'corruption.' Nature was regarded by the medieval mind as a hostile place that needed to be tamed. The clergy taught that because the world is broken and evil we must look forward to the comfort of heaven after earning a place, and churches that eulogize the Rapture at the end of the world are sanctioning careless stewardship of it today. There never was a deep theology of human ecology until very recently, and the gospel of prosperity preached by some denominations and the zealots of Ayn Rand are at odds with a kindly society that cares for and shares with its disadvantaged and vulnerable members. Caring for the environment goes hand in hand with a natural justice that embraces more than our own kind.

When Charles Darwin enrolled at Cambridge University in 1828, the plan urged by his father was to take holy orders because, although never a fervent believer, it would provide a respectable position in society among many parson-naturalists of his day. The Church of England offered a comfortable living to those men, many of them Deists who did not take religious observance very seriously, and some who wanted the sinecure for the freedom it offered to pursue a hobby or idleness. The dusty records of Victorian homilies ranging from parish to cathedral pulpits, and from high churchmen like Cardinal John Henry Newman to Baptist Charles Spurgeon, reveal few examples of clerics exhorting their congregations to be good stewards of the creation. Some men, like the Rev. William Paley, looked for the signature of a divine creator in nature, as if to ask what nature can do for theology but never the other way around.

Charles drifted away from theology to a deeper love, but I doubt if he had graduated to wear a dog collar, cassock, and surplice he would have proselytized for nature conservation. Preaching about an apocalyptic Sixth Extinction or climate change was implausible before environmental anxiety was borne in our lifetime. The long struggle of civilization to tame wild nature for human needs and wants was still underway and, despite the pleading of poets and mystics, nature still looked vast and threatening.

When Rachel Carson's *Silent Spring* was published in 1962 and the green movement was sprouting, there were young naturalists like me who hoped religions would lend their moral authority to conservation sensibility. But still absorbed in biblical exegesis and focused on human congregations, many denominations continued to overlook the natural systems that preserve all life. It didn't help that the scriptures offer so little encouragement for green preachers, although the Old Testament commandment comes close to an environmental ethic if we construe, 'Thou shalt not steal,' as a decree to protect our common wealth and the interests of unborn generations. Clerical vacuity was so alienating that it triggered a fit of writing, which was published by the Church of Scotland as *What on Earth does the Kirk think about Ecology?* As a layman, I knew it would never stir the church hierarchy, but there was the consolation of letters from dear old ladies in the Women's Guild who were concerned about their grandchildren's future.

Since those days, there is 'greening' across the Abrahamic religious traditions. Never a member of the Roman Catholic tradition, I am drawn to its fringe writers, and particularly to Thomas Berry (*The Dream of the Earth*) and Matthew Fox (*The Coming of the Cosmic Christ*), whose radicalism broke with his Dominican fold. Their beliefs have much in common with the panentheism[7] of Christian mystics, such as St. Francis of Assisi, Hildegard of Bingen, Meister Eckhart, and Julian of Norwich. Thanks also to artists and musicians, creation spirituality was kept alive during the joyless centuries of the medieval church and the materialistic tide of the Enlightenment that followed.

The Eastern contemplative religions were always better 'naturalists' than their Western counterparts, and they influenced the Celtic Church before its absorption by Rome. There is now a 'Green Patriarch' at the head of the Orthodox Church, and Pope Francis struggles to change the heart of a church that was dominated for centuries by patristic doctrines. He often mentions his namesake as an inspiration.

> The vocation of being a 'protector,' however, is not just something involving us Christians alone; it also has a prior dimension which is simply human, involving everyone. It means protecting all creation, the beauty of the created world, as the Book of Genesis tells us and as Saint Francis of Assisi showed us. It means respecting each of God's creatures and respecting the environment in which we live.
> Homily of Pope Francis, March 19, 2013

His call to action has an optimistic ring to counter the deep pessimism of our times, which is circling back to resemble the social mood under storm clouds in the 1340s and 1940s. Some of our brightest minds have the darkest thoughts, for why else would they plan to invest in future colonies of the Red Planet instead of care for the Blue[8] one that has always been our home? Call me a planetarian! The pontiff's appeal is based on moral authority not scientific gravitas, and will drown in public amnesia as the stream of other urgent matters forces attention. Those who look back on our era won't applaud a noble era, and will notice how vested interests trampled wise and patient vision. Business continues as usual from the drag of lobbying, corruption, vested interests, and an American Administration that shows no sign of acknowledging environmental perils, and threatens to aggravate them.

If we are honest, we are hypocrites to point fingers at others, accusing them of causing climate change, environment degradation, and species extinction. We are not exculpated by recycling household waste or filling bird feeders, for they are measly efforts that cost us nothing compared to a radical surrender of consumerism, which is painful beyond imagination. And, besides, the poor are really carrying the burden of care, albeit involuntarily, because the heaviest carbon footprints are made by the privileged among us who can afford luxury foods and vacations in the Caribbean. The Canadian psychologist Robert Gifford calls our excuses for failing to act, 'Dragons of Inaction.' His list runs to over two dozen dragons, all starting with the personal pronoun, and my first four are:

> I'm only an individual so my impact on climate warming is a drop in a bucket.
> I will try when richer folks reduce their consumption first.
> I'm tired of news about the environment.
> I'm too busy at work to listen.

Pessimism is a most unattractive demeanor, but are those who maintain a sunny optimism whistling in the dark? Planetary health is such a complicated subject and the stakes are theoretically so high we dare not look too closely or put full faith in forecasts. Such doubts feed controversy and partisanship. Divisions about what actions to take, if any, run so deep that they are a large part of the problem. A willingness to listen to the opposition and cross the aisle is the key for wise policy. The early church fathers had a Greek word for this resolve. They coined *koinonia* for a fellowship of believers whose endeavors transcended their differences, and surely that is what Pope Francis was driving at.

At the beginning of this essay I offered a broad definition of *naturalist*, and didn't restrict it to cliques of birders or volunteer conservationists. I think it should embrace everyone who loves the earth, even if their entire lives are dwelt in cities surrounded by human artefacts and never see a wilderness. My definition includes ladies I met at the Women's Guild who could not tell an eagle from a vulture, a disabled man who only saw wildlife on TV, and Ann Frank who never lived to hug her chestnut tree. Everyone who loves the earth, and anyone who helps to protect its bounty or teaches the care of our natural heritage, has the heart of a naturalist.

GREEN FIRE

Aldo Leopold was a forester employed to protect game for hunting in the American South-West in the early decades of the 20th Century. He rode through hot, rugged terrain to track and exterminate the big three predators — wolves, bears, and cougars. One day while resting on a rocky bluff he spotted wolves heading in his direction. They were unaware of him crouched behind a boulder from where he drew his gunsight on the leader as it splashed out of a creek onto a bank a couple of hundred yards away. It was out of range, but a chance shot felled the target and the pack scattered.

> We reached the old wolf in time to watch a fierce green fire dying in her eyes. I realized then, and have known ever since, that there was something new to me in those eyes—something known only to her and to the mountain. I was young then, and full of trigger-itch; I thought that because fewer wolves meant more deer, that no wolves would mean hunters' paradise. But after seeing the green fire die, I sensed that neither the wolf nor the mountain agreed with such a view.

From *A Sand County Almanac* by Aldo Leopold

Many years later he recalled how the experience affected him more than almost any other before or afterwards, but why it was different was hard to explain. It was like a religious conversion experience, an ineffable change of heart when he knelt beside the mortally-wounded animal to gaze in its flickering eyes. Killing was a common action, but this time it had an uncommon reaction. He questioned wildlife management policies he was paid to enforce, as well as the assumptions he had grown up with since his father taught him woodcraft and how to hunt.

> I personally believed, at least in 1914 when predator control began, that there could not be too much horned game, and that the extirpation of predators was a reasonable price to pay for better big game hunting. From the movie *Green Fire*[9]

There were so many questions challenging the wisdom received from bosses and elders, and he knew it would court trouble to express them openly. So, he pondered privately. Would ridding big predators create a booming population of deer and elk for hunters? Might game herds then overgraze their food supply and die of starvation? Would the genetic stock of game suffer when weak and unhealthy individuals were no longer weeded out by top predators? Can carnivores serve key roles by preventing unintended consequences that might throw the ecosystem out of whack? These questions struck at the root of wildlife management policy, but few people were moved by his theorizing, which needed decades of research to validate.

Leopold wrote to the National Parks Service in 1944 outlining a program to reintroduce wolves to Isle Royale, a remote island wilderness in Lake Superior where they were declining. This was a dramatic turnaround for a man who had been employed to extirpate predators. The proposal was panned. Over the past 70 years, there have been wild fluctuations in the number of healthy packs on the island, depending on the abundance of moose to prey on. Inbreeding played a part. The accidental introduction of canine parvovirus by a visitor's dog and tick-borne diseases further aggravated the parlous status of the wolf population. Only two individuals are known on the island today, while booming numbers of moose are decimating the balsam fir forest, impoverishing the habitat on which their survival hangs. A lone wolf occasionally ventures across an ice bridge from the mainland, but human help is needed to restore packs and refresh the genetic stock.

Leopold would be delighted to see policies he dreamt of now succeeding at the Yellowstone National Park, where gray wolves were reintroduced from 1995. I was thrilled to see the Lamar Valley pack this summer. Within a few years of arrival, wolves were already bringing beneficial changes. Cutting down the deer and elk herds, most particularly by weeding out the old and weak, was reducing damage to the lower boughs of trees and overgrazing winter foliage, but there were also cascading effects that wildlife biologists hadn't foreseen. Carrion left by sated wolves helped to feed bears, eagles, ravens, and coyotes through the lean months. Wetland vegetation improved as beavers returned to build dams and lodges, which offered, in turn, more habitats for fish and wildfowl. Old notions were flawed, and human hunters never provide the same service because they harvest prime, trophy specimens on which the continuing vigor of game herds depend. Biodiversity benefits from outsize impacts of top predators, which is why wolves are called a 'keystone species.'

Leopold forsook his rifle when he moved to Madison, WI, in 1924, where he later became the nation's first professor of game management. Some years later, he bought a worn-out farm at $8 per acre that had been abandoned by homesteaders in the Dust Bowl years. A chicken coop was converted into rude living quarters for family visits on weekends, which they called the 'Shack.' His frustrated attempts to grow crops and trees in the bleak landscape taught him how to care for the land, and shaped his journey to become a national spokesman for conservation. Toward the end, he moved to live full time at the farm, where he wrote *The Land Ethic*. It was published posthumously and continues to inspire and challenge us. When I read that, 'conservation is a state of harmony between men and land,' it made me wonder about my own backyard. Is it as harmonious a semi-natural environment as I assumed, or are my gardening efforts aggravating an ecologically dissonant landscape?

After Hurricane Isabel ravaged south-east Virginia in 2003, we hired a landscape designer to plan a new garden for us to enjoy and for visitors to admire. We brought in topsoil and mulch, planted sapling shrubs and tree, seeded lawns, prepared flowerbeds, improved drainage, and spread gravel on paths. It was patient work and now, over a decade later, the yard is attractive and there is shade from the torrid summer sun. But in striving for a pretty garden and curbside appeal we paid no heed to the interests of critters that share our land. It was delusional to think we could be nature's physicians, healing land impoverished by an old history of tobacco farming and ravaged by hurricanes and invasive plants by turning it into neat lawns and cheerful borders. It was a deceit, like a ruddy face we say means a healthy body because we only look skin deep.

A healthy body has no need of a physician because it can tackle common ailments and repair minor wounds without help. Optimal physiology is allostatic because it restores the body after stress or exercise. Likewise, the native oak-hickory forest that grew here until it was felled for farms and towns withstood the assaults of climate, geology, and blight for eons.

Hardwood trees were the climax vegetation of a self-regulating biome. Decomposing animal and vegetable matter on the forest floor was the base of an energy pyramid for nourishing green plants at the next level that fed animals eaten in turn all the way to the top carnivores. When a wildfire or storm leveled a patch of forest, it regrew by a succession of pioneer plants, shrubs, and finally woody perennials, like scabs healing a wound to make the body whole again. What can be better than a system that heals itself? Teddy Roosevelt wrote when he was struggling to save the Grand Canyon from developers and resource extractors: 'You cannot improve on it. The ages have been at work on it, and man can only mar it.'

He might have been writing about the great eastern forests, but they were already logged to fragments before his time. Within a few generations of European colonization, the creative work of evolution was transformed along our seaboard. A land as bountiful as Virginia was never going to be left virginal. The Peninsula is now a mosaic of farms, gardens, and woodlots, but thankfully it is still blessed with semi-natural state parks along with private and public forestland. The new landscape is picturesque, even romantic (roadside billboards announce *Virginia is for Lovers*), but it is no longer in harmony with nature, nor is the small patch we loan from nature that we call our own. Even parks that look 'natural' are far from pristine when we look closer.

Park rangers and volunteers struggle to push back a tide of invasive species and diseases introduced accidentally in foreign shipments or deliberately imported and escaped from gardens and nurseries. Virginia's soil and warm climate encourage aliens: bamboo is marching, kudzu is smothering, and Japanese stiltgrass is spreading across the 'goodly land.' Changes in vegetation and land use have upset an ancient balance, setting competitors against native stock, and encouraging some species to spiral out of control: ticks, tent caterpillars, Japanese beetles, and the cloven-hooved locusts we call deer. To say the land is disturbed is a gross understatement. It is a battlefield. We will never achieve a lasting conquest against the insurgents, and the original living treasures will continue to struggle. We live in a man-made land.

In striving to dominate nature and eliminate the enemies of our needs and pleasure, we unintentionally eliminate many critters that are beneficial allies. I mean insectivorous birds, bats, amphibians, and reptiles. Some formerly common birds that eat garden pests have declined by over two-thirds since the 1960s, some butterflies and native bees that do magisterial pollination services are rare or extinct. I could take you to places where 40 years ago you had to raise your voice over the din of crooning frogs, katydids, and crickets, but no longer. A landscape groomed and poisoned to look tidy and pretty is paid for by the elimination of wonderful friends.

Before reading Leopold's book, I started to taper off the use of chemical fertilizers and weed-killers, reserving Roundup® for spot treatment. An experiment revealed only a quarter of the manufacturer's recommended concentrations are needed to be effective, except for the toughest weeds. This sounds a feeble and half-hearted effort, but it takes a first step to begin a hike of a thousand miles, and I now gaze at land more wisely and eager to advance. Pretty flower borders and green lawns look like sterile deserts, as they do to critters that used to live here. I bite my lip when I recognize alien plants in garden centers. Evolved in different environments, they replace the native plants I have lately come to appreciate, although some offer rich pickings for insects come for nectar and pollen.

The local plant eaters that co-evolved with food plants find most aliens unpalatable or even poisonous. Butterflies, bugs, and creepy-crawlies are diminishing in number ('Insectageddon'), opening niches for hardier species to take hold if they are less picky eaters, and leading to population explosions in the absence of competitors or predators.

In the late spring last year, I tested a hunch that native plants are preferred for invertebrate grazers. I collected leaves from a wide range of plants, both native and alien, to examine which had been nibbled. It wasn't a perfect study, and I ignored less discriminating eaters like browsing deer, groundhogs, and squirrels, which are another story. But the data were so clear-cut I did not need a larger sample to convince me that grazers choose native leaves by a wide margin. I want to know if the diners were insects or mollusks, and what kinds, but rarely saw them because they mostly fed at night. The bottom line was that most leaves in our yard were left untouched because we have grown a mostly inedible landscape. I doubt if Leopold would be surprised.

It takes thousands of generations of natural selection for mouths and guts to adapt to unfamiliar fare so that animals can digest it and tolerate plant toxins. For example, an aggressive Eurasian subspecies of the common reed *Phragmites australis* is colonizing wetlands and shorelines up and down the east coast because it is inedible to most herbivores. One day in the distant future grazers will find 'phrag' appetizing, but the evolutionary mill grinds slowly.

Doug Tallamy has brought these notions to wider attention in *Bringing Nature Home*. This ecologist at the University of Delaware has a vision of revolutionizing gardening for a sustainable partnership with nature. Too late to preserve wilderness in the Mid-Atlantic, there is still lots of 'spare land' in backyards and 40 million acres of lawns, some of which might be converted into semi-natural habitats if we have the will. They can be just as attractive, or more so, if we open our eyes to a more expansive definition of natural beauty.

He urges private and public landscapers to cast aside ingrained, esthetic preferences for showy alien plants and, instead, encourage the cultivation of more native species. That doesn't mean turning the clock back to the old forest, which has gone forever, but choosing plants that have thrived here since the Ice Age. Many of them are spectacular perennials that require limited care or water: rose mallow, sneezeweed, black-eyed susan, beebalm, and birds-foot violet[10].

When Tallamy revels in attracting more insects to his garden I wonder if his neighbors say, "Yikes, is he crazy? Don't we have enough bugs already? We'll have to buy more sprays from Home Depot!"

Setting aside butterflies and honey bees, which are welcome, it is hard to sell the idea of encouraging more bugs and creepy-crawlies in our backyards. But the most annoying ones are often alien, and our irritation is trivial compared to the interference we tolerate from human sources like noise and pollution, or the waste of topsoil covered by concrete and asphalt. If we balk at the obstacles before weighing the benefits we never start anything worthwhile.

I began my garden revolution with timid ambitions, knowing how easily New Year resolutions collapse before the end of January. I scatter clover seed across the lawn in the fall and raise the mower blades in spring for pollinators to feed on the white blooms. Homeowners ask lawn care companies to eliminate clover but, if you stop to consider for a moment, clover is more attractive than fescue and nourishes the soil by fixing nitrogen. It stays green all winter and when lawn grass goes brown in summer drought; it is a red-letter day when you show a four-leaf clover to a child. But here's the thing, clover is not a native Virginian. Compromises are needed when we try to nurse land back to better health.

I have a new immigration control policy. Aliens are not barred here (I too am an immigrant), but I have a bias to natives. We now have a butterfly garden with milkweed for monarchs, spicebush for swallowtails, and violets for fritillaries. We have more redbud, dogwood, crab-apple, black-eyed susans, coneflowers, sneezeweed, joe pye weed, wild asters, and possumhaw. They burn my cheeks with green fire.

RETURN OF THE NATIVE

A bird soaring over our yard caught my eye. It was not tipping from side to side on ragged wings to catch an updraft like a buzzard (*sic*); it was an eagle floating over the tree-tops and heading across the Virginia Peninsula toward the James River. It glided straight and true like a cross on outstretched black wings, and its white head and tail caught the sunlight. Although 'baldies' are common again, they are still an arresting sight. Maybe there is somewhere a patriotic American who salutes when he sees his national emblem flying overhead like Air Force One, but there is another and grander reason for being proud — it is a native come home.

The bald eagle population in the Chesapeake Bay watershed has been climbing since a nadir in the mid-20th Century to reach, or even exceed, pre-colonial times. As predators of fish, fur, and feather, eagles were in the gunsights of watermen, fur trappers, and duck hunters, even after the *Migratory Bird Treaty Act* of 1918 protected vulnerable species. Conviction now carries a maximum penalty of a $100,000 fine or a year in jail, for which a man has been arraigned here this year, but the law was always hard to enforce.

When the ornithologist Bryan Tyrell surveyed the extent of eagle persecution in 1936 he had no difficulty finding evidence, because there was little shame in shooting eagles and only pathetic efforts to prosecute offenders because the authorities had limited resources during the lean years of the Great Depression. Muskrat trappers shot eagles for taking their catch and duck hunters took pot-shots for snatching wildfowl, although only the remains of fish were found in their stomachs. When Tyrell inquired about a corpse lying under a dying chestnut tree on the banks of the Potomac River, local people told him 50 other eagles were dispatched at the same perch.

Rolling forward to the 1950s and 1960s, bald eagles suffered a greater catastrophe than they ever did from shooting or the lead shot ingested from scavenging deer carcasses. Their woes were aggravated by loss of nest sites to waterfront development and the failure of naïve birds to navigate power lines and road traffic, but pollution was the greatest foe. An industrial plant on the James River disgorged *Kepone*, an insecticide related to the organochlorine DDT, but it was the hazard to human and not avian health that prompted the Governor of Virginia to prohibit fish consumption for a hundred mile stretch of the river. No respecters of human law, eagles still fished up and down the river. *Kepone* entered the food chain in plants and invertebrates, and thus became concentrated in these top predators.

The upshot was that eagles laid fragile eggs that broke under the weight of a brooding parent. Hardly any chicks hatched in those years. Forty years ago, you would be lucky to see an eagle on the James, and fewer than 30 pairs nested across Virginia.

The river remained unhealthy until after 1972 when the EPA banned toxic effluents. The cleanup enabled fish stocks to slowly improve, and progress was sufficiently encouraging that the US Fish and Wildlife Service launched a program to reintroduce eagles. It is the most dramatic and successful American conservation story for a single species.

At the last count, the number of breeding pairs in the state is over 700, and they have been delisted as an endangered species. Their nests are monitored by ornithologists in light aircraft flying over breeding territories. As I write this essay, there are two active nests a couple of miles from here on Jamestown Island, and the bird I saw today may have been taking its catch there to feed an eaglet.

Not everyone welcomes back a bird that competes for sport fish or a fishing livelihood, but most people love it as an inspiring symbol of wild nature and for national pride. The eagle is depicted on the escutcheon of the Great Seal of the United States, and occasionally one can be seen in Washington DC, which is a sight that should please even congressmen who put business before conservation.

After the great bird disappeared, my thoughts turned to other returning natives. I mused about the mixed fortunes of Clym Yeobright, the chief character in *The Return of the Native* by Thomas Hardy. It was the book title that brought his name to mind as I was searching for a metaphor of the eagle.

Clym returned to his birthplace on Egdon Heath after successful years as a businessman in Paris. His childhood on the heath was hard and the future there looked bleak, but he felt a pull back to the bosom that nurtured his ancestors and laid a foundation for his late success. He could afford a comfortable life in a familiar landscape where old neighbors would celebrate the hero's return, and he could find a pretty wife to build a family and grow the community.

There is never a guarantee that turning back the clock will restore a native to the life and security he or she once knew. Likewise, animals returned to habitats in their former ranges require good timing to be successful even with the help of human hands, which are often the very hands that extirpated them in the first place. Bringing back top predators and animal engineers is especially challenging if their interests clash with ours. There is an uneasy co-existence between gray wolves and ranchers after they were reintroduced in the West, and landowners protest when rebounding beavers cause flooding in their meadows. We are, likewise, hearing murmurs against bald eagles.

As more people migrate to cities, urban life makes us forget our dependence on the land and the benefits of biodiversity. Then, the disappearance of a non-economic species, like the eagle, goes unnoticed by the majority. The raw sources of our food, clothing, medicines, and manufactured products are cast to the back of our mind, if we think about them at all. Without companion animals in our homes or watching nature programs on TV, city-dwellers might rarely muse about the host of creatures that share our planet. There is then little engagement with nature, or nothing more than swatting a fly or baiting a mouse trap.

Even if we say we care about the loss of iconic species, like elephants and pandas, it is hard to stay attentive to the creep toward their extinction, which gets little notice until they are gone like a melting glacier. That is why I should be more anguished about common songbirds in my yard because national surveys show they are in a downward spiral. Besides this myopia, we have a shameful lack of care about environmental threats because, if we think about them at all, they look overwhelming, and we hope someone else is working on them.

This is the Decade of Biodiversity, an admirable-sounding attempt by the United Nations to draw attention to environmental health, even as politicians are distracted by the latest humanitarian disaster (caring for one species instead of all). When I ask someone if they have heard about this global initiative the reply is usually a blank face or puzzled stare. Nature conservation is more of a political football in America than most countries, with vested interests cheering on politicians who would erode past progress by opening national forests and parks to commercial mining and logging, and remove legal protection afforded to threatened species.

The IUCN monitors the status of wildlife around the globe and coordinates programs to reintroduce species to their old habitats. It publishes the famous *Red List* of species in a range from *Threatened* (population decay) to *Endangered* (seriously imperiled), and records animals and plants now extinct. Perusal of the list is sobering when you read 41% of all amphibians are 'threatened,' along with 34% of conifers, 33% of corals, 31% of sharks and rays, 25% of mammals, and 13% of birds. Wildlife management and hunting regulations help to stay the decline, and that is why there are still good numbers of lobsters and wild turkeys.

It is a sad commentary on our character that both the UN and professional conservationists feel it is necessary to appeal to self-interest to win public attention. As an example, the preservation of tropical jungle is urged for the cornucopia of commercial products and medical remedies that might be hauled out, rather than for its importance in stabilizing global climate and preserving natural bounty. I wonder if we would curb our greed if we had the longevity of an oak tree or a California redwood, for then we would feel impacts that are sometimes too gradual to notice in an 80-year span. Posterity will judge our responsibility for climate change and presiding over the Sixth Extinction, the first great annihilation that cannot be blamed on geology or an asteroid. The cancer of greed and materialism still grows, as if the planet has unlimited resources, and the self-absorption that alienates our roots in nature has swelled since a poet lamented early in the Industrial Age.

> The world is too much with us; late and soon,
> Getting and spending, we lay waste our powers;
> Little we see in Nature that is ours;
> We have given our hearts away, a sordid boon!
> From a sonnet by William Wordsworth

We make human ecology our priority, but it is braided with the rest of nature. Of course, there will never be enough resources to protect every threatened species, and, although most deserve attention if we take biodiversity seriously, only a few can be helped. Habitats come first because without a home range to thrive in animals can only be preserved in menageries, and then in tiny numbers. Animals that are given most attention are the most beloved and iconic, and there are rousing narratives of successful reintroductions to homelands where they were extinct. Stories that make us cheer include golden lion tamarins in Brazil, Siberian tigers in Asia, and black-footed ferrets in the Great Plains. The publicity helps to prime the pump for funding new projects.

But what about lowly species we care nothing about, or even despise? There are a half-million coleopterans, which prompted the physiologist J.B.S. Haldane, an avowed atheist, to jest that God must have 'an inordinate fondness' for beetles. They have a vital role in the web of life, both as decomposers for humus to fertilize the soil and for providing food to animals we cherish. Edward O. Wilson gave invertebrates the tribute of calling them 'the little things that run the world.' But who will help beetles and their kin? Most people will only offer a hand to animals they like, which are not necessarily the most valuable but chosen for esthetic reasons or the services they give us.

I remember when one of my favorite birds, the red kite, was endangered in its native land. In student days, I drove for hours across country to watch them at Cors Caron[11] nature reserve in mid-Wales ('Tregaron Bog'), a redoubt for the last dozen and in jeopardy from inbreeding. Kites were common sights before Victorian gamekeepers used them as targets, but further back in history they were welcome, even in London where they cleared streets of rotting carcasses that bred disease.

On that visit, I had a fleeting glimpse of rusty-colored birds with forked tails flipping acrobatically over the wetland. I wondered on the homeward journey if I was one of the last to see them. If anyone had predicted kites would return from the brink of extinction in my home country I would have called them mad. But reintroduction and conservation efforts backed up by law enforcement have grown a nucleus of healthy birds to a throng of over 2,000 pairs across Britain. I recently saw one flying in Hardy's Wessex and hear they have spread to the outskirts of London. It's a rare example of a returning native, especially for another raptor.

If we take greater care of habitats and their wild inhabitants, there will be fewer needs for reintroducing animals and birds. But the price of biodiversity is eternal vigilance, to rephrase an expression attributed to Thomas Jefferson. For good or ill, the fate of many creatures is now in our hands. Although habitats were never static before our footprint, the pressures are so much greater today, and the draughts of a warming globe are being felt. Conservation efforts and reintroduction programs are bound to become more arduous and politicized as human populations grow and habitats bow from climate stress. Developers gripe, farmers grumble, and ranchers reach for their shotguns. I even heard a British student complained that a red kite swooped to steal his sandwich! The strains ahead will not be so funny.

Thomas Hardy was lucky to live in less anxious times, and his countryside counted more wildlife because it was less intensively used. The Victorians were a more optimistic people than the current generation, although the life of his fictitious Clym did not end well. The returning native never enjoyed lasting happiness in his former birthplace, and found himself at odds with his wife and neighbors. His belle was dissatisfied as they drifted down into poverty, and he had to take a job as a laborer cutting furze on the cruel heath.

We want our favorite characters in stories to be rewarded with contentment and harmonious lives after struggling to succeed, but that does not always happen in the Hardy world where fate often trumps hope. The author called himself a realist, but he sent Clym back to his birth place where his fortunes went into a tailspin. Pessimism is the author of self-fulfilling prophecy because it quenches the energy needed for growth and progress, and must be bravely denied.

I chose Clym as a metaphor of the struggle to bring natives home to where they belong and can thrive again. It is an arduous task, especially if their home has changed, but my eagle and kite days give me hope that more natives can come home for good. We love stories with happy endings, like the one in which Mr. Darcy brings Elizabeth Bennet home to Longbourne after a long ride out of Hardy country.

A ZOO-TO-GO

For kids growing up in London in the post-World War II decade, it was a special treat to be taken to the zoo by parents or school teachers. It attracted crowds because the city offered little entertainment for tots after our rounds in the playground. We were hoisted on our fathers' shoulders for a better view of the big cats pacing in their cages, or to wave at Guy the gorilla looking bored across the moat. We harbored no guilty feelings about their cramped quarters and social lives because we knew they existed only for our entertainment, for why else would they be there? We felt the same about the circus, but think differently now.

There were no lessons about wild nature or the habitats they were taken from, apart from one-line labels on the bars. We thought it would be cool to be zookeepers when we grew up, so we could slide joints of meat to tigers, toss herrings for sea-lions, and lock our schoolmarm in the reptile house at the close of day. In hindsight, there was not much difference between the zoo and Wormwood Scrubs, the high security prison, except for the species incarcerated. There was Whipsnade Park with its rolling meadows for large animals to roam more freely, but the Duke of Bedford's Woburn Safari Park was still years away from opening.

Zoos have come a long way since those days, but it took years for them to wake up. The author Gerald Durrell (1925-1995) was considered a maverick when he called for zoos to be centers for breeding endangered species instead of public exhibitions of unhappy creatures. As often the case with radicals and pioneers, especially those without the 'right' professional credentials, he had to tolerate ridicule before he became celebrated as a visionary for putting animal welfare ahead of human interests. The Durrell Wildlife Conservation Trust[12] on the Isle of Jersey is his memorial, but there was one thing he never changed — you still had to go to his zoo to see the animals.

One of my friends in the Virginia Master Naturalist program is a zookeeper, but not the kind we ever met as children. Clyde was more radical than Durrell when he created a portable zoo he could take to kids in their classroom or the park. He collected creepy-crawlies and other critters in his neighborhood or the local churchyard under an official collection and exhibition permit. After the class, he returned the reptiles and amphibians to where he found them, but he kept the six- and eight-legged critters at home with permission from his wife.

He transported the menagerie in Tupperware boxes and glass jars piled into the trunk of his car. There were none of the larger predators or venomous snakes that boys drool over, but even small critters were nevertheless tremendous hits that enthralled his audience. Since Clyde's zoo opened in 2007, it has been exhibited to over 13,000 children and adults across five school districts in our region. He deserves a medal.

His primary mission was education rather than conservation, although a deeper knowledge of wildlife encourages people to care about our native animals and the places they thrive. Clyde was concerned that children are less connected with nature than when he was a boy roaming the Pennsylvania countryside. His parents' generation allowed boys and girls to explore within boundaries beyond the garden gate, to build camps and treehouses, and discover wildlife. Fewer kids now grow up on farms or even walk to school. Parents are more vigilant than a generation or two ago, and to let kids 'range' is to invite condemnation for being a bad parent.

Despite tiny statistical risks of being harmed (which mostly happens in the home), paranoia about child safety outdoors is widespread and tragic incidents blazed in the media are magnified in our minds. Parents chauffeur their kids to school in beefy SUVs and yellow buses, and weekend hours are booked with music, sport, and other structured activities. Any gaps in a feverish week are rarely open for idle exploration or running free in woods and fields, although there is always time for TV and the tiny screen. Children are watched by 'helicopter parents' hovering nearby, or 'lawnmower parents' smoothing their path. George Monbiot, who writes for *The Guardian*, laments: 'Without a feel for the texture and function of the natural world, without an intensity of engagement almost impossible in the absence of early experience, people will not devote their lives to its protection.'

It seems unlikely that a newly-minted generation alienated from nature will care as much about the environment as the meager boasts of their predecessors, but the chances are better for those who have seen Clyde's zoo and listened to his stories. To watch them is to feel your heart glow.

Clyde and his 'Zoo Cru' of helpers haul out critters from their containers on the front desk of the classroom. On Earth Day and at other outdoor events in parks, he displays them on picnic tables. The children strain to see the beasts—beetles and butterflies, mantises and millipedes, slugs and snails, salamanders and skinks, toads, and turtles. On another table he exhibits skins, scales, and shells from creatures that are too precious or too dodgy to let loose. As the kids shuffle closer, he holds out a bucket.

"Want to stroke the spotted salamander?" The tiny hand of a girl shoots up.

He rests a hissing Madagascar cockroach on his sleeve to challenge the front row.

"I dare you to hold the giant."

A boy with an open palm steps forward. Others shrink away, gaping and giggling. A pair in the second-row peer in boxes offered by Clyde's assistant. A boy tickles the roly-poly to make it curl into a ball, and a girl pokes a centipede to make it scurry for cover under a leaf. The creatures are familiar to some of them, but new to a surprising number. As their confidence swells Clyde is jostled by a chattering melee of small bodies stirring with curiosity, raising voices with disarming questions that are more penetrating for their innocence.

He explains every species has its own story. One of his favorites is about the community that lives under logs, where he catches many of his critters. He asks the class what they expect to find when they roll a log over. A boy looking over his shoulder shoots up an arm to be the first to answer: "Beetles, sir." A girl chimes: "Spiders." Clyde grins. He starts to spin nine yards of his ecology lesson at a level they can understand, and I doubt any other lesson that day will keep such rapt attention or be as memorable.

When he talks about beetles he leans forward to share a dark secret.

"Have you ever wondered why trees that fall down from old age or after storms don't heap up to make ever bigger piles of wood? Do you know what makes logs disappear?" As the kids look at each other, he has an owlish smile.

"It's a mystery, boys and girls, but I'll tell you what I know. Some of these creepy-crawlies spend their whole lives under logs where they chew rotted wood as happily as you eat Cheerios at breakfast. Yum, yum." There is another small explosion of giggles.

He reaches for a plastic Ziplock bag to show them an ounce of brown, granular matter. The audience is not impressed, but his tales have taught them patience will be rewarded.

"You won't guess, so I'm telling you it's beetle poop!" A chorale of laughter almost loses control of the class, and he raises his voice. "It's not really dirty stuff because it started as bits of leaves and wood the beetles ate, but that's not the end of the story. Other living things we call decomposers, so tiny you need a microscope to see them, change it into healthy soil for growing plants and trees as well as our crops."

Clyde hopes the children will begin to understand how everything works together to preserve the diversity of life, but he can't leave them to think everything under the log is rosy. He tells them about miniscule predators as voracious as lions and sharks. Beetles, slugs, and spiders are eaten by salamanders, frogs, and toads, and a black racer winding under the log gobbles them all up. Nature has a raw side.

"One last thing," he says, lifting his voice again to keep order as two children drift away to dance whirligigs. "After we look under a log, we must roll it back again." There are puzzled looks. "If we leave the patch exposed, creatures that need a damp, dark place will dry out in the sun or be eaten by birds. We mustn't be careless or wasteful because all things are connected to everything

57

else. That includes you, me, and your parents." It is a strong message to close the session.

Clyde loves the book that made Rachel Carson famous and gave momentum to American conservation, but at the end of her life she wrote an essay to celebrate a child's sense of wonder. It perfectly captures his mission with an urgent message for mentors to encourage children to discover an innate sense of joy and wonder at the natural world.

Most children in our district have had only one chance to meet Clyde and see his zoo. Without repeated performances or an encouraging mentor his lessons may never stick. You might wonder if his stories are crushed by layers of experience and knowledge laid down like geological strata in young heads instructed in other subjects at home and in the classroom. I hope his lessons are never forgotten, even if they rest unvisited in deep underground caves of the mind for years or even decades. Memories from childhood can be like a lost tangle of hyphae until, at some unexpected or propitious moment, they sprout above ground like mushrooms to broadcast fruitful spores.

Clyde is now a retired zookeeper, but others are carrying forward his program that school curricula have no time for, so the next generation is a little less alienated from nature. Thank you, Clyde, for life lessons.

REHABILITATING RABBIT

I found a sodden ball of fur in the pool skimmer one morning. When laid gently in my palm it was cold and still, so I peeled back an eyelid to check for the glazed globe of the dead. It winked.

It was a cottontail bunny barely a month old, yet already independent of its mom. After falling in the pool overnight, it had scrambled (or swam as rabbits can) to rest its head on the skimmer ledge above the water.

Wrapping him in a towel, I laid Peter in a cardboard box with the lid folded over to make a warm, dark place. All our wild bunnies are called 'Peter' for sentiment's sake, notwithstanding serious doubts about *his* sex. As a boy, I learned the distinction between male and female rabbits is tricky, and once (but never again) made the mistake of keeping two 'brothers' together in the same hutch.

After he had dried out, Peter was still limp and looking lifeless. My wife started nursing the furry bundle, hoping her body heat would help to revive him. His adrenal glands were pouring out corticosteroids and epinephrine in a shrinking attempt to generate heat in his body core. His energy stores were becoming depleted and he was tipping into hypoglycemia from which his physiology would lean into heart block and fatal ventricular fibrillation. What can one do to save a hypothermic rabbit, or any creature in those straits?

> Peter Rabbit was not very well during the evening. His mother put him to bed, and made some camomile tea; and she gave a dose of it to Peter. From *The Tale of Peter Rabbit* by Beatrix Potter

I prized Peter's mouth open to drip warm, diluted honey from a blunt pipette to strengthen him. We had timid hopes of finding him alive in the morning.

I thought what a strange species to care for a varmint when the sight of a rabbit browsing in our garden can provoke murderous thoughts. Herbaceous borders and veggie patches are cultivated for our benefit, not for raiders to dine at all-you-can-eat salad bars. There are no free lunches in our yard, not if we can help it, though there are exceptions. When a critter is promoted in our estimation from varmint to patient, it draws down violent thoughts to compassion and responsibility to nurse it back to life and feed it as we would a beloved pet. We would even dig in our pockets for a vet bill if it helped the animal to survive. When a creature falls on bad luck we feel our heart-strings pulled, even if it had been stealing our crops or murdering the songbirds we love. We are like a neighbor who bails an offender out of jail after he robs our home, and then offers him supper and a warm bed for the night. Should we congratulate ourselves for kind hearts, or ought we to worry about our false nature and sentimental perversion?

The unlucky rabbit was not the only creature that won the kindness of a stranger that week. I unwound a garter snake from a nylon net protecting frogs in our pond which had become caught in the unintended snare. And the following day I violently steered to avoid something crawling across the road, but was too late to rescue it from becoming turtle soup under the wheels of the following vehicle.

Our ambiguous relationships with nature puzzle me. We want to control nature, yet celebrate wildness. We like pretty birds, cheeky chipmunks, and cute squirrels if they don't conflict with our interests. And when they fall casualty to road accidents and window strikes, or become orphans or victims of domestic pet attacks, it makes us feel good to be merciful. We adopt the hapless creature like a dutiful parent; but, aside from some strange myths like Romulus and Remus, a wild animal never feels a duty toward us.

Our hearts are touched by the *individual* that falls into misfortune, but rarely by an unlucky herd, swarm, or shoal. A bunch of anonymous rabbits would not draw the same warm feelings Peter evoked. We spare the individual and shoot the masses. When wee Peter dropped into our lives his mortality appealed to our compassion, and we welcomed him without hesitation. It was against our nature to rescue a garden raider (an edible one at that), but it was natural and attractive to be kind. Someone might have urged us to euthanize him by a blow on the head, but the thought never crossed our minds. Peter was lucky not to have his accident in the yard of a neighbor like Mr. McGregor.

> "Now my dears," said old Mrs. Rabbit one morning to the young bunnies, "you may go into the fields or down the lane, but don't go into Mr. McGregor's garden; your Father had an accident there; he was put in a pie by Mrs. McGregor.
> From *The Tale of Peter Rabbit* by Beatrix Potter

Compassion for animals is partly owing to our peculiar tendency to anthropomorphize them, and this may account for the greater tenderness of young children. Peter Rabbit in the Potter *Tales*, as well as Hazel, Bigwig, and Cowslip in *Watership Down*, are all sympathetic characters modeled on our better selves. They are like decent citizens who happen to be dressed as animals. But for every story of natural goodness and bonhomie, there is a villain. Napoleon, the Stalinist tyrant of *Animal Farm*, is a caricature of our grotesque side, although George Orwell's depiction of pigs should deeply offend the honorable porcine community.

Dreamers and writers have told utopian stories of humans making peace with the kingdom of wild animals. Isaiah dreamt of the wolf living with the lamb and the leopard lying with the kid; St. Francis delivered a sermon to the birds; we grew up with stories of animal friends of Tarzan, Mowgli, and other heroes; and we have been entertained by a host of cartoon stories in which we subliminally identify the triumphs and tragedies of animal lives with ours.

Those are deep reasons why our sentimental selves might be roused by the sight of a sick or dying animal. I think Mr. Lockley in *Watership Down* put his finger on it, because, when tragedy struck, he shared with animals the mystery of mortality and the struggle to rise above the terror of dying.

But to return to a more practical, and I dare say legal, matter as a law-abiding Virginian, I ought to have handed Peter over for professional care. According to the Virginia code: 'All persons caring for sick, injured, orphaned, or displaced wild animals are required to have a permit from the Virginia Department of Game and Inland Fisheries.' It is illegal to raise or treat wildlife without a permit. It seems odd that critters that can be shot, poisoned, or trapped with impunity cannot be cared for and rehabilitated except by official authorization. Admittedly, there is a public safety argument (all mammals can carry rabies), and it is understandable that rare and endangered species need special protection, but bunnies?

Rabbits are among the species most frequently transferred by the caring public to licensed 'rehabbers.' Across the state, over 300 people are trained to care for injured, sick, orphaned, and displaced animals with the goal of returning them to the wild, or euthanizing those beyond help. Those kind hearts provide services for the love of animals at their own expense, and only call on veterinary backup when surgery, medication, or mercy killing is required. Since every species has its peculiar dietary and housing needs, rehabbers can't offer 'Ark' services for every critter presented at their doorstep by the gentle public. Some rehabbers specialize in hawks, owls, and eagles; some care for reptiles and amphibians; some are devoted to the furry-fold. And when large creatures need long-term care or cannot be released to the wild they are transferred to centers where there is specialized care for life.

The Wildlife Center of Virginia[13] in Waynesboro has cared for 65,000 patients of many kinds since it opened in 1982. Some of the residents have lost the power of flight and others the means to forage for food, but the lucky ones go home. Most years, a bald eagle is released in a state park nearby after it recovered from an accident, like colliding with a car or a power line. When the veterinarian gently lifts the bird on a gloved hand from a cage out of the back of his van, the crowd that gathers for the launch is hushed, apart from crazy clicking of cameras, until an audible sigh when we see the bird aloft. It circles majestically to find its bearing before heading over the woods. The audience is rewarded not only with a spectacle but a quiet sense of paying nature back for what we take away.

Our Peter needed tender handling too, because rabbits are easily stressed and can die from shock. We would have been crushed if he died in our care. The fictitious Bigwig was less sentimental about the mortality of his leporine relatives than we were for Peter. He argued that extreme measures to save life are not called for when animals reach a point at which they no longer have a reason to live, but direct remaining energy into dying. It reminds me of a palliative care physician who said my relative was 'actively dying,' by which I presume he meant her organs were no longer striving to keep her alive but collaborating in a merciful process of death. It does not make biological sense to me, but accounts for why a rabbit caught in an eagle's claws quickly stops the struggle and goes limp, as if submitting to its fate.

I wonder if Peter had given up hope before I fished him out the pool. But if he was yielding I refused to accept it, and our determination brought his story to a happy ending. We will never know if it was the warmth of strangers or the taste of honey that revived his spirit, but we did something good that day. Later in the week we released him in the garden to rejoin his kind. He sped into the veggie patch and disappeared.

IN A NUTSHELL

After a horseback tour of the Corsican mountains, Professor J. Russell Smith of Columbia University wrote a little book called *Tree Crops: A Permanent Agriculture* to record his impressions of a land rarely visited in the 1920s. The book is now forgotten, but it still makes interesting reading if you can find it. I love his account of chestnut forests.

> This chestnut orchard (or forest as one may call it) spread along the mountainside as far as the eye could see. The expanse of broad-topped, fruitful trees was interspersed with a string of villages of stone houses. The villages were connected by a good road that wound horizontally in and out along the projections and coves of the mountainside. These grafted chestnut orchards produced an annual crop of food for men, horses, cows, pigs, sheep, and goats, and a by-crop of wood. Thus, for centuries trees had supported the families that lived in the Corsican villages. The mountainside was uneroded, intact, and capable of continuing indefinitely its support for the generations of men.

Russell Smith was amazed to see vigorous chestnut trees on stony mountain slopes where no crops could be grown. The trees did not need irrigating, fertilizing, and plowing, or indeed hardly any attention before September when the villagers harvested heavy crops of nutritious chestnuts. They called them "the food of laziness."

Chestnuts were staples of the local diet and versatile ingredients for numerous recipes. They were milled to make flour, although chestnut bread must be supplemented with gluten to make it rise. The trees provided surplus nuts for hogs in winter, imparting a delicious woody flavor to meat. Logs from the forest were hewn to make sturdy furniture, house sidings, roof shingles, and fence posts that resist rotting. But nuts are the signature images of these trees.

Nuts and nutrition sound euphonious, although they have different roots in the English language. All kinds of nuts are rich in proteins containing essential amino acids, and are excellent sources of antioxidants and fiber. They also have beneficial minerals and vitamins depending on the species—vitamin A in butternuts, chestnuts, pistachios, and hickory nuts; C in chestnuts; E in almonds; K in cashew and pine nuts; folate in ginkgo nuts and peanuts. They are gluten-free for the growing number of people who are sensitive to glutinous proteins. Chestnuts are particularly rich in carbohydrates, which would be a drawback if their carbs had a high glycemic index. Acorns have a similar nutritional profile, but the bitterness makes them inedible unless the tannins are first extracted, as American Indians did before grinding the nuts into flour.

To be botanically accurate, not every 'nut' is a true nut: almonds are drupes and peanuts are legumes. We might expect all of them to have impressive food value because, by parallel with the highly nutritious eggs of birds, they are investments for the next generation for which only the finest materials will do. Nuts and eggs are almost perfect foods, and both are ingredients of the renowned Mediterranean diet.

Russell Smith's visit to Corsica left a deep impression that set him thinking when he got home to Connecticut. If a single species of nut tree had sustained Corsicans in their mountain fastness since the Roman Empire, why did Appalachian farmers struggle in their rugged terrain? There is an easy answer. After felling the virgin forest along the mountain chain to grow corn, potatoes, and other annual crops, there were no deep roots to hold the topsoil from washing down to streams and creeks in winter storms. He predicted those farms would never prosper without returning goodness to the dirt, because the style of farming 'didn't fit the land.'

Tree Crops was published the same year as the Wall Street Crash, and coincided with the last of a series of wet years before a drought visited the Great Plains and the Great Depression afflicted households across the nation. The American Prairies were originally a stable biome with topsoil anchored by dense grass roots and fertilized by bison and other grazers. Like the mountain men of Appalachia, prairie farmers cultivated their land according to traditions passed down by their forefathers in Europe where agricultural practices evolved over centuries in a different climate and terrain. After plowing deep furrows and harvesting cereals or cotton, the ground was left bare without a cover crop in winter, and dirt exposed to drought blew away in great swirling clouds. Some of the dust was said to settle as far away as New York. The word dustbowl gave new meaning to the pejorative label 'dirt poor farmer,' and the calamity forced the Joads and real-life Oakies along with farming communities from neighboring states to abandon Grapes of Wrath country. After heading west on Route 66 with hopes and possessions piled in caravans and old trucks, they left the farm gates swinging in the wind until modern agribusiness arrived on an industrial scale.

The human and environmental tragedies were deep and vast and, with the benefit of hindsight, predictable. Russell Smith believed it was folly to incessantly grow annual crops on that kind of land and in that climate. The Corsicans were lucky they did not have to impose alien crops on reluctant ground because they had permanent agriculture waiting to be managed. America needed a large farming industry to feed a growing population, but he was sure it was on the wrong track and had overlooked the potential for tree crops as 'permaculture.'

He called for more orchard trees of all kinds, and even low-yielding species can serve as 'shelter-belts' to protect fields from erosion. Some nut trees can thrive in mountains where the ground is too rocky or steep for annual crops or prone to flooding. They can be harvested annually without care and chemicals, and don't need irrigation from underground aquifers. Moreover, they would help to stabilize the soil and improve nitrogen naturally, as well as offer perennial shelter for wildlife. There was the admitted economic drawback for cropping when trees undergo unpredictable cycles, yielding superabundant harvests in mast years but mostly a succession of lean ones, but he denied this would be an obstacle to the advancing science of horticulture. And, indeed, plant breeding technology now offers a wide range of cultivars for almonds, walnuts, pecans, pistachios, apples, pears, cherries, nectarines, et cetera.

The professor would be sad to hear we are even more dependent on annual crops today, and only plant a tiny number of species and varieties of mostly corn, wheat, and soybeans. He knew that dependence on a few high-yielding varieties of the big three is a policy that puts food security at risk. In his day, many agronomists were warning that food production would eventually fail to keep up with population growth and trigger catastrophic famines, as predicted by Thomas Robert Malthus (1766-1834). Those men who lived to the 1960s saw their warnings repudiated by a Green Revolution introducing better irrigation, pesticides, and fertilizers, along with new crop varieties that have kept the world fed and a Malthusian crisis at bay.

The statistics for agriculture are particularly rosy in America viewed through the lens of economics. Cereal costs are a much smaller fraction of the domestic budget than at any time in history, and provide a larger proportion of our dietary calories. US farmers pride themselves on efficiency, although commercial success rides on the back of federal subsidies for commodity prices and crop insurance to the tune of $300 billion between 1995 and 2010. But as shoppers we seldom pause to think about small family farms that struggle and sink into bankruptcy, while the big producers enjoy the lion's share of public dollars.

The USDA has little reason to steer a new course in agronomy while food is cheap and abundant, and the nation is sheltered from the volatile draught of international prices. Nor does it pay great heed to the long-range impacts of intensive agriculture, which we bury for future generations. As for tree crops, they never had the political gravitas of the cereal oligarchy, and their passionate advocates are regarded as 'nuts,' except in one state.

Viewed from the air, the almond orchards of the Central Valley of California stretch between horizons in rows so long and straight they look like lines of longitude. California produces 80% of the world harvest of shelled almonds, amounting to two billion pounds annually and a gross value of nearly $3 billion in a good year. As the state's top agricultural export, almonds are an enormous success story, but the industry follows the philosophy that made oceans of cereals in the Midwest, namely, the creation of a monoculture in a landscape purged of other life. This is not how permanent agriculture was originally envisioned, nor by its contemporary advocates like Philip Rutter in Minnesota or Peter Kahn at Rutgers University.

Climate change is a warning that orchards and thirsty annual crops are not forever in the Valley. Irrigation is an acute challenge and growers are too dependent on cheap water from aquifers and ill-prepared for chronic drought. There are other strains too.

Unlike grain crops, almonds need insects for flowers to fruit. Early in the year, commercial beekeepers converge on the orchards from across the country, conveying millions of hives on semi-trailers in the largest controlled pollination program in the world. Nut harvests depend on them because wild pollinators are too scarce for the job. But the services provided by honey bees are being seriously undermined by colony collapse disorder, which is hard to address when there are multiple causes.

The other side of the world in the Sichuan province of China, pear trees failed to fruit in the 1990s after bees were wiped out by profligate use of pesticides. Fruit harvests were restored by orchard workers stepping in to dust blossom with pollen on brushes and swabs, which was as effective as insect pollination, but the ancient contract with insects no longer looks so dated. Since wages have risen and hand pollination is uneconomic, orchard owners mourn their bees.

Rather than trying to heal the root problem by promoting healthy apiaries, we automatically reach for a technological fix. We hear that drones are being considered as pollinators. I don't mean the lazy males whose raison d'être is to fertilize queens and never work in the flower garden, but the aerial vehicles guided by GPS that retailers are testing for shipping goods. The analogy between delivering food to a customer's doorstep versus pollen to flowers is elegant, but biotechnology may make drones redundant before they are launched if fruit trees can be hybridized or made transgenic for self-pollination.

As much as I admire marvels of engineering, I wonder if ascending a technological spiral to solve a biological problem is the best solution for crops and other natural resources. I expect Russell Smith would agree. The higher we climb the further we stray from the genetic bedrock that evolution built. If we take a track that leads nowhere, it may be time to dust-off abandoned practices that were effective in the past and are needed again. Farmers used to leave fallow areas around fields for perennial herbs and trees to protect ground crops from erosion and provide food and shelter for pollinators the year round. If we no longer need to move beehives around the country, the risks of spreading insect diseases and parasites will surely decline.

The wonderfully productive American chestnut tree was never cultivated as an orchard tree and has become a ghost in the landscape. It was already retreating from assault by an Asian blight in Russell Smith's time, and ink disease has a long history of devastating European sweet chestnut trees, and invaded Corsica. Many other forest and orchard trees are now succumbing to diseases carried from foreign lands by accident or our foolishness. Trees were the permanent living features of many landscapes, but they are now threatened in many places.

Russell Smith's dream of permanent agriculture was doomed even as his book was reaching bookshelves. He was too late to warn about threats to the prairies or encourage more orchard crops, though he was more prescient than he knew when he promoted forests and silviculture. Trees are more than food crops and lumber, and are winning more hugs as we realize our destiny depends on an ancient interdependence. Not only do trees inhale carbon dioxide and exhale oxygen, they moderate climate by retaining moisture and shielding a torrid sun, their roots protect the soil and support underground species in a wood-wide-web. They provide renewable fuel and materials for fabrication, offer supposed healing properties from 'forest bathing[14],' and make homes for animals and quality food for all. We need a new vision for this old ally.

GHOST ON SANCTUARY MOUNTAIN

W e have tramped up a gently sloping meadow to a plateau where we are stopping to gaze through the gloaming at a fuzzy forest border 50 yards ahead. Looking west, there are thunderheads dispersing into ribbon clouds braided with gold from a sun that has already rolled over the world's edge. The sky has broken open through another bank of clouds for the first stars to twinkle, with a half-moon peeping down. The valley below, so green and speckled with wooly sheep this afternoon, is now washed with burnt umber and the lines of hills have turned into gray waves furling back to the purple horizon. Middle Earth is going to sleep as the evening wears on, apart from a few lights in the direction of Hobbiton.

The scene flashes memory back to boyhood. I would take off after supper with a camera to photograph badgers or foxes emerging from their dens in the twilight. In those days, I headed for a twenty-acre wood where the orange glow from London never sets at night; we are now on the side of a small mountain crested with forestland as the day retreats into a primal blackness. In the London suburbs it was the North Star I traced in the sky from pointers on the Plough (or Big Dipper); here it is the Southern Cross that guides navigators. Then, I passed a village pond on my way to the woods where a startled moorhen splashed across the surface; now I look down at the murky shape of a reposing giant in the valley that was Lake Karapiro, sparkling with spray from Olympic rowers in daytime.

My son Tom and I came for wildlife in the New Zealand night, and hope to see kiwis. We came for prejudice sake, favoring native feather and beak over foreign fur and fang that were introduced by human colonists. The closer we draw to the forest the further behind we leave the deer, rabbits, hedgehogs, stoats, ferrets, possums, feral dogs, rats, and cats that take native fauna and change habitats. We too have come to the 'Maunga' as aliens, but also as friends and will tread the forest lightly, respectfully, even reverently.

A Maori Queen who owned Maungatautari opposed its development, and her wish has been honored since her death in 1927. This surviving fragment of a vast forest was already profoundly altered from its primeval state by animal and plant invaders and commercial logging. It became Sanctuary Mountain some years ago when unsung heroes of conservation created a mainland island as a refuge for native wildlife. A community-driven project supported by public subscriptions and grants inspired a throng of volunteers who work the equivalent of 37 full-time staff. By 2004, they had completely encircled 3,400 hectares (8,000 acres) with an eight-foot fence stretching for 47 km (30 miles). It is the longest pest-proof fence in the world, and was dug deep to discourage burrowers, strong to keep out marauders, and tall to deter climbers. An agile possum will be fried if it climbs on the top wire. All the non-native predators, browsers, and pests inside the enclosure, except for mice, were eliminated by trapping.

No doubt there were discouragers and doubters, as there always are with pioneering endeavors, but the investment is already paying off, and the outcome is better in every way than a conventional zoo. Native vertebrates, mostly birds including some endangered species, have increased four-fold and many are breeding here—kaka (parrot), takahe (rail), hihi (stichbird), karariki (parakeet), tieke (saddleback), and kokopu (fish). The tuatara (the world's oldest lizard) and the giant weta (the largest insect) are here too. Native flora fared better than indigenous fauna because the forest was never completely logged, and mature trees in inaccessible places have avoided the axe.

The sanctuary is an experiment for restoring a native forest, a laboratory for public education, and an inspiring example of community achievement. The Maunga might become a model for the future as the last great forests are shrinking. Since it is impossible to restore ancient habitats after land is degraded, efforts must be redoubled before it is too late to save indigenous species in parcels large enough to support them. Sadly, animals that require large home ranges, like African cheetahs, will not easily find accommodation in terrestrial 'Arks.'

New Zealand is investing in wildlife preserves on land and offshore islands because it has a bad conscience. For millions of years before humans arrived, this calf of the supercontinent Gondwana was an evolutionary laboratory where strange forms evolved, yet there never was a serpent in this Eden. Some species of birds found the power of flight an expensive luxury, and among those that chose to be grounded a few became flightless giants because few predators could kill them. But some 800 years ago when human colonization began, the moas and other amazing creatures were quickly driven to extinction, and their smaller relatives barely clung on.

Tom is leading me to a pinpoint of red light in the blackness at the northern entrance to the preserve. He looks for a switch on the fence to open a security gate, so we can step inside a wire cage to enter the forest through an opposite gate. I turn on my LED headlamp to look around, and tilt it to shine on a board displaying a map of footpaths and history of the project. What looked like the perimeter of a prison camp from outside now melts into an elven Lothlórien as we begin our hike into the peaceful forest and inhale its sweet and unfamiliar perfume.

> That is the fairest of all the dwellings of my people. There are no trees like the trees of that land. For in the autumn their leaves fall not, but turn to gold.
> Legolas speaking in *The Lord of the Rings* by J.R.R. Tolkien

I am following a lighted ellipse cast by Tom's lamp as he leads me along a narrow trail of bone-dry dirt. We wind between stands of tree ferns whose fronds lean on stout stems like enormous fans, and walk under trees I have never seen before. Is the famed kauri here? The trees are under 50 feet tall in this part of the preserve because the forest is still regenerating after clear-cutting, but giants exist elsewhere. When the kakapo is re-established here, the rimu will offer nutritious fruit for the chicks of this giant, flightless parrot with Victorian sideburns. It is only found wild in tiny numbers on offshore islands, but one day it will cry out again in the Maunga, and make visitor's hair stand on end. A green parrot, it symbolizes the green movement on an isle green as Ireland.

BIOPHILIA

There's an Isle, a green Isle, set in the sea...
From *St. Patrick's Day* by Jean Blewett

The bush grows densely on rich volcanic soil in this ideal climate, and we are careful to keep on the path to avoid getting lost. Great lianas dangle like hawsers dragging from ships in a harbor. Other epiphytes are coiled around boles and boughs in chummy embrace. I lean to throw light on the underside of graceful fronds of silver ferns that curve overhead like relics of the Carboniferous Age. Along with other large pteridophytes, they provide a protective shield from rays pouring through the ozone hole, but it takes a light shining in the darkness to appreciate their full beauty. They are silver umbrellas that would grace the throne of a South Pacific queen, but the fern pattern was rejected for the design of a new national flag.

The forest is silent apart from a rattling stream beside the trail and the occasional call when we disturb a roosting bird. We stop to listen and turn off our lamps. After plunging into black, Tom is invisible only 15 feet away, and, yet, I know in less than a half-hour our eyes will see each other's ghostly outline and our path ahead, however faintly.

Suddenly he breaks the silence. "Hey, Dad! Look." He has better night vision, but I soon share the spectacle of hundreds of beads of turquoise light lining the bank alongside the trail. The word awesome is too hackneyed for the emotion of being surprised by a sight that was never made for our pleasure but given abundantly all the same. I feel as if I have parachuted into a movie set where elves string fairy lights to guide walkers to a mysterious destination. Perhaps if we hurry we will catch sight of Frodo further up the trail.

The lights remind me of the glowworms I saw as I floated through the Waitomo caves. They are not worms, not even beetles, but the larvae of a gnat that uses light to attract unwary prey onto the sticky threads they dangle from cave roofs, like the 'wreckers' of yore flashing lights on the English coast. When I turn on my lamp again and bring it very close to a glowworm it switches off its light and a brown grub crawls away. Dark radiates the beauty, and light betrays the grotesque.

We have tramped a mile without seeing or hearing a kiwi. Tom seems determined our visit will not be wasted and is examining an oblong box fixed to the bole of a tree.

"It's a weta refuge," he explains, and twists the outer cover to show me a narrow passage under the acrylic inner lining. "No one's at home," he sighs.

The giant weta is a cricket four inches long and heavier than a sparrow. My disappointment is only brief because he has found something inside the hollow of the same tree. He smiles in the glow of my lamp. "That's huge!" he exclaims, pointing from a safe distance at a black tunnelweb spider, which scuttles away before I see it.

If the unexpected is the most memorable part of a journey, embracing the most anticipated is often the sweetest. We came for brown kiwis, which are breeding here again after a century of absence, but there is still no sight or sound of them tonight. I imagine one shuffling on the path toward us like a shaggy specter, too short-sighted to notice us and too distracted to look up as it sniffs for grubs with nostrils at the end of its absurd beak. There is still a chance we will hear females after they emerge from burrows to call their chick to go hunting, but the males have stopped whistling now that courting season is over.

Brownies are the only kiwis on the mountain. They are the commonest of the five species in the country, but nowhere are they abundant. I guess an encounter with a kiwi will feel like being flung back to when their cousins roamed as avian counterparts of the dinosaurs. I am sad to miss the moas by the blink of a geological eye. Kiwis are the smallest members of the ratite family, and small is beautiful if it helped them to evade the fate of their relatives, which only come alive when children gaze at giant bones in museums.

> The skeleton of the great moa on iron crutches,
> Broods over no great waste …
> Not I, some child born in a marvelous year,
> Will learn the trick of standing upright here.
> From *The Skeleton of the Great Moa in the Canterbury Museum, Christchurch*
> by Allen Curnow

The first kiwi hatched on the mountain in modern times was named Huatahi, which means in Maori 'first of the new fruits.' Building on this success is a challenge for conservationists, who need fresh genetic stock to avoid inbreeding. A warden comes here in the breeding season with a muzzled sniffer dog to search for kiwi nests, and takes a few eggs away to raise chicks in a 'crèche' for populating other havens.

As the chance of seeing kiwis is fading, I strain again for night sounds. There is a distant, drawn-out *ee-wee* which reminds me of a recording I heard last week of a weka (a kind of rail). Surely, it can't be a bird that is unknown here. Hope is the thing with feathers. Perhaps it is only the voice of a frog or toad, because night sounds are treacherous. But *wait*! I hear a bird overhead calling *quor-quor* with gossamer softness.

"Tom, I think we have a morepork!"

Peace will reign again in the preserve after our last footfall at the gate. To walk in woods after dark is to be a stranger in the dominion of secretive creatures that eke out lives unknown and unwatched. Nocturnal visitors come to see what chance offers, and dare not harbor expectations. To stand quietly in a forest at night is a more moving experience than tramping by day because, as light yields to night, I feel a progressive absorption with the trees and bush, and the senses grow more acute. A primitive imagination tricks me to think I am invisible, all-seeing, all-hearing.

In the blindness and silence there is ineffable reward, and hope does not perish. I wonder even now if a kiwi is lurking nearby and making fools of us. Next time I will try my luck by hiding a few feet off the path with my back against a tree, as I did watching badgers in an English wood.

What's that I hear? It sounds guttural or retching, turning on and off monotonously, and further away another makes a reply. Tom is pulling out a smartphone. The screen lights his face as I watch him punch the tiny keyboard. The *3G* icon glows as he searches for a website he knows has mp3 bird recordings.

He holds the phone between us. "Yes, Tom. That's it!"

It is too much to hope the weird bird will strut in front of us like a shrunken ghost of its relatives. And, anyway, how dare I be dissatisfied with sound without sight when the spirit of the moment will last in my memory, thanks to the Maunga.

PART II. ORIGINS

SPERM ARE FROM MARS AND EGGS FROM VENUS

There is no chemistry more marvelous or more mysterious than when two microscopic dots of protoplasm, so similar in elemental composition but so different in size and form, unite to create an entity with potential to make a new human being. Is the turning of base metals into gold more amazing? Could a chemist with a laboratory stocked with bottles of every kind of molecule ever replicate what happens naturally every minute around the clock? No explanation is needed for why I chose a career in reproductive physiology and embryology. My cup of curiosity was always full.

Our biological origin is like no other story, but the cast involves only two players and one of each sex. Their union is, however, but a moment in a continuing drama for making a new creature with decades of potential life ahead. It is like the first kiss of a man and woman that flowers a long union.

Heavenly bodies have been portents of human destiny, and the sperm and egg (or the male and female essences representing them before cells were known) are characterized by two planets.

Mars is the aggressive, energetic player, the male form symbolized in astrology by a shield crossed with a spear (♂). Alchemists chose iron as his metal for its strength. Venus is the lovely, fecund female, symbolized by a circle with an inverted cross (♀). Beautiful copper ore represented her.

These dimorphic symbols originating in Antiquity were adopted and formalized in the 1750s by the father of taxonomy Linnaeus for the sexes of every animal and plant. The identity of gametes, however, was still controversial in his time (see next essay), but the principle of joining two dissimilar but complementary entities to create something novel was understood. Although iron and copper cannot be alloyed to make gold, when sperm and egg are joined to make an embryo they start a genetic lineage that may be passed down through countless generations as an organic Philosopher's Stone.

The distinctive appearance and behavior of the male sperm and female egg are their most arresting features, although in many ways they are similar. Reduced to chemical ash, they are indistinguishable. Both halve their chromosome number to prepare for fertilization and restoration of a diploid set; both have limited lifespans of around a day after their release from the gonads. One of the greatest marvels is how the union of two brief lives makes a product that can live over a century. As we grapple to understand this transformation, their biology still seems close to magical.

The egg is the more complex and enigmatic of the two. Although far smaller than eggs in other vertebrate animals, the eggs of humans and most mammals are huge when compared to somatic cells. Sperm cells, by comparison, are rudimentary dwarfs apart from the exceptional length of bat spermatozoa. The difference in scale between mammals and other animals is easy to understand because the yolky eggs of birds and herps are incubated in nests where they have a payload of yolk to nourish embryos stranded inside their shells until ready to hatch. We mammals have no need of yolk as we are 'tube-fed' via a cord that conveys food, dissolved gases, and waste products across a placenta.

Sperm have a more absorbing appearance than eggs because they are animated with a motorized tail to propel their bolus of DNA inside a nuclear head. They remind us of frog tadpoles we watched in jam jars as children. The random thrashing of tadpoles is purposeful, and sperm too have a goal, though very few reach it. Swimming sperm can absorb our attention under the microscope for ages, but we quickly get bored looking at plain and sessile eggs. Appearances are deceptive, though, because eggs are the more intriguing of the two gametes.

The philosopher Denis Diderot had an uncommon appreciation of them for someone in the 18th Century when no one had seen a mammalian egg.

"See this egg?" he exclaimed to an audience. "With it you can overthrow all the schools of philosophy and all the churches of the world!"

He used the egg as a rhetorical device for Materialism, but the cell has its own galvanic story. Remember the Great Sphinx of Giza with a human head and a lion's body that guarded the temple secrets? Eggs are sphinx-like. Next time you have one on your breakfast plate, pause to reflect on one of nature's greatest inventions before you smash it open with a spoon.

Eggs have the contradictory character of arch-specialists and ultimate generalists at the same time. On the one hand, they are the only cells in the female body in which meiotic divisions create genetic diversity and the only ones capable of fertilization. On the other, they are the ancestors of every other cell in the body. That is why they are called 'totipotent,' to acknowledge their supreme role as mothers of nations of cells.

Besides the biological paradox there is another conundrum. Eggs have a double nature. The genetic material of sperm is inactive until a couple of days after fertilization, whereas eggs are genetically active and inactive at the same time. They are like a coin in which images on the head and tail tell different stories that are nevertheless united.

Eggs silence their genome during the final stages of ripening before ovulation. Genetic silence is rare in cells, but necessary in this case because genes cannot keep housekeeping and other functions going while DNA is reprogrammed with software to prepare for an embryo. They manage this shutdown by storage of proteins needed for the cellular fabric and RNA molecules for instructing development. RNA is like the family archives bequeathed by a mother to her child to manage the family estate. But an embryo inherits more than a bunch of files from the mother cell: it acquires membranes, ground substance and organelles. It swallows the voluminous cytoplasm.

Sperm too are genetically silent before fertilization because their DNA is highly condensed, and their body is redundant after injection into an egg. They are dumb-asses. Negligible amounts of their cytoplasm and RNA are transferred because eggs own all the instructions for unfolding development. But despite this inaction males are not useless because embryos need their set of chromosomes, and sperm kick-start development otherwise eggs slumber into death. Sperm are like Prince Charming awakening the Sleeping Beauty with a kiss.

Since so much is invested in and dependent on eggs you might wonder if they can divorce from sperm. Can't they manage their role alone by keeping a double set of chromosomes, or if they must undergo meiosis to repair DNA can't it redouble after the splitting division of meiosis? Wouldn't it be even easier to 'bud' babies from ordinary somatic cells in the body instead of engineering complicated egg cells for the vagaries of mating with the opposite sex? Animals like aphids and Hydra manage perfectly well by budding without a buddy, or only occasionally consort with another individual. If more animals had 'virgin birth' (parthenogenesis) they could bypass courtship, which is troublesome and comes at a price. It sounds like a win-win scenario.

There is an unfortunate snag with adoption of a solo life. Endlessly dividing and replicating DNA encourages genetic errors to creep in because DNA copying is not perfect. The genome becomes slowly corrupted by gaining or losing DNA letters, which is disastrous in protein-coding segments of genes and regulatory regions of the genome. Meiosis offers an opportunity to repair sex cells, and throws the genetic dice for natural selection in the next generation. But if two sexes are good wouldn't three or more partners be even better?

Hijras in the Indian subcontinent are regarded as people belonging to a third gender, but not in any fundamental genetic sense because they are either eunuchs or male→female transgender individuals. Other groups and cliques have also been called a third sex, but their distinction as a separate gender is socially defined or simply a wisecrack like Oscar Wilde's label for priests if they were chaste homosexuals. Those stories are beside the point, anyway, because a third genetic contribution is disastrous. When conceived with a double genetic contribution from the female or male the triploid embryo is inviable and usually disappears without notice. Two is company and three's a crowd.

Eggs can be jolted to develop on their own by an electric shock or acid treatment or by flooding them with calcium. My late colleague Matt Kaufman found alcohol is a powerful trigger in vitro, but there is not enough for an effect after binge drinking. Sometimes, human eggs that fail to fertilize in an IVF lab undergo spontaneous parthenogenesis, which is a sorry waste of precious cells. They look the same as fertilized eggs, apart from missing a male pronucleus which tells an embryologist to discard them. Parthenogenones from mouse eggs live only 7-10 days, and if any are conceived naturally in women they always die before the next menstrual period. If it is an iron rule of nature that two parents of opposite sex are needed to make a baby, why is there a biological obstacle to virgin birth?

An explanation arrived in the 1980s with a discovery by another old colleague, Azim Surani, and simultaneously from James McGrath and Davor Solter in Philadelphia. They asked what happens if an embryo inherits the right amount of DNA but only from one sex. They obtained a clear answer from experiments with nuclear transfer in mice. When there was a double maternal or double paternal genome present the embryos always died in pregnancy, although at distinct stages and in diverse ways.

With a double female contribution, embryos start to grow normally and reach the stage at which a heart and circulation form, but die soon afterwards because their placentas are under-developed. This is like parthenogenones made by triggering eggs artificially without sperm. When a double paternal genome was present, the embryos called androgenones soon perished despite an abundance of trophoblastic placental cells. The abnormal placenta was reminiscent of molar pregnancies in women where a cystic mass of trophoblast cells spreads to invade the uterine wall, sometimes transforming to metastatic choriocarcinoma.

These experiments explain why we need a biological mom and pop. The fate of fertilized eggs depends on the provenance of

DNA, even though (apart from the X and Y chromosomes) the coding sequences are indistinguishable. DNA in a gamete knows the sex of its parent, and after fertilization executes genetic programs accordingly by switching on some genes and silencing others. When a gene from one parent is shut down while its matched copy from the other is active the cell is functionally haploid at that locus, and said to be 'imprinted.'

Having only one gene of a pair turned on may seem trivial, but it decides if pregnancy will be successful, the health of the baby, and even the risk of some kinds of cancer. Imprinting is part of the ascendant field of epigenetics, which is revealing how sophisticated software operates the DNA hardware. The take-home message is that imprinted maternal genes are needed for the embryo, and paternal ones for the placenta.

We need both to make a baby, a conclusion confirmed by Tomohiro Kono in Tokyo. He twiddled with imprinted genes to create a mouse with one parent, called 'Kagura.' Geneticists like to give unique animals a personal name, and this one means 'the girl found in a bamboo stump.' His striking conclusion was that only two genes bar the path to parthenogenesis.

If no more stand in the way of an all-female society, what does it portend for men? Whatever our feelings about the matter, we will need males for a long time (the author discloses self-interest as a male!). Dr. Kono's methods cannot be adapted for humans, although the gene-editing technology *CRISPR* brings genetic modification of embryos closer.

Does imprinting exist because of a fundamental advantage of mixing DNA from different individuals compared to solo reproduction? No! Two sexes are found in everything from bacteria to ourselves, while imprinting occurs only in species with a placenta, i.e., mammals. In the competition to pass genes to the next generation, it is in the interest of males to promote their own fertility with multiple mates; it helps to have imprinted genes to boost placental growth to the limit of female capacity, even if careless of placental overgrowth in an occasional partner. It looks unfair to pit male success against female health, although males pay a price for their maleness in other ways, during courtship and risky behavior. Females are more heavily invested in their own pregnancy because they can't theoretically have as many offspring as males, and have balancing mechanisms to offset the male effect. This is another aspect of the yin and yang between the sexes.

Finally, where do cloned animals like Dolly the sheep stand in this tale, and what planet represents her in the zodiac? The first is a hard question to answer because she is an outlier. She didn't need Mars to fertilize her, and the original egg from which she was made had its genetic material hollowed out. We should make her planet Pluto as the most distant orb and the last to be discovered, although some astronomers deny it is a legitimate planet.

Dolly looked like any other sheep at the research farm in Roslin, a small town outside Edinburgh, except for her plumpness from pampering by visitors. She nuzzled my pocket for a treat. Cloned from an udder cell of another sheep, it was understandable that the research team named her Dolly after the celebrity with a famous profile.

Clones are formed when embryos split into tiny balls of cells to make twins or quads, but Dolly was created by a method that can make many copies. She was not the first clone made by her creators, the late Keith Campbell, Bill Ritchie, and Ian Wilmut, who started down that road a few years earlier with cloned lambs. They kept Dolly's birth such a closely guarded secret that visiting researchers like me were not aware of the unique conception until a journalist called one day in 1996 after news was leaked from an anonymous source. The story deserved global attention because time's arrow was reversed in the clone made from an adult cell.

Dolly had a peculiar parentage. Besides the surrogate mother that carried the pregnancy, there was the sheep that donated egg cytoplasm and the genetic contribution of a six-year-old ewe born from a normal mating that provided DNA from an udder cell. In a sense, she had four parents that contributed differently to her existence.

Cloning first dazzled scientists in the 1960s when the Nobel Prizewinner John Gurdon made identical copies of frogs by injecting tadpole DNA into their eggs stripped of genetic material. It was proof that genes don't fade away irreversibly after their role in early development, and can be reactivated when exposed to cytoplasmic 'goo' inside eggs. Development is far more plastic than we assumed. Few embryologists dared to suggest that adult mammals can be cloned, and most thought it was a law of nature that development walks in one direction and can never turn back. That is what I was taught in college and passed down, in turn, to my students until Dolly came along. She proved that eggs are more equal than sperm because she did not need a conventional father.

She created waves. The news media had a field day, for who would not marvel at a beast created from an egg jolted into life by an electric shock in a Scottish laboratory close to where Grail stories were hatched at Rosslyn Chapel? There was negative fallout, as often happens when a dearly held theory is crushed. Some scientists were scornful at first, and a couple of doctors made phony claims they had cloned a human baby. Sadly, there was even a falling out in Dolly's team. Acrimonious breakups in science are like marriage divorces, and more regrettable when so much was achieved together.

Mammalian cloning is one of three dominating reproductive technologies of the 20th Century, along with the contraceptive Pill and IVF. It no longer commands newspaper headlines since what was sensational has become commonplace, following the usual history of technology. Clones have been made in dogs, cats, cattle, horses, mules, rabbits, and mice. Farm animal clones have been engineered for agricultural and pharmaceutical goals. Pets have been cloned too, although they never look the same as owners hope for the original Max or Molly. The technology encourages wild hopes of recreating extinct animals, and we will hear more rumors of cloned children.

An egg looks calm and boring beside the energetic sperm, but, remember, it is the mother of controversy.

MYSTERY OF MYSTERIES

The origin of human life was hailed as the 'mystery of mysteries' long before the label stuck on the origin of species. Aristotle was the first biologist we are aware of drawn to the question, and I have enormous sympathy for someone who, as long ago as the 330s BC, had no microscope to observe cells or the faintest idea about genetics. He was only armed with elementary knowledge of anatomy, and knew nothing of physiology. He was more of a naturalist than a true scientist and his deductions were guided by observations without the benefit of experiments.

I imagine the bearded philosopher strolling beside Theophrastus with sandaled feet over the flagstones of the Lyceum, a heavy mantle thrown over a shoulder, and a chiton girding his waist. There is a throng of pupils around them. While Plato had his head in the clouds, Aristotle was more grounded with a curiosity that led him to places rarely dignified by Athenian aristocrats. He visited fishermen drawing their nets on the beach and took home samples of their catch to examine fish anatomy by dissection. He also stopped at barnyards to collect fertilized eggs for cracking open to study embryo development, a phenomenon everyone was familiar with and knew nothing about.

On the first day, he saw the yellow sac of yolk floating in watery jelly attached to the shell by a gelatinous cord, as every cook knows. A couple of days later, a red spot appeared on one side of the yolk from which vessels radiated like tree branches, and soon afterwards a tiny heart pulsated. A recognizable body was not yet discernable, and the form of a chick gradually emerged from the mush, growing a head, legs, and wings sprouting sheathed feathers as the day of hatching approached.

Aristotle grasped that life originates with an undifferentiated egg that struggles through a series of stages to make a complex body for living outside the shell. This knowledge is mundane to us who grow up with the story, but the revelation upset traditional belief in his generation. It was believed that every new creature is preformed, perfect and complete, and the latest model in a series is like a nesting Russian doll (*matryoshka*) harboring inside itself smaller copies for making future generations[15]. His insight trounced the preformation theory and is not so very far from epigenesis in modern embryology, but, as we will see, later authorities cast it aside for the ancient dogma.

Aristotle did not study fertility in mammals as thoroughly as birds, because the wise man knew his limits. It is so much harder to study embryos in a womb, and research on human pregnancy is still an immense practical and ethical obstacle. But if he had visited farms at slaughter time he might have learned something from the carcasses of sheep or goats.

A 'tupped' ewe is an economic loss if a farmer sends a pregnant animal for slaughter unknowingly, and it still happens. At Edinburgh University, we used slaughterhouse material to teach undergraduate classes until health and safety regulations banned the practice. After students got over the sight of blood and gore, they were fascinated when they saw a gravid uterus opened to reveal a perfect fetus (sometimes twins) floating in its fluid-filled amniotic sac and attached by a cord to a polycotyledonary placenta.

At earlier stages of pregnancy there is only a hemorrhagic corpus luteum in the ovary to signal a mating has occurred because the embryo is too small for the naked eye. If we flushed it out of the uterus or Fallopian tube we needed a microscope to see it, and found it does not look anything like a miniature lamb. There is no simple extrapolation from the form of a fertilized egg to a newborn baby, much less than the transformation of a lump of soft dough to a crusty loaf from the oven. Development seldom takes our breath away because of its familiarity, but when thoughtfully considered it is the most awesome marvel in nature.

Aristotle used a carpenter and plank of wood to illustrate the respective roles of male and female, which was not such a shamefaced sexist metaphor in his time. The craftsman was the mysterious impulse in male semen to energize a new creation made from a plank representing menstrual blood. To his credit, the theory was not wholly paternalistic; he involved elements of both sexes to make a baby, but had no notion of complementary halves to make the whole. His conclusions should not have shocked citizens because the concept of life emerging from a bloody exudate was not so far from the widespread belief that no special 'art' is needed for worms and flies to be created in dunghills. Indeed, belief in spontaneous generation persisted until Pasteur, and the Georgian hymn writer Isaac Watts did not scandalize congregations when he composed the lyric, '…for such a worm as I!'

Aristotle overlooked the ovaries and Fallopian tubes because the first thing he noticed in pregnancy was an egg-shaped swelling in the womb where he presumed conception takes place. As for the testes, he dismissed them completely because it was general knowledge that bulls can impregnate cows after castration, if only for a few hours. The balls were weights for kinking the long seminal ducts. Such blunders were understandable and mostly went unchallenged because of his unrivalled authority and the lack of experiments to test speculation.

Five hundred years later, the Greek physician Galen published notions that were only slightly closer to the truth than his predecessor. He suggested 'female semen' formed in the blood was strained through the 'female testes' (ovaries) before it passes through the Fallopian tubes to the uterus where it makes a frothy admixture with male semen. At least he gave the ovaries some credit.

Aristotelian and Galenian theories held sway for centuries until the miracle of the Italian Renaissance when bold individuals launched the study of anatomy and ignored proscriptions against dissecting human cadavers, which was sacrilegious in Medieval Europe. Padua was the center of a new school boiling with intellectual ferment as brilliant citizens questioned old verities. Andreas Vesalius published the first accurate textbook of anatomy, the *Fabrica*, in 1543. When I examined an original copy in London's Royal College of Surgeons I plainly saw the ovaries he depicted. There were cysts bulging from their surfaces, representing either a follicle containing a single egg or a corpus luteum that forms from ovulated follicles as a source of progesterone and estrogen.

Vesalius mostly drew attention to large organs that looked important. His pupil, Fallopius, took a closer look at the female

96

generative organs and described the tubes named after him, but he never realized they were partners of the adjacent ovaries, and suggested they were merely exhaust pipes for eliminating vapors. Fallopius was the mentor of Fabricius, who had a greater interest in reproduction than the other two men and repeated Aristotle's study of chicken eggs. He published the first drawings of embryos and portrayed eggs in hens' ovaries like little bunches of grapes, which he called the 'ovarium.' In deference to Aristotle, however, he relegated the ovary to a part of the uterus instead of giving it the status of a separate organ.

The rest of the story continues a scientific relay race. The next runner was a young English doctor whose name we know. William Harvey studied under Fabricius from 1598 for four years in Padua where his tutor showed him valves that direct the course of blood flow in veins, and inspired the revelation of vascular circulation around the body. After returning to his Oxford chambers, Harvey took up the study of chicken eggs, but was distracted by other eggs he had to fry.

When King Charles appointed him Physician in Ordinary in 1632, Harvey followed the royal personage on travels around the Kingdom, even during the conflict of the Civil War. This appointment gave him the chance to dissect deer after regal hunts in the Royal Parks, and during the rutting season he could observe the progress of pregnancy. We might expect the man who discovered the circulation of blood would have arresting insights about reproduction too, but loyalty to Aristotle closed his fertile mind. He thought a clot of blood and semen would be the first sign of new life, so he was perplexed when he found the uterus still empty after a doe was covered by a male.

This alteration in the womb when I had often discovered to His Majesties sight and having likewise plainly showed that all this while no portion of seed, or conception either was to be found in the womb, and when the King himself had communicated the same as a very wonderful thing to diverse of his followers, a great debate at length arose.

The King helped Harvey by granting permission to keep deer in one of his paddocks. They were euthanized at weekly intervals after mating, but he never saw any signs of pregnancy until several weeks later in mid-November. He then observed 'white filaments like spider-webs, becoming … membranous or gelatinous sacs.' A few days afterwards, there was a ferment of tissue he construed was making a fetus.

Harvey concluded that semen was not making a direct contribution to conception, and didn't even reach the uterus. He thought it evolves like a vapor to stimulate the uterus to secrete an egg, a strange preternatural theory for a scientific genius. He worried that critics would ridicule his idea, so he sat on the manuscript for years, as Darwin postponed publication of his magnum opus two centuries later for fear of an offence. His friend, Sir George Ent, eventually prevailed on him to publish under the imposing title, *Exercitationes de Generatione Animalium*, which appeared a few years before his death in 1657. Among the more valuable insights, he affirms epigenesis and the doctrine *ex ovo omnia* (everything comes from an egg), but he was lucky not to live to hear scorn poured on his theory.

The story of conception migrates across the North Sea to the Netherlands. It was a golden age of Dutch art and science when the 'generation question' was an absorbing interest for a brilliant trio of anatomists in Leyden. They grasped that the enigmatic 'female testes' corresponded to the ovaries of hens and, hence, were sites of egg production. The Danish anatomist and geologist

Niels Stensen reached the same conclusion and might have played a greater role had he not taken holy orders to become a bishop.

A fourth Dutchman working solo was also making brilliant deductions and publishing lavish drawings fit for an art exhibition. Regnier de Graaf was 26 years old and a neighbor of Jan Vermeer in Delft when he sent a short letter to a fellow scientist in which he equated 'female testes' with ovaries. In those days, an article of correspondence between scientists was accepted as evidence of precedence.

Jan Swammerdam, a brilliant and impetuous member of the Leyden trio, impugned de Graaf's reputation when he heard the news. He claimed precedence for his own team: he said their theory had been plagiarized and the honor of discovering the ovaries was theirs. Fortunately, de Graaf could defend the charge against him by revealing a letter in which his challenger had already acknowledged the discovery was made independently, and even urged de Graaf to publish it. Competition is beneficial as a driver of science, but becomes counterproductive when it breaks codes of civility and cooperation. Swammerdam's mental health had affected his judgment, and it is a pity this episode cast a cloud over his legacy because he made other important discoveries. Besides describing metamorphosis in insects, he proved the large bee in a hive is not a king, as contemporary paternalism dictated, but a queen bursting with thousands of eggs in her body.

All these talented young men died a few years later, and de Graaf's friends lamented the bitter controversy contributed to his passing. Had he lived longer than 32 years, he might have solved the great mystery that absorbed them, as he suspected the grape-sized cysts in human ovaries (named Graafian follicles) are equivalent to eggs in chicken ovaries. This is inaccurate because follicles are too bulky and inflexible to negotiate the narrow passage of the Fallopian tubes, but I am sure that logic did not escape his notice. He came close but unfortunately never suggested the egg was a tiny speck inside a follicle.

His choice of rabbits was luckier than other researchers who studied other species. When he flushed out the contents of Fallopian tubes of mated animals he realized the tiny spheres floating in the dish were embryos traveling to the uterus. This was a momentous finding that scuttled Harvey's mystical theory and set the course to a correct conclusion. Had he met Antonie van Leeuwenhoek, a tradesman in his town who became a famous microscope maker, he would surely have found eggs after bursting open their follicles.

Authority figures used to carry so much sway that an opinionated elder statesman of science could set it on a false trail until overwhelming evidence forced a correction. Albrecht von Haller was an acclaimed 'father of physiology,' but he championed a theory that morphic rudiments of life materialize in the uterus from an amorphous fluid released by the ovary. This was a faint echo of Harvey's speculation, but both men made unfortunate choices for study because deer and sheep embryos grow lanky and slowly. Rabbit embryos are better models for human embryology but, little studied, so confirmation of de Graaf's insights had to wait until late in the next century. The story then transferred to London and William Cruikshank, a student of the famous obstetrician William Hunter.

When Cruikshank had completed formal training in the summer of 1778, he asked his mentor for permission to repeat de Graaf's experiments. Hunter agreed and purchased rabbits from a cuniculture dealer in Chelsea. They were housed and killed humanely, a care that was rare among experimenters in those times, and autopsies were performed up to three weeks after mating. Two animals yielded momentous results.

> ... at last, by drawing a probe gently over the Fallopian tube ... I pressed out several ova, which seemed to come from about its middle ... (in the next specimen) ovaria had the appearance as if the ova had not yet gone out; however, many of them were found in the uterus, and many in the tubes ...

It is not clear if Dr. Hunter was convinced by his student's findings, but Cruikshank has rarely been given credit for drawing close to the fact that eggs are shed by ovulation from ovaries and fertilized in the tubes. He could not publish his results for another two decades, so I hope the junior researcher enjoyed the reward of a thrilling discovery, which, although not original, was crucial confirmation of de Graaf's keen observations. Experimenters engage their subject in a spirit of hope but without assurance of success, for if they were sure of the outcome there would little reason to start a project and less joy at achieving their goal.

There were other false starts and wrong turns before the story climaxed. The draper of Delft, Antonie van Leeuwenhoek, was an unlikely scientist and he believed that 'animalcules' observed in seminal fluid through his simple microscope (really a high-power magnifying lens) were miniature embryos. Confirmation bias led him astray because he adhered to the view that the female contribution to babies is the 'fertile ground' on which embryos take root. Others held that a child is already fully-formed inside the nuclear head of the father's sperm, a 'homunculus' theory that dismisses the ovaries from any part in reproduction. Those ideas are farcical today, but then there was a heated debate between 'spermists' who thought the male contribution was all, and 'ovists' who argued that life originates solely from an egg.

The controversy festered until 1824 when two young doctors in Geneva almost made a breakthrough using the latest achromatic microscope. The principles of fertilization were already understood when Jean Louis Prévost and J.B. Dumas combined eggs and sperm in a dish to make frog embryos, which was first realized by the remarkable Italian priest Lazzaro Spallanzani. The Swiss pair turned their attention to internal fertilization in mammals, which was a huge challenge that could not be observed closely before 1959 when M.C. Chang in Massachusetts developed IVF in rabbits.

They found sperm in the uterus of dogs soon after mating, which is obvious now but Harvey's claim that semen stays in the vagina still lingered. Taking great pains to search fluid flushed from the Fallopian tubes and uterus, they saw glassy spheres resembling those described by de Graaf. These were the embryos they hoped to find, but the spherical bodies recovered from punctured follicles in the ovaries were dismissed as debris. *Arrh!* They were so close, but never realized they threw away the very objects that had been sought for so long by so many outstanding researchers. Dumas recalled their disappointment three years later:

> Although we have easily cleared up many minor problems, the fundamental point of the whole question escapes us, and when we reach the crux of the matter, truth eludes our every effort, and all we do serves only to attest our weakness and ignorance.

The last chapter opens soon afterwards in another city. There was a German nobleman and professor of Königsberg (now Kaliningrad), Karl Ernst von Baer, who was by general account a modest man with an uncommon breadth of scientific interests. Charles Darwin paid him compliments for a penetrating understanding of evolution, and we still sometimes hear about von Baer's Law of Development, but he is celebrated for one great discovery he declared was lucky. Surely it was more.

He searched for eggs and embryos in mated dogs and rabbits like his predecessors with one key difference. Instead of starting chronologically from the day of mating, he began at a later stage of pregnancy when embryos were known in the uterus and large enough to be easily seen. He then worked backwards one day at a time from the uterus to the Fallopian tubes and finally to the Graafian follicles on the day of mating, which coincides with ovulation. This reverse strategy gave him confidence to publish a shining report on his *die miracula*, May 1, 1827.

> I opened one of the follicles and took up the minute object on the point of my knife, finding that I could see it very distinctly and that it was surrounded by mucus. When I placed it under the microscope I was utterly astonished, for I saw an ovule (egg) just as I had already seen them in the tubes, and so clearly that a blind man could hardly deny it. It is truly wonderful and surprising to be able to demonstrate to the eye, by so simple a procedure, a thing which has been sought so persistently, and discussed ad nauseam in every text-book of physiology, as insoluble!

It was a long, bumpy road to discover where mammalian eggs are made. Some travelers had a clearer vision of the destination than others who led followers into blind alleys from where science had to reverse to find a sure highway to home. The story involved perseverance, competition, errors, and flashes of inspiration, as well as a shrewd choice of subjects and microscope technology. Few endeavors in biology have had such a long incubation or faced more stubborn problems, but discovery is often tortuous because the course of true science—like love—never did run smooth.

103

WHO'S AFRAID OF ARTIFICIAL GAMETES?

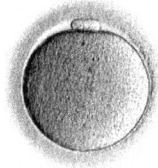

In the dystopic society imagined by Aldous Huxley, the World State forces the population to replace natural fertility with reproductive technology and production line management of human character and ability. But he never invented artificial gametes, perhaps because the idea was too outlandish in 1932, and, yet, they may be used to help people build families long before his Brave New World in the 25th Century.

When I ask what people think about artificial eggs and sperm, I get blank stares. They imagine daring biologists coiling DNA around silicon chips to make 'Frankeneggs' with orifices for 'Frankensperm' to dock payloads of DNA propelled by tiny motors. Biologists are not that creative, although the concept of artificial gametes attracts us.

The technology will be accepted when eggs and/or sperm can be engineered to be *biologically* indistinguishable from 'wild types' generated in ovaries and testes or, in other words, if they make healthy babies. This achievement will virtually complete the conquest of infertility and make donor gametes obsolete for people born sterile or prematurely sterilized by age, surgery, or cancer and its treatment. Then, patients will be offered the chance of that dearest gift, a genetically-related child created from their own cells fertilized with an egg or sperm from their partner.

The public reaction to the first fertility revolution (IVF) was a mixture of joy and horror, and the pioneers had to endure condemnation from the Establishment and press misrepresentation. But the story now in its 40th anniversary year is positive for over six million people born to date, some of whom are parents themselves and seldom need to repeat the technology that was necessary for their own conception. History will repeat with artificial eggs and sperm after a rough ride. The social omens are looking encouraging.

Forty years ago, we heard that contraception should be a priority because of overpopulation, and *The Population Bomb* by Paul Ehrlich was recently published. Infertile people were blamed for bringing the condition on themselves, and those who would help them were accused of aggravating the world problem. But isn't it cruel to stigmatize people for a disease that is not their fault? Attitudes to fertility have changed and conception has become more a matter of choice than chance. Smaller families are desired because of the costs of raising children, and more people choose to stay childless.

Private decisions about fertility have public consequences. Many governments are becoming nervous about the demographic transition underway, with birth rates falling below replacement levels and populations getting grayer. They are encouraging parenthood, offering more childcare services and longer maternity and even paternity leave. Europe and Japan are in the vanguard, and China has relaxed its one-child policy. In a 2016 poll of Western countries for *The Economist* magazine, people in all but one of them thought the average family size of their nation was lower than ideal. This reversal from anti-fertility to pro-natality may augur political encouragement for services to help people who are involuntarily childless, including the provision of artificial gametes one day.

Gamete engineering is the biggest technical challenge faced by reproductive science. IVF was accused of bending nature in the 1970s ("Playing God"), although its goal was to mimic the environment of conception in the body, not subvert biology. Working with nature should be reassuring that babies will be born healthy, or at least with no more abnormalities than occur otherwise. But converting a somatic cell from, say, skin or another organ into an egg or sperm is not a fate that nature intended, even though it gives us permission to try. This is the goal for artificial gametes and will need even greater diligence.

It requires no less than turning a cell back to its early history and then running the genetic program forward on a track to make germ cells and mature them to gametes. The process overlaps reproductive cloning, but the products are completely different. Artificial gametes must undergo reduction divisions with the double effect of swopping chunks of DNA to prepare for fertilization. The game of making gametes encourages genetic diversity, whereas cloning strives for uniformity.

A cell returned to its primal condition becomes 'pluripotential,' which means it can become the mother of other cell types in the body, including gametes (but not placental cells). If I liken all cells to a pack of cards divided into suits (for organs and tissues), a pluripotential cell is a joker that can join any suit it chooses. Once on its journey of development, the cell loses pluripotency to switch to another 'suit,' and never looks back. Lineages branch and differentiate so nerve cells stay committed to being nerves, heart cells to heart, and so on. Somatic cells cannot switch to become germ cells under natural conditions, so we must fool them. We currently have two routes.

The first track requires injecting the nucleus of a somatic cell into an enucleated egg. Apart from the cost and availability of donor human eggs, it has a low success rate but when successful the injected DNA is reprogrammed by cytoplasmic 'goo' to begin growing into a ball of cells looking like a tiny embryo. It must be admitted as a clone (another problem) which will be sacrificed to extract its tiny cargo of pluripotent stem cells. Next is the immense challenge of directing the pluripotent cells along a developmental path by dexterously controlling the culture conditions toward making germ cells instead of a somatic cell fate. A decade ago, a South Korean scientist engaged in cloning human eggs set progress back when he reported fabricated data. That episode even cast doubts whether the enterprise can, or should, succeed, but after the storm new research indicates this track is possible, although there is another way that is more acceptable and likely to flourish.

Induced pluripotent stem cells, universally known as iPS cells, are pluripotent by definition and made with uncontroversial somatic cells. They don't need the magic offered by eggs, and because the somatic cells come from the recipient who uses them they will never provoke an immune reaction after transplantation. This is very important when iPS cells are needed to repair nerve, muscle, and bone marrow, but not a problem with gametes.

In a nutshell, the technology involves treating a bunch of somatic cells with a cocktail of special molecules called transcription factors to turn their genomes back to a ground state in which they 'think' they are embryonic. The original mix contained four factors of which two were oncogenic, but safer molecules were found. This process is extremely inefficient, but since the starting cells are abundant a few make the switch to become pluripotent and, because they can multiply indefinitely large numbers can be harvested. This is not trivial, and it is a marvel that cells can revert to an earlier state, but the next stage of driving them forward is the greater challenge, like the one described above. Under the influence of a special brew of molecules in the culture dish, epigenetic switches in the cloud of proteins surrounding genes decide the fate of cells, whether they become a nerve or heart cell or a sperm. The subtlety of these changes is profound, and the goal of replicating what nature does with ease all the time is breathtaking, but there is, nevertheless, amazing progress at Kyoto University where iPS cells were originally discovered.

Fibroblast cells engineered to make iPS cells have already produced fertile mouse gametes. This is proof of principle, although a very long way from helping sterile patients to conceive using their own genetic material. The Japanese scientists caution their methods are not suitable for humans, and the goal of making gametes for clinical use will be far harder than the pioneers of IVF faced. There are many technical hurdles to negotiate known hazards, plus known unknowns waiting in the background.

There is headway toward making human sperm from iPS cells. A wise researcher chooses the most tractable path, and in this case, it is with sperm because they are easier to make than eggs. The male gamete does not need a large and complex cytoplasm, and after its mother cell has halved its genetic content to a haploid state the proto-sperm is ready to go into an egg, even if it is still too immature to swim. It can be injected directly using a technique which is used daily in IVF clinics all over the world.

As spermatogenesis rolls forward with an innovative technology and egg production lags, we have the latest example of inequality between the sexes, and this time at the most tender stage of human development.

Some readers may worry this essay paints too glossy a portrait of artificial gametes. They are right that radical departures from natural conception can have potentially unpredictable consequences. They might point out that, although there are exciting prospects for iPS cells to cure degenerative diseases and treat trauma, we are opening the door to widely-feared germline therapy and a dystopic future (Pandora's Box). Aldous Huxley imagined how reproduction might be drafted for social manipulation, and the advancing tide of technology has never stopped, for when it is dammed in one place it overflows the banks elsewhere. The aims of this research are humanitarian and to satisfy curiosity, but the spinoffs could be capricious or unpredictable, just as they were for nuclear physics, the silicon revolution, and recombinant DNA technology. In the face of risks, we must have faith in wise leadership and live hopefully.

THE STRANGE TALE OF A CHIMERA

The monstrous chimera had a serpent's tail, the head of a lion, and the body of a goat. That was in a Greek myth, but chimeras really do exist.

I created a bunch of mouse chimeras in my laboratory by fusing pairs of tiny embryos at the 8-cell stage to make a single embryo with 16 cells. First, I had to remove shells which normally prevent them from sticking to each other or to the Fallopian tube. Larger numbers of embryos can be combined to create a giant chimera, up to a size limit for inserting into the uterus, but after implantation the growth rate is downgraded to ensure the baby is a normal size at birth. All my chimeras looked healthy and intersex pups were rare, although some combined male and female cells. I knew they were blended because a few days after birth they grew hair in random patches of white and brown inherited from their parents with corresponding coat colors.

Human chimeras could be created in the same way, even from different pairs of parents as I had with mice, but why would anyone want to make a baby with four genetic parents? Two is enough for any child!

A human male chimera was identified recently in California while undergoing fertility treatment with his wife. They had a son after she received intra-uterine insemination with his sperm (IUI). There was nothing unusual in the case until a routine blood test revealed the boy had a blood type that did not match either parent, which was as much a cause for suspicion as amazement. How could a third party be involved in conception without casting doubt on the mother's fidelity? They checked for mix-ups in the birthing center, but there was no doubt she was the boy's biological mom, so the husband opted for a genetic test to compare buccal cells with his son's specimen.

When they did not match, they were retested with the same result. Still trusting his wife had never been with another man, it looked like the fertility clinic had accidentally exchanged his semen sample with another patient the same day. Technocuckoldy happens. In 2016, for example, the University Medical Centre in Utrecht admitted about two dozen women undergoing IVF treatment had received the wrong sperm by mistake, and there have been deliberate cases of fertility fraud elsewhere. The American couple asked a geneticist for a more extensive evaluation before consulting their lawyer. She suggested they send samples from the father and son to a personalized genomics company in California (23andMe[16]) which offers cheap and direct services to consumers, mostly for genealogical research. The genechip analysis changed the story from alarming and litigious to interesting and reassuring.

Father and son's DNA matched 25%, not 50% as expected with normal paternity. At face value, this suggested the boy was not the man's son but his grandson or nephew. But the dad really was his biological parent because careful analysis of his semen in another lab showed 10% of his sperm corresponded exactly to the boy's DNA; the rest was from an unknown relative! He was then found to have a similar mix of DNA in his buccal cells, and likely to be the same elsewhere in his body.

The geneticist deduced he was harboring cells from a twin brother conceived at the same time but unknown and unborn. He had rendered a limited organic existence to his vanished twin when he was born, with cells from both colonizing his testicles as mother cells for making sperm after puberty. Dad was a chimera.

A chimera may sound weird, but it is not as unusual as you might think. Anyone harboring cells from more than one fertilized egg qualifies. Strictly speaking, when someone receives a transplanted organ or bone marrow from a donor they are chimeras, though they never have as much cellular diversity as the man in this story. Chimerism also occurs naturally, and it is not only a normal process but a necessary one in a few species.

The strangest case is the angler fish occasionally hauled out of the ocean depths. It is unmistakable since no other species has a dorsal fin modified like a fishing line to lure prey to its jaws. Those are the females. The males were overlooked for a long time because they are comparatively small, and the species is far more sexually dimorphic than black widow spiders. Instead of a male mating in a conventional way (he doesn't dare), he fuses skin with a female and is gradually absorbed into her body. The angler fish in matrimony takes the Episcopalian Book of Common Prayer quite literally ('A man cleaves to his wife and they become one flesh'). But the male fish is not yielding to death, or not exactly, because his blood vessels hook up with hers so that some of his cells can be nourished for survival, including the all-important sperm precursors. Females then become chimeras from receiving the sacrificial male transplant, which enables her to be self-fertilized with genetically distinct gametes. Smart work!

Most mammalian chimeras that originate spontaneously share a placental circulation. Blood is exchanged between siblings before birth, and it was that kind of intimacy that made the man chimeric. In transfusion syndrome, a competition is set up between a pair of fetuses that becomes harmful or even fatal to the weaker one. Cross-circulation is exceptional in monkeys, and the common twins and triplets of marmosets are born healthy. In cattle, on the other hand, twinning has economic consequences when there are opposite sexes in utero, which is expected 50% of the time without identical twins. It is dreaded by farmers because a male calf perverts the development of his sister, which becomes a sterile freemartin.

They were known in Ancient Rome, but the toxic impact of a male twin was not recognized until John Hunter reported it in the 18th Century. Conceived as genetic females that are identifiable from cells with a Y-chromosome, freemartins are molded by higher levels of testosterone and the hormone AMH carried over from their twin to masculinize the female body and shrivel the primordial uterus. They have non-ovulating ovaries and behave like males.

Medieval artists and craftsmen played on superstitious beliefs by illustrating centaurs, gryphons, harpies, and mermaids, but gargoyles are the most enduring chimeras. They stared down from church roofs on past congregations of sinners to frighten them into repentance. There was also a tradition of rustic stories of human freemartins, but never any scientific proof they existed.

In *Brave New World*, low caste females were made into sterile, bearded freemartins by a chemical process at the London Hatchery & Conditioning Centre. The author's images should remind us of our history of privileged people using physical differences to debase and abuse others. Fortunately for true chimeras, they are not targets for prejudice, and I never heard the word used as an insult. Surely, that is because they go unnoticed until a question of paternity or an unexplained variation in skin color or sensitivity prompts a request for a genetic test.

I vaguely wonder if I, too, am in the chimera club because I was told I shared my mother's womb with a twin who vanished before birth. It does not necessarily follow that his or her cells would find a safe harbor in my body. And even if it was true, knowledge of their existence, so many decades after my sibling died, would never give me the spooks, not even if I learned that some alien cells colonized my brain. That would be a great deal more natural than being a chimera from a donated organ. I would only muse how different life would be if my twin had lived.

A WOLF COMES HOME

There is something incongruous about the notion that the golden retriever lying at my fireside is mostly wolf. Don't wolves dread fire? How much shaggy wolf remains inside her doggy nature?

Dogs and wolves are members of the same species, share a common ancestor, and most of their DNA. There are, however, over 20,000 years of domestication in the making of dogs, offering plenty of generations to mold the appearance and behavior of every modern mutt. But it matters how much wolf still lingers in them because it affects our attitudes and their training.

Humans never had a good relationship with wolves. It is paradoxical that the closest wild relative of our best friend, the dog by our hearth and Old Yeller in the movies, is one of the most reviled creatures? They have been our arch-enemy from time immemorial: first for taking game from hunters, then for stealing livestock from shepherds and farmers. The prejudice is reinforced by stories like the Grimm's *Little Red Riding Hood* and a fount of myths about blood-thirsty wolves and werewolves.

Even biologists who now know better upheld heartless views of wolf society. Packs were regarded as strict hierarchies dominated by an alpha male and female, who had the first rites to a carcass and ruthlessly disciplined the lower ranks. Peace was barely preserved by a mien of threatening behavior until subordinates cowed in submissive gestures. This fierce portrait was like a feudal society in which the vassals paid homage to their king in exchange for gifts and privileges. So inured are we to the belief in a cruel reign that our attitudes change slowly, even while research is painting a different picture of wolf society that ought to make us more respectful of wild intelligence and canine virtue. That should also inform the way we regard and train our pets.

Cesar Millan bases his dog training program on a portrait of wolves that is outdated. If it seems unfair to pick on him as an example of widespread attitudes and practices it is the price paid for winning celebrity status. There is no doubt he has an admirable talent for handling difficult animals (*The Dog Whisperer*), and his endeavors to save and rehabilitate abandoned dogs deserve respect. But he makes no apology for practices that are contradicted by modern science, and vigorously defends them. He claims that when we play the alpha role our dogs will stop fighting for dominance because they will then see us as their "calm-assertive pack leader."[17] He warns if our pets succeed like young wolves in striving to assert themselves we lose control of them and they are the winners.

This philosophy is at odds with behavioral science, and has sometimes gotten him into hot water with humane societies, despite being so obviously an animal lover. Of great concern is the risk that less caring people can twist this thinking to justify the harsh and even cruel treatment that pets have suffered down the ages at the hands of some owners. Sadly, the victims often don't understand why they are being punished, and it is heart-rending to know that even grossly-abused animals often stay loyal to the abuser. How many humans have you heard of who remain faithful to their torturer?

Not every dog is well-behaved or friendly, of course, and some need tough love. It is not only the postman who is confronted by growls and bared canine teeth at the gate. Some animals are bad-tempered by nature, and aggression is deliberately selected by some breeders. We have notions about which breeds to give a wide berth when they are loose in the street, and take care to gauge the circle of a strained leash. American pit bull terriers, Rottweilers, Alaskan huskies, German shepherds, and Doberman Pinschers are among the top ten for aggression, although the only dog that ever bit me was a toy poodle! You never can tell until you know the dog, and that goes for its owner too. Threatening behavior is a territorial response in many animals, which goes for us too and explains the aphorism, 'Good fences make good neighbors!'

Victoria Stilwell is another TV presenter and author (*It's Me or the Dog*), but she trains dogs in the opposite way, as the name of her website implies (*Positively*[18]). Her policy is to shower them with rewards for every good behavior, something we call positive reinforcement and behaviorists call operant conditioning. According to Victoria, most trouble with dogs is not their fault but their owner's (i.e., ours), so we are in as much need of training as our pets or more so. A sharp cameraman for her show occasionally catches a dog looking 'sympathetically' at its owner being chastised by the bossy Englishwoman. Her students are thrown back to days when they were under the rule of a sassy schoolmarm.

Of the two philosophies, Millan's is the harder to reconcile with the new understanding of wolf society. Simple extrapolation from wolf to dog is to exaggerate a relationship that has evolved by twists and turns of genetic selection over millennia more than any other domesticated animal.

The first close studies of wolf behavior were in zoological parks, but captive packs are mostly loose associations of individuals, often without a common family history and forced to live together in a contrived environment of confined space. Anxious behavior is expected in animals that are estranged from close relatives and constantly face the fangs of alien wolves. Besides, in trying to interpret their gestures we can easily misread them. It used to be thought a bowed head was a submissive posture when a wolf was approached by another of higher status, although it never made much sense because it is an excellent position for grabbing the 'boss' by its throat. The new explanation is that it conveys trust and cements a social bond.

Wolf society is looking quite different to woof society in the light of studies of wild animals tracked with radio-collars and GPS technology. Blood samples taken from darted animals for genetic fingerprinting reveal their relationships. Contrary to the belief that a wolf pack is a bunch of rangy bushwhackers led by a brutal leader, it turns out to be mostly a family group. Its members are usually close relatives, mostly adults that grew up in the same pack and never split from their parents. Individuals will occasionally leave for a solo life or join another pack to refresh the genetic stock, but for greater personal and food security they stick together to hunt big game, like moose and bison.

We ought to expect more cooperation than competition within a family, even acts of altruism. Loyalty to insiders and less aggression to outsiders increases hunting and breeding success, and reduces the risks of injury from fighting. The evolutionary rationale is kin selection because where genes contribute to harmonious behavior reproduction will benefit and, hence, more of those characteristics will be represented in succeeding generations. Nothing succeeds like success. Moreover, there is little evidence of rigid hierarchies in wild wolf packs, except for Mom and Pop keeping on top of unruly 'teenagers.'

Dogs have a consciousness of status that is entirely different to wolves, and they don't jostle for superiority over others as we do. When they go feral they don't return atavistically to be wolf-like, but form a fractious group of individuals. There are no scientific teeth for the belief that we must play the tough alpha role to train our dog successfully, and as my pet cozies up in the firelight I don't want to.

Is it the familiarity of our furry friends that blinds us to the marvel of why dogs are so companionable? Their cousins are much less trusting and terrified of fire, even if they have been raised in captivity from birth. While there are minor differences between the two in intelligence, there is a gulf of chumminess. Most dogs love to please. Once a trick is learned, it is not necessary to always reward them with a treat: pleasing their owner is a sufficient satisfaction. Wild animals must look after themselves and rarely care for others, but remarkable stories are told of courageous dogs saving the lives of people and other animals at their own risk. YouTube videos of services rendered by dogs offer almost unlimited entertainment and attract some of the highest 'like' scores, perhaps because we believe their enduring virtues are mirrors of our better selves.

John Bradshaw's book *Dog Sense* describes the search for a better understanding of canine character and traces its genealogy to an origin five million years ago. He uses the Swiss Army knife as a metaphor for the canid genome, which has provided flexibility for the descendants of proto-dogs to colonize six continents and evolve into jackals, foxes, coyotes, and wolves. It was this adaptability that made domestication possible, with the emergence of a beast with greater loyalty and willingness to please than any other.

After drafting this essay, I lay down my laptop beside the armchair. Lilah woke from dozing at my feet and cracked open an eye. She was not casting an anxious glance at her alpha male or waiting for instructions: I think she was just checking her 'Dad' was OK.

THE HERMIT OF DOWN HOUSE

The gleam of a great idea often glows first in the eye of an unknown face in some obscure corner. How many college dropouts and loners tinkering in garages have become celebrated silicon entrepreneurs? How many great writers, painters, and composers created their finest works in garrets or *en plein* air instead of academies? Even in the sciences, the elemental factor for a breakthrough is a roving and penetrating mind instead of a large, well-funded laboratory. Prestigious schools and universities were not designed as nurseries of genius: they value absorption, transmission, and conservation of knowledge, and sometimes discourage radical thought. The originators of scientific revolutions are freethinkers and often outsiders. Jolts to established belief, like the discovery of the quirky nature of elemental particles and the blind force of natural selection, don't fit the tidy lessons I was taught about how science advances, so I found Paul Feyerabend's seductive theory a revelation. The Berkeley philosopher argued that the process of discovery is more anarchical than we want to believe, and we tend to play down the irrational and quixotic turns of discovery for the sake of telling a splendid scientific story.

I was musing about Charles Darwin's revolutionary theory when I recently toured his old home again. Down House is a quaint Georgian property a mile outside a village in the Kent countryside, and less than 20 miles from central London. It was walking distance from my childhood home. As a teenager pondering college options for biology, I visited the house one day with a school buddy and we got into a heated argument about the theory of natural selection. I maintained it was incontestable, but Steve snapped back with the certainty of a sixteen-year-old.

"*The bible* and *The Origin of Species* can't both be right: you have to choose one or the other, Roger!"

It is a familiar contest that has never been put to rest in America, but I think it is a false choice. I flipped through *The Origin* that summer to prepare for another spat, but how could I recruit to my defense the vast number of observations and deductions Darwin marshalled so meticulously in his weighty tome? A few years later, I was a more confident debater as a college student after reading an essay by Theodosius Dobzhansky titled, *Nothing in Biology Makes Sense Except in the Light of Evolution*. I missed the chance to cheekily point out to Steve that the author was not only a famous Darwinian but also a lifelong communicant of the Orthodox Church. Too late, I found a quotation from Feyerabend appealing to keep our minds open: 'Human life is guided by many ideas. Truth is one.' *Q.E.D.*

On my latest visit, I wondered how much had changed over 50 years since I first stepped across the threshold of Down House. Charles Darwin had been dead for the better part of a century, but I recall feeling as if the owner had just stepped outside for an hour to check experiments in his garden or stroll along the Sandwalk he called his 'thinking path.' The house and acres of garden on the North Downs were unfaithful to my memories. They have evolved from a hallowed place in history preserved on a shoestring budget for pilgrim naturalists and scientists to become something of a tourist destination after the house was adopted by English Heritage and the district was nominated as a World Heritage site.

I remember when I would pull the doorbell a bent custodian appeared like a Victorian butler, a relic of an era when visitors arrived on horseback or took a surrey down from London to consult with Mr. Darwin. An ostler would lead the horses away while guests were ushered into a drawing room where they would sink into the Chesterfield and gaze at portraits of Darwins and Wedgwoods in heavy gilt frames hung on walls covered in green and puce patterned wallpaper by William Morris. How different today. I was welcomed with a cheerful smile by a lady at the ticket desk and stopped in the lobby turned into a gift shop to look at glossy magazines and imitation Darwiniana. The house still has the air of a family home, but most rooms are loaded (I cannot say 'graced') with information boards and even dioramas. I prefer the more authentic, if dowdy, interior from memory, but I wasn't disappointed with the Old Study.

That room always mattered most to me, and it was a relief to find it had hardly changed. Heavy with dark mahogany furniture and dreary walls, it could make an atmospheric setting for a Charles Dickens novel. Daylight struggled to penetrate the windows and the air had the musty odor of the flint church down the lane. At center-stage, there was a table strewn with old books, stamped envelopes, yellowing papers, and a feather quill in a dry inkwell beside an upturned glass goblet. Cabinet shelves were crammed with books from every department of knowledge. You may wonder if the room is a museum reconstruction, but it is mostly authentic with some additions from the same period.

My attention was drawn to the black leather chair with horsehair poking through holes in its arms. It rested on castors slightly askew to the table, as if waiting for its owner to return. I imagined a Victorian parson leaving for a break after drafting his Sunday homily, or a writer resting his quill to light a pipe and pace up and down to break a mental block. Only the magnifying lens, dissecting instruments, and portraits over the marble fireplace hinted that a man of science once occupied the space. The piles of pillboxes might lead you to think the owner was an apothecary or a hypochondriac (he was that), but you would only find dried beetles and butterfly wings inside. Naturalists have modest needs because their passion is pursued outdoors to fire curiosity with observations they bring home to ferment in minds long after the trip is over. And what a mind Darwin had!

He had none of the usual qualifications for scientific greatness, and the Ph.D. degree did not exist in his day. Dr. Robert Darwin thought his son's lackadaisical attitude to scholarship and love of hunting and horse-riding would make him a worthless loafer. He prodded Charles to sign on to the family profession of medicine, but the young man dropped out of the Edinburgh Medical School when he saw what surgery demanded. The wayward son was encouraged to enroll at Cambridge for training as a Church of England parson, but a college don he befriended steered destiny in another direction. He joined the *Beagle* expedition as the ship's naturalist, which changed everything and launched the first great revolution in biology. Darwin's genius flourished during the five-year voyage, but his talent was entirely different to the intellectual fireworks of Newton, Pascal, and Einstein, and we struggle harder to explain it.

He came from a radical intellectual tradition through his grandfather Erasmus and in marrying his cousin Emma Wedgwood. The two families had influential ancestors in the Enlightenment who embraced scientific progress, opposed slavery, and backed the grumbling American colonies. Charles returned from his world voyage in 1836 to settle down to family life, first in London and then as a country gentleman for 40 years at Down House. He inherited the family's activism, and a Whiggish background fortified a radicalism that would offend staid Victorian society. Unlike his Grandpa, though, he never sought the limelight, and admitted when he came to doubt that species are immutable he felt like "confessing a murder." Chronic ill health dogged his endeavors, but it had a silver lining as an excuse to avoid social distractions and live a semi-hermit's existence. He kept his head below the parapet when the storm called Darwinism broke.

Charles was ever painstaking and cautious in his research, and took the greatest pleasure in exploration and discovery at a pace of his own choosing. The watchword for contemporary scientists is 'publish or perish,' for they must rein in temptations to be intellectual wanderers to focus on minutiae defined by research grants. They must hurry into print with their findings before they are beaten by ferocious competition in hot fields of research. Darwin had the advantage of great amateurs in bygone ages. He had no need to earn an income from his vocation, no graduate students to supervise, no research costs he could not afford, and no drag on working hours. His friends cared more than he did about the risk of being scooped by competitors, and he stubbornly accumulated mountains of data until he was confident in them.

His early interest in beetles expanded to the whole realm of nature, embracing biology and geology, extant and extinct forms of life. He devoted years to classifying barnacles, converted his lawn into experimental beds to study earthworms and wild flowers, inquired about artificial selection of animal breeds, and maintained a vast correspondence with other naturalists.

The idea that all living things are related started as a hunch during the *Beagle* voyage, and long before *The Origin* was published he sketched in a journal the form of a tree with branches linking species into a common genealogy, and scrawled beside a note: 'I think.' His theory of natural selection took another 20 years to be distilled from observations and experiments, and wore down a lot of shoe leather on the Sandwalk. The news that Alfred Russel Wallace was returning with the same theory after roaming the Malay Archipelago (Indonesia) forced his hand in 1858, and they published a joint paper. But a glacial pace prepared him for the professional and public reaction. He had left no stone unturned, no detail too slight or arcane to be ignored, and even barnacles helped to rock the world. There was never a risk he would be forced to an intellectual retreat, like too many recent scientific 'discoveries' that has required a new breed of scientific watchdogs[19] to monitor authenticity.

Darwin loved to sit by the hearth to ponder his latest experimental data and read letters from correspondents all over the world who wanted to share theories and observations. Unencumbered by paid employment and with servants to help his beloved family and home, he withdrew for long hours to his notebooks, specimens, and magnifying lens, like a St. Jerome in his cell except there was no bible, cross, and skull in the Old Study. Within those four-square walls was the quality time he needed and a peace that is harder to find today as we are bombarded with electronic beeping, flashing screens, and urgent ringing for attention. Thinking is such a natural process that we hardly give it much thought or any training, and as attention spans shorten we become feebler thinkers.

If the Sandwalk was Darwin's thinking path, the black leather chair was his thinking chair. It has always been a source of wonder for me. A tattered object, you would overlook it in a cheap antique store—as you might walk past the unprepossessing garage of a Silicon Valley entrepreneur. But it became the seat of an extraordinary personage, and the launch pad of one of the greatest revolutions in human thought. That revolution continues to roll forward and explain what was inexplicable—fossils embedded in mountain tops, elaborate male plumage in birds, organ vestiges like the appendix, DNA sequences shared across the spectrum from flies and worms to humans.

Once upon a time, a brash student was tempted to leap over the security cord at Down House to sit in Darwin's chair. He was inspired by another young man who tried to plonk himself in the Coronation Chair at Westminster Abbey for a royal moment before a copper hauled him away. But the student realized the eminent chair would never inspire great thoughts again because it has become public property, and great ideas ferment in obscurity.

PART III. PERCEPTIONS

SHIFTING BASELINES

Captain Smith sailed a crew of fourteen men to the 3,000 mile waterways around the Chesapeake Bay in 1608. They set out from the Jamestown fort in the new Colony of Virginia in a shallop made of oak planks with a sail and oars brought over from England in the hold of the *Susan Constant*. When they entered the estuary from the King James River, they could see down to four fathoms, and it was often shallow enough to see the bottom. Vast reefs of oysters filtered the entire bay every week, and some shells were the size of dinner plates for serving a hearty meal. Smith anticipated huge harvests from hunting and fishing.

... the oysters lay as thick as stones ... (there are) more sturgeon than could be devoured by dog or man ... (and) grampus, porpoise, seals, stingrays, brits, mullets, white salmon (striped bass or rockfish), trouts, soles, and three sorts of perch.
From the Journal of John Smith

I imagine awestruck sailors gazing from the boat across a territory so much vaster than the England they knew, and stranger too. They saw bald cypress trees with boles rooted under the high-water mark, and, beyond their green wall, the forest stretching to a purple horizon. The trees were taller than cathedrals, and different to the mixture of oak, elm, and beech they knew at home. When they moored at the shoreline the mysterious forest was alive with strange calls and songs, and pug marks and scat along the trails told of a wealth of animal life lurking close by. No person should go hungry with so much good fishing and hunting. The crew padded along trails with muskets at the ready when they came to clearings burnt by Indians to grow corn, beans, and squash. Smith noted the land was fertile and the country was 'very goodly.'

The explorers never found gold or any other precious minerals that investors at the Virginia Company of London hoped they would haul back to England. They never realized the real wealth in the Bay lay under their boat all the time. If you walk along the shore or examine riverbanks eroded by high tides and hurricanes, you can see a history of natural wealth laid down inch by inch over eons far deeper than humankind. A thick stratum of shells including the occasional shark tooth and whalebone fragment is exposed. The largest and most beautiful fossil is *Chesapecten jeffersonius,* named after America's third president as the state fossil of Virginia, and, four million years later, these scallops have not yet been rendered to stone and look as fresh as if they were served to diners yesterday. They testify to beachcombers how the Bay once teemed with life and as John Smith recorded in his journal. Seafood harvests from the Bay remained light for the first couple of centuries, but the 19th Century 'Rush' took such a heavy toll that shellfish became scarce, and the dearth was compounded later by pollution. It is slowly recovering from multiple assaults on its bounty.

A fisherman coming here the first time may still be thrilled with his catch if it beats experience he had fishing elsewhere. There are still plenty of croaker and catfish, striped bass and summer flounder in due season, and other sport fish to take home to fry or grill. His catch of the day draws the baseline or mental norm of what the Bay can offer, but its original abundance defies his imagination if he tries to picture it at all.

We define 'normal' from the experience of what we see for ourselves rather than from a deep knowledge of a past that is barely known and hard to fathom. We are careful to filter stories further back than those we were told first-hand by our fathers, knowing how the fog of memory makes accounts passed down by remoter generations untrustworthy. The best sources of fishing stories are from commercial watermen whose families have plowed the Bay for yore. James A. Michener wrote about these men in *Chesapeake*. Watermen inherit their boat and fishing license from forefathers going back a couple of centuries, and will tell you how fishing has changed: "You oughta seen catches in the old days, Boy!"

The pristine state of the Bay and its watershed was only lightly impacted by Indian tribes because they had a low population density and only basic technology. They left no written accounts of the bounty harvested from land and water, and the English explorers only left us meager descriptions. To an ecological archeologist this is a depressing poverty of knowledge, but does it really matter what the Bay or indeed any natural environment looked like in time before memory? Surely, to dwell on the remote past is a sentimental luxury when we have urgent work to manage the man-made present in a fast-paced world? History is bunk, isn't it?

One person who disagrees is the marine biologist Daniel Pauly[20]. He believes knowledge of the deep past is necessary for informing the present. Every generation creates its own mental map of what is 'normal,' like the fisherman who draws from a day of sport or a waterman from a life casting his nets and lobster pots, but their expectations are so much lower than if they really knew how rich and diverse the Bay was in its original glory. We draw expectations from our impressions, and where ecological poverty is escalating our norms step down generation by generation. This is social amnesia and we never circle back to define richness from its original state. Dr. Pauly calls this a 'shifting baseline.' He had ocean fisheries on his mind, but there are plenty of other examples in which baselines have shifted, and not only in the environment but all around us with consequences for consumers and all citizens. My brief list begins with shifting waistlines!

1. Consider how the average 20 lb. of extra body mass has stealthily promoted enormous numbers of middle-aged Americans and Britons into the clinically overweight/ obese category, yet in a Gallup survey many of them declared they felt "just right."

2. If you think a Golden Delicious, McIntosh or Fuji apple is delicious, you never knew the flavor of heirloom varieties going extinct, like the Ashmead's Kernel, Calville Blanc, and the Spitzenburg grown by Thomas Jefferson. Fortunately, the scrumptious Cox's Orange Pippin is still sold at English markets.

3. A community proud of its public park and fine trees, and never casts back to think how much grander and more venerable were the specimens growing there before.

4. Ask gardeners who struggle to grow flowers and vegetables in thin topsoil and they may sigh it was always that way, never realizing

the dirt was highly fertile before tobacco farming impoverished the land.

5. Newcomers tolerate traffic delays with a greater equanimity than long-term residents who remember times when our highways were uncrowded.

Ocean biology and chemistry offer some of the sharpest examples of shifting baselines, but changes are grinding so fast now that we notice them happening in our lifetime. Yet, we slowly rouse to action and give too little heed to our impacts. With the rise of sea levels, tide of floating plastic, and decline of fish stocks and shore birds thrust to our attention, we are less inclined to recoil as environmentalists than as consumers feeling hurt in our pocketbooks by higher prices and taxes.

At the top of the food chain, large, predatory sport fish are especially vulnerable to overfishing and pollution. They were never abundant in commercial fisheries, but their numbers have plummeted to less than 10% of harvests 40 years ago, and to the point of endangerment for some species. More importantly, many fish species that used to be superabundant are harvested unsustainably, and the disastrous drought of cod from the Grand Banks[21] of Newfoundland is very slowly reversing. That some of our most nutritious food is becoming a luxury only the rich fraction of the world can afford is a tragedy, and one might say a social injustice, calling for protest and greater regulation, yet governments are often slow to protect collapsing fisheries, blinded by baseline shifts and more responsive to industrial lobbying.

A better knowledge of marine archeology, which Dr. Pauly appeals for, might help to protect the oceans, and stabilize harvests by understanding the original environments that were sustained across vast sweeps of prehistory. In those ecosystems there was never stasis, but a dynamic balance existed in which everything was linked to something else. When something changed or was threatened the effect was felt elsewhere, like a spider's web sensitive to vibration from the remotest corner of its orb, and return to a more calm and steady state.

John Muir understood this from having planted his feet firmly on the ground he was studying. He wrote, 'When we try to pick out anything by itself, we find it hitched to everything else in the Universe.' This is not a modern revelation and was understood by mystics in the ancient East and West who lived closer to nature than we do. The native wisdom of American Chief Seattle (1780-1866) chimes with modern ecology.

> All things are connected.
> Whatever befalls the earth
> Befalls the sons of earth.
> Man did not weave the web of life,
> He is merely a strand in it.

It is hard to image how the landscape of his namesake city looked before it became a bustling place of concrete, asphalt, and neat gardens, hosting a huge aerospace and silicon industry. Even if we pore over the journals of contemporary explorers, fishermen, and whalers, and especially if we turn back to prehistory by excavating geological strata, former environments challenge our imagination, and there are fewer pristine places to serve as mirrors of the past.

I thought about shifting baselines in my home state of Virginia after perusing Captain Smith's journal and other early records. I knew that most eastern forests are secondary or tertiary growths that are now regenerating after farming and logging started to decline in the late 19th Century. The comforting impression was misleading because I assumed the land would evolve as a facsimile of the original virgin forest, harboring a similar range and abundance of native species if spared further human inference. I dreamt a few centuries hence people might again have the spectacle of huge boles supporting towering canopies as if we never trampled the land. And, moreover, I thought the tiny stands of old-growth forest that remain and are protected by *The Wilderness Act* are perfect examples of the pristine state.

When President Lyndon Johnson signed the Act into law in 1964, he said something that used to strike a chord. "If future generations are to remember us with gratitude rather than contempt, we must leave them a glimpse of the world **as it was in the beginning**..." (emphasis added).

I wish it were true, but I know it is a naïve hope because we cannot turn back the clock to rewild nature without leaving our footprints. Nor, even, are the many wilderness areas so carefully protected by federal offices completely faithful to the past.

When hiking anywhere from the coastal plain to the Shenandoah Valley to the spine of the Alleghenies, I see lots of trees and shrubs that have seeded naturally on former farmland that was originally part of a green canopy stretching to the Mid-West. There are pines, oaks, hickories, maples, hemlocks, and other native species whose return I can celebrate. As a naturalist, I have faith in nature's ability to heal itself, and as someone who cherishes landscape I hope that left to itself a 'natural forest' will claw back, although I won't live to see it. But an old forester scolded my confidence as we sat in a regenerating grove on the Blue Ridge.

He pointed at a invasive tree of heaven I hadn't noticed and reminded me of the kudzu smothering trees and shrubs on the country road where I parked. He told of a battle with introduced species and diseases as well as changes in soil drainage and fertility from past land use that have changed the proportion of natives versus aliens and molded a new norm for the forest. I held too woodenly an optimistic theory of forest recovery that natives will always win because natural selection guarantees an optimal fit to a niche, so no foreigners can withstand them in the end. If only ecology was that simple. If only I had reckoned on the changes wrought by human industry and mischief, and taken account of climate change. I should have considered the analogy that no matter how firmly a human civilization is entrenched with fortresses and weaponry a kingdom can be overthrown by barbarians by craft or superior technology, or even the whims of nature.

We are only satisfied with the appearance of nature if we are blinded by shifting baselines and never imagine the original state. But if we aim for an outcome closer to that state our helping hands are needed for conservation and rewilding, and this is harder when habitats and ecosystems are fragmented and invaded. I had to toss aside an optimistic belief in wilderness taking care of itself to grasp that dramatic action is occasionally required and human fabrications are sometimes beneficial to pluck a kind of triumph out of disaster.

Fire lookout towers standing over forest canopies are monuments to battles fought against the great destroyer, but there is an irony that fire can be wise forestry policy if its extent and location are controlled. There were always wildfires started by lightning or people, but too much fire suppression risks a greater conflagration from burning underbrush in dry western states and holds down biodiversity in forests in other places. Lodgepole pine forests in the Rocky Mountains are an example because their seeds need fire to germinate, and in its absence forest gaps are filled with other species. Across country in the South-east there were vast stands of long-leaf pine, but unless the brush is burned to remove competitors its saplings won't grow into mature trees and offer homes to the rare red-cockaded woodpecker and other creatures that are fussy about their habitat.

Regimented easements for firebreaks, power lines, and pipelines through forests and bush country can provoke local opposition as eyesores, but even they can be a blessing, if a mixed one. Those ugly reminders of violated nature can encourage greater diversity of life. Since sun-loving plants can't survive under a dense canopy the woodland floor offers poor pickings for browsing animals, but where light breaks through a greater variety can thrive. The logging industry is abhorrent to tree-huggers, but when light reaches a formerly shady floor it stimulates a temporary flourishing of wild flowers and wildlife before forest succession if clear-cutting has not caused too much soil erosion.

It is a general assumption in conservation circles that most human interference is pernicious because bad farming practices impoverish the soil and wildlife, dams and mills disturb floodplains and vegetation, and asphalt and concrete bear down mercilessly on the ground underneath. There are, however, silver linings where careful land management promotes natural diversity, and nowhere is this better understood than by people responsible for national and state parks. We only fool ourselves when we think we can restore an original state, or know what it was like.

The American chestnut tree was my blind spot. I could not imagine it gracing eastern states where it was beloved by country folks who dubbed it 'king of the forest.' For a long time, I didn't know what we had lost because I hardly knew it existed until I read Susan Freinkel's book.[22] It provided early settlers with timber lighter than oak yet robust for furniture, roofing shakes, sidings, and fences. The large harvests of sweet nuts were good for eating, and those left scattered on the forest floor were mopped up by hogs for fattening in the fall. The tree had vanished up and down its range by the mid-20th Century after the accidental introduction of a foreign blight. Some four billion trees have gone, and when the few remaining rootstocks thrust out sprouts the blight soon cuts them down. It is hard for those who never saw the 'kings' to picture them flowering and fruiting magisterially almost everywhere, and I admire programs[23] that strive to create a variety resistant to disease for our grandchildren to see.

Captain Smith would have known the chestnut tree, whose nuts may have sustained his fellow colonists at the Jamestown Fort. If we could resurrect him from a tomb in a London churchyard, he would spin yarns about a primeval forest he knew that is foreign to our ears. But it is no good fawning over the loss of old forests that will never come back. It is as futile as when Nick Carraway stared across the water to the green light at East Egg after Gatsby passed, dreading change but wanting to 'beat on, boats against the current, borne back ceaselessly into the past.' Most of our land passed a tipping point long ago, and drivers of change, both human and natural, continue to mold the landscape for its inhabitants. Generations hence may look back in envy at sights we casually enjoy today before we wreak more changes for them, and better informed by history than us they will be less blinded by shifting baselines and hold us in a contempt that President Johnson warned.

IN CANNIBAL COUNTRY

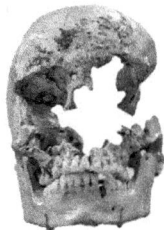

The cannibal nibbled the last scraps on the femur, and cut the juicy calf muscle off the bone. The girl's skull was reserved for last. He cracked it open with a rock to scoop out gray matter on the tip of his knife to taste if it was edible. Left another day, the maggots would have gotten the cadaver, but it was still fresh and would stave off hunger another day. This was not modern plunder of a victim in New Guinea or the Amazon jungle but long ago in Virginia, and a short walk from where I sit.

Archeologists named the teenager 'Jane' when they found her bones during an excavation of the old Jamestown fort. A curator bleached her skull for display at the Archaearium[24] where I jostled one day in a small crowd for a better view of the spectacle. Old bones seldom attract much interest in museums unless they are from dignitaries or devils, but cannibalism is sure to draw attention. As soon as her remains were exhumed, Jane became a historical celebrity, attracting public attention the same year as the bones of King Richard III were dug from under a carpark in the Midlands. His skull was fractured by blows inflicted during a battle that changed English history; a starving man broke hers after she died.

Cannibalism is not so much a forensic as a morbid curiosity, and our absorption grows with knowledge of its circumstances and the identity of the victim and her diner. When we peered at Jane's remains in a glass cabinet we wanted to see the hole in her skull and where it was scraped, because they nourished our fascination and horror. There is the irony that we are repulsed when cadavers are eaten to save life but approve when they are professionally dissected. Is this contrariness because the bodies lying in anatomy halls once gave permission for medical education and research but would never offer themselves for a feast? But I must be careful not to stray into treacherous territory by sounding like an apologist for cannibalism!

Jane made a perilous sea voyage from England around 1609, shortly before the 'Starving Times,' to join the Jamestown pioneer settlement as an indentured servant. The community sheltering in the fort then numbered a few hundred souls and her first winter tested the endurance of poor and privileged people alike. Food stores were exhausted when storms prevented ships from resupplying them, and the colonists of a strange and hostile land had not yet learned how to efficiently grow crops, hunt and fish or forage for food in the woods. It didn't help that relations with Indians turned sour. Barely a quarter of the colony survived to the following summer, and Jane was one of the casualties.

It is hard for us who have never known famine to imagine what it feels like to starve or understand how hunger hollows out character. After the salted pork, chicken, and vegetables were gone, the people were so desperate they ate rats, gnawed boot leather, and looked ravenously at each other and at unburied stiffs like the skinny girl. There was no justification or mercy for the man who killed and ate his pregnant wife. George Percy, who took charge after Captain Smith, recorded their plight.

> And now famin beginneinge to looke gastely and pale in every face that notheinge was spared to mainteyne lyffe and to doe those things wch seame incredible ...

There are other lurid stories from more recent times about the breaking of one of society's most ingrained taboos. The Donner Party is a signature story about the hardships of American pioneer families migrating to new lives in California. Their wagon train was trapped in the Sierra Nevada Mountains in the ferocious winter of 1846-47, and when survivors reached their destination they admitted the bodies of those who died on the way were eaten.

In another tragedy made into the movie *Alive*, an airplane carrying the Uruguayan national rugby team crash-landed while trying to cross the lofty Andes. When aerial search parties failed to find the wreck, the survivors thought they had to surrender to starvation when the paltry snacks in the plane's galley were eaten. To make matters worse, they had no warm clothes for insulation at that frigid elevation. That anyone survived the ordeal of four months and two made it out to find rescuers is a testament to the overwhelming instinct for survival, an instinct that sometimes trumps sensibilities of civilized conduct. They struggled against a natural revulsion to eat their own kind, which was harder because the source was their deceased friends and team mates, but in yielding to it they survived.

Animals have no such scruples, but the motivation to eat their own kind varies. Spiders and mantises engage in 'sexual cannibalism,' bacteria resort to 'stress cannibalism,' and chimpanzees practice 'tribal cannibalism.' You may have seen a parent feasting on its live pups if you kept pet mice or rats at home. A behavior that seems perverse is often a reaction to disturbance or threats, and makes sense to recycle scarce nutrients for a new litter in more propitious circumstances.

Sand tiger sharks offer a stranger story. This is an ovoviviparous species in which embryos are fed inside the mother's body, like a mammalian pregnancy without a placenta. The most advanced babies use precocious dentition to gorge on their siblings before they are born, but what looks like wicked fratricide is more understandable from an evolutionary perspective. Female sharks are promiscuous and the first males to mate are strong, dominant individuals, so their offspring develop in the belly of females ahead of Johnny-come-lately subordinates that become dinner. Thus, the fittest are born, latecomers are selectively eliminated, and nothing goes to waste in the amoral womb.

Human cannibalism is a harder sell, of course, except in dire circumstances where the meal was already dead. In some places it was a custom to gain spiritual power over fallen foes. Observing the Fore tribe of Papua New Guinea, Daniel Gajdusek noticed cannibals paid a heavy price from consuming human brains because some were infected with kuru, a prion disease related to mad cow disease. The risk of disease is greatest when we are exposed to tissue from our own kind, as we know from calamities when blood transfusions and organ transplants transmitted HIV and hepatitis C to recipients.

I have never dined with cannibals but before making solo visits to the Highlands of West Papua (then called Irian Jaya) in the 1990s my friends half-joked I was carrying my fresh meat for 'brutes' to enjoy. It was phooey, of course, and I waved off tall tales about Cannibal Valley told by earlier trekkers boasting to home audiences of their pluck. Years earlier, there were lurid newspaper reports that blamed (some say in error) head-hunters for Michael Rockefeller's disappearance after the Harvard-Peabody Expedition, but the Papuan Highlanders have changed dramatically since the 1960s, except for their poverty.

My first visit coincided with a terrible drought in the Highlands I should have anticipated because it was an El Niño year. As our plane flipped over a mountain range, a small town appeared in the valley below through a haze from small fires burning in the open. A Javanese passenger crammed in the next seat explained in broken English. "People hungry. Smoke make clouds for make rain." The Dani who only connected with the outside little more than a generation ago still clung to traditional beliefs, and they were desperate.

No amount of preparation can prepare a wed-fed man for the sight of profound poverty. On the dusty, dirt street outside the ramshackle airport, there was a slow stream of diminutive Papuan women whose arms protruded like sticks out of smelly rags. They bowed under bundles of firewood or carried string bags of sweet potatoes slung from their foreheads. The men, too, were skin and bone and carried a parang (machete) or a digging stick for cultivating gardens of sweet potato crops that shriveled up that year. Many of the men were traditional dressers wearing only a penis sheath made from a gourd, and sometimes a large leaf covered their rear cleavage. Were these the cousins of Gajdusek's cannibals and close relatives of the fierce warriors Robert Gardner and Karl Heider photographed at that very spot for their book, *Gardens of War*?

There were hundreds of tribespeople dying of famine in the backcountry, but I never heard a story of cannibalism or saw any violence. There was a gracious dignity of endurance in hardship, and later they offered me hospitality with great tenderness. The memories still blaze in my head.

The following day I climbed in the back of a rusty pickup truck to go to the start of a journey on foot into the bush. Two women piled in beside me, the younger one nursing a naked infant in her rags. Her grin revealed orange gums from betel juice to ease toothache. Her companion, who was more my age and I guessed she was her mother, looked forlorn and wasted, her skin stretched tightly over her skull and eyes staring out of dark sockets on a hard world. She had chopped off two fingers on hand and one on the other as traditional signs of mourning, one for every child or spouse lost. The men slice off part of an ear lobe as their sign. I saw numerous amputations, some far worse, which cast thoughts back to home and my family. I wanted to hold the old lady's hand, to share a little warmth of common humanity, but I waited too long wondering whether I should or if I could until the chance was lost. She drew her hands over uncovered breasts that flapped like loosely fitting shoes when we drove over bumps. How did she bear to go on? Did she have a kind of peace I could never understand?

> Poor naked wretches, wheresoe'er you are,
> That bide the pelting of this pitiless storm,
> How shall your houseless heads and unfed sides,
> Your loop'd and window'd raggedness, defend you
> From seasons such as these?
> From *King Lear*, Act 3, Scene IV by Wm. Shakespeare

Lear only knew wealth and power and had to experience for himself the destitution and hunger of his poorest subjects to understand and feel for those who endured them day after day. It's the same for us.

So many years later, memories of the Highlanders are still challenging. If I always knew in my head the only difference between people across the globe is the chance of time and place it was my time with the Dani and Lani tribes that made me take the lesson to heart and reinforce it on a return visit. Through my encounters and first steps toward friendship I realized they had a comportment that I would fail to match if I found myself in the same adverse circumstances, and any morbid curiosity I had about their forefathers' dietary habits was bad taste. We regard eating our own kind as the most monstrous and unforgiveable act, but should abandon this reflex revulsion to comprehend the circumstances. If I had succumbed to the temptation to ask villagers in the back country when they had their last cannibal feast it would have been crass, and why would I except to assert my superiority? If anyone ever asks me about cannibal country I think about Jane and point out the window toward Jamestown Road to tell them, "You're there!"

MY BIG FAT NEANDERTHAL FAMILY

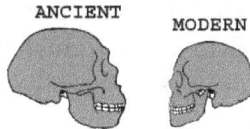

ANCIENT   MODERN

I wonder how long there have been 'others' targeted for discrimination and used as scapegoats? Prejudice has a prehistoric pedigree that seems hard-wired in the human psyche. I submit Neanderthals were the first victims to bear the stigma and endure barbs from our ancestors coming out of Africa thousands of years ago. We still picture them as oafish cavemen thirty millennia after they mysteriously died out.

At least we recognize them as distant members of our human tribe, while ridiculing their long noses, brow-ridges, and prow-mouths. I think we define our prejudicial attitudes and are tempted to deny their humanity because we have so much in common with them in our genomes and anatomy, and look down on them with a special contempt reserved only for other humans. We give apes greater tribute for being noble beasts instead of despised cousins. In looking down our noses at different races of archaic and contemporary humans we are revealing insecurities about our assumed superiority, and the fear of being swamped by the 'others.'

Even some social scientists and anthropologists have from time to time held other tribes and races in very low esteem, if not outright derision and denial of their humanity. There is a dark history of pseudoscience justifying prejudice and persecution from the record of imperialism and eugenics, and there never was a researcher who concluded his own race or gender was inferior in character or intelligence to another, or, if so, he was never published!

That conviction is partly borne out by a conversation I had about Neanderthals many years ago. I was attending a reception for a distinguished British anatomist visiting Edinburgh as an external examiner for our commencement (graduating) class. When the conversation flew from Cabernet and canapés to Neanderthals, I asked him if he thought their slightly larger cranial volume (and brain) meant they were at least as intelligent as us. I was stunned when he denied it was bigger, which I knew as a fact, but a young faculty member won't win an argument with a 'Sir' who is a Fellow of the Royal Society. I try to understand his attitude without justifying it because we are now living in an era when conviction sometimes trumps evidence, and there seem to be fewer people who care about facts. That accusation is deeply wounding for a scientist, of course, and I could have drawn a truce with him if he said the Neanderthal brain is only larger because of a bigger body, but the conversation ended in a sulky silence. I maintain the 'others' might have been our intellectual equals, although I can't see how that can be tested.

Despite bounding progress in recent years, there is still so much we don't know about Neanderthals, and may never understand. Were they nomads or did they live in caves? Did they eat mostly animals or plants or enjoy a mixed diet? Was their culture a monotonous round of hunting and gathering or was it rich in art, symbolism, and mysticism? And did the first great encounter between the two people begin with a handshake and exchange of gifts or with scowling faces and pointed spears? According to an old story still told, when our brilliant ancestors arrived late on the scene the dim Neanderthals were doomed. We flatter ourselves. But such are the triumphal tales of conquest over native people in the name of civilization and religion, and assumed superiority was ever the rude and cruel excuse for abuse.

Among so many historical records of abuse, I will choose one as an example of attitudes toward aliens when they are first encountered. For the first expedition of H.M.S. *Beagle*, the young aristocratic officer Robert FitzRoy was promoted to ship's master after his predecessor fell into a deep depression and shot himself. While he was surveying Tierra del Fuego at the southern extremity of South America, he ordered the crew to take hostage two adults, a boy and girl from a band of natives after they tried to steal a small boat. He treated them well on the return voyage, which I assume was against their will, and arranged to teach them his language, instruct them in his Christian faith, and dress them to look English like him for presenting at the Royal Court.

They were sensations at home and regarded as wild curiosities, but to his credit FitzRoy wanted to return them to their homeland and at his own expense. An opportunity presented when the Admiralty commissioned him for a second five-year voyage, embarking from Devonport in 1831 with Charles Darwin as the ship's naturalist. As soon as the Fuegians were released, they threw off their clothes, painted their skin again with pigments and reverted to their old customs. These are natural reactions for people who want to reunite with their own community, but the behavior vindicated FitzRoy's belief that a permanent gulf exists between native and civilized people. Savages will be savages, and always inferior to European man.

Darwin too was born into the gentry and accepted contemporary notions of a hierarchy of human races with his own kind at the apex. But there were political differences between the two men, for the captain was a high Tory whereas the naturalist was an old-fashioned Whig or liberal with a social conscience. Charles recorded in a journal his first encounter with free Fuegians in their own land.

> It was without exception the most curious and interesting spectacle I ever beheld: I could not have believed how wide was the difference between savage and civilized man: it is greater than between a wild and domesticated animal, inasmuch as in man there is a greater power of improvement.

He was deeply curious about the tribes he met on his travels and, although acknowledging a pyramid of humanity, he didn't think it was fixed forever and might crumble to a heterogeneous mixture when people are brought out of isolation through education and socialization. Brutes could be dukes. FitzRoy always regarded them as uncouth, but this harder attitude was mild compared to the European colonists who arrived in the next couple of decades. They brutalized the natives, calling them feral and hunting them like wild beasts in spates of genocidal violence. Adding to the horror, the Fuegians succumbed to epidemic diseases to which they had no resistance, and this was the last straw for their society. We don't have the extinction of Neanderthals on our conscience because we have no knowledge of what happened so long ago, but many people think our ancestors had guilty hands in one way or another.

Many years later, Darwin was shown a strange skull recently excavated from a cave in Gibraltar and now exhibited at the Natural History Museum in London. This was the first fossil of an adult Neanderthal, predating by some eight years a specimen in the Neander Valley of Germany which has given the people a name. The general opinion was the skull belonged to a primitive creature from an epoch before our species emerged, but it turned out to be wrong. He chose cautious words that anticipated the difficulty of connecting branches of the human tree: 'Light will be thrown on the origin of man and his history.'

Studies of human ancestry began with fossils, but molecular paleontology is making most of the running today and challenging old assumptions. The bonanza of new knowledge is owing to the remarkable stability of DNA and the extreme sensitivity of the polymerase chain reaction (PCR) for amplifying traces of the molecule from fossilized bones. The Neanderthal genome was mapped and sequenced in 2008. Experts were amazed when they found a 1-4% overlap with modern Europeans and Asians. People with a pure African background have none of it, which implies that the Neanderthal fraction inherited by the rest of us is not a residue predating the split of lineages from our common ancestor (*Homo heidelbergensis*). It was acquired by our intermarriage (call it what you will) with Neanderthals in the Middle East after our ancestors came out of Africa about 50,000 years ago. We coexisted for 5,000 years, giving plenty of time for integration, and although we cannot say how fraught the relationship was, it seems that our Neanderthal heritage arose consensually rather than from sporadic mating with stolen women. It is hard to imagine Neanderthal women carted off against their will from their menfolk who were beefier than today's NFL players. But I digress.

When I sent a specimen of my DNA to a commercial genomics company, it revealed I had inherited a whopping 2.7% from Neanderthals. That is close to average for my ethnicity, and more DNA than I share with my third cousins. The news amused me. It must be 'good DNA' for why otherwise would it have been passed down through 2,000 generations of my family tree. Some segments have persisted longer than others. Some is associated with skin and hair for adapting to a colder climate after our ancestors came out of Africa. We have, however, also clung to Neanderthal DNA linked to some common diseases, although it too may have been beneficial in the past. In lean times, 'thrifty DNA' encouraged more fat storage for survival, but we pay for this former benefit with the modern tendency to diabetes and obesity in times of plenty. Hardly any of their DNA is found in genes expressed our testicles, which suggests we were at the limits of interbreeding.

Our genomes have been drifting apart for thousands of years through the accumulation of mutations and natural selection. After the first cross of 50:50 sapiens and neanderthalensis DNA, back-crossing again and again by preferential mating with our own kind diluted the Neanderthal fraction, eventually stabilizing at a low level in the population from whom we descend.

Of all the puzzles about Neanderthals, intelligence is the hardest to measure and DNA offers limited help, but Victorian phrenologists had no doubts about their theories. Those men trotted around the globe recording dimensions of heads to see if their shapes and sizes predicted the differences they believed to exist in character and intellect of rich versus poor, saints versus sinners, and civilized nations versus primitive tribes. The results were foregone conclusions. Skull dimensions were trustworthy yardsticks to distinguish dummies, who were preponderant in socially disadvantaged groups, from superior minds like themselves, white upper-class males. When Neanderthal fossils were discovered they had another opportunity for skullduggery, and summarized their conclusions in an 1880 issue of *The Phrenological Magazine*.

> The Cro-Magnon skull is superior to the Neanderthal skull in regard to intellectual and moral development ... he was indeed a savage.[25]

I doubt Neanderthals were dim people or any less bright than us, and hope that opinion isn't weaker for sounding politically correct in an age striving to correct old biases. I admit it looks contradicted by the apparent failure of their technology and culture to advance much over eons, but neither did ours until the Agricultural Revolution after thousands of years. I wonder if Neanderthals struck an unconscious deal with nature by opting for a stable and sustainable relationship whereas we spoil the very foundations of everything that sustains us in air, earth, and water. Yes, I think Neanderthals were smart, except when they married us.

The German lion of Darwinism, Ernst Haeckel (1834-1919), deserves much respect for his scholarship that it pains me to dishonor him, but I cannot ignore his low estimation of Neanderthals which he called *Homo stupidus* to distinguish them from our brilliant selves, *Homo sapiens* (literally 'wise man'). His proposal is a study of prejudice, but our cousins had already been given the name *Homo neanderthalensis*, and precedence counts in taxonomy. They are sometimes designated as a distinct species, but I favor the status of subspecies based on our conjugal relationship. The genetic gap was greater than between modern races of humans, but they were inside the fence that defines species by reproductive isolation. Mating between distinct species is rare, and when it happens the offspring are often sterile, like mules and hinnies conceived from horses and donkeys.

Popular images and stereotypes of Neanderthals are now turned upside down. We know they were fair-skinned with reddish hair; they were never strict carnivores but ate a mixed diet and cooked food; they spoke a language instead of grunts to communicate; and they created symbolic art on cave walls and decorated their bodies with images as people still do. Most moving of all are clues they were not emotional icebergs, but

157

expressed tenderness to each other, and the survival of individuals to advanced ages with physical disabilities surely proves they had a family or friends who cared. Finally, their corpses were not casually left to scavengers as animal carcasses are, but given a respectful burial. Were last rites performed by a Neanderthal shaman?

I wish I had this information at the cocktail party with the professor in Edinburgh to condemn the vulgar images in old books. The American paleo-artist John Gurche[26] has made sculptures based on careful studies of the physiognomy of archaic humans, and the profile he created for a Neanderthal man is imposing, almost handsome, even noble.

BADGER BOTHER

Some years ago, I was walking along a trail in a Yorkshire wood when I came across a gang of four in muddy boots and jeans offloading shovels and pickaxes from the back of a rusty gray van. In the back of a pickup truck a bunch of terriers barked furiously, as if I had trespassed on their territory. Luckily, none of them tried to jump the tailgate because the breed has a reputation for nipping the calves of strangers. I guessed their roughneck owners had not brought them for a run in the woods, but as little gladiators for a cruel blood 'sport.'

I could have strolled past and ignored them, or pretended to be disinterested, but on the spur of the moment I decided to confront them, for which my companion later scolded me for being reckless.

"You're not digging for badgers?" I asked a man who gave us a furtive glance from under his flat cap.

When he turned to his mates I guessed he was making a grimace because they grinned back at him. The attitude was meant to make us feel uncomfortable, nudge us on our way, but I stood my ground, looked curious and stared closely at the shovels leaning against the truck. I could not think of another reason why men would give up a Saturday afternoon when Sheffield Wednesday[27] was playing a home game, and there was circumstantial evidence a few steps away. I saw the yawning entrance hole of a badger sett that was obviously occupied because the soil was padded down. I was sure because I have spent hundreds of hours watching badgers since I turned thirteen.

"What's going on?" I urged the man, lowering my voice an octave to impersonate authority. "I hope you aren't planning to set your dogs on badgers."

When he turned, he took a step closer and stretched a broad grin under a ginger mustache. "Heck no! An' what's yer business 'ere? Yer no Tyke?"[28]

I told him the land belonged to a friend who wanted wildlife to be left in peace. It was not true, and I wasn't even sure if it was private or public land. But I spoke with good intent, and there would not be any danger of rebuttal because those types hailed from the city and had little rural knowledge. I should have heeded my companion tugging my sleeve; she was right to worry it was risky to accuse someone of a crime punishable with a custodial sentence. That kind of cruelty has persisted for centuries in England, especially in the north where animal welfare groups say it is rising.

I guessed the baiters would dig out the sett until they reached the blind end of a tunnel where terriers stop the badgers from burrowing away by biting their legs and hide. Exposed in a pit, the spectacle of dogs and badgers fighting provides entertainment as men stand round betting on which will survive the contest. My sympathies are with both species. Dogs are often injured or mortally wounded because badgers are great fighters. Their jaw muscles are attached by tendons to a thick midline crest on their heads, and it is almost impossible to dislocate jaws from articulation in a ball joint under the broad zygomatic arch. Despite a strong and spirited defense, badgers always lose in the end and are dispatched with the edge of a spade across the skull.

I succeeded no more than confusing the men whether I had any business there, or was just a passing busybody. When they went into a huddle, it was our cue to beat a diplomatic retreat. I have read that unsavory badger diggers have attacked people who challenge them, and I dreaded the responsibility of bringing a companion to harm. I left the scene boiling with anger, but the next time I passed that way the sett was still undisturbed, and had a swelling sense of pride that quashed the memory of a gutless retreat.

Eurasian and American badgers are distant relatives that belong to different genera (*Meles meles* and *Taxidea taxus*, respectively). Both are peaceable beasts and powerful diggers that only turn ornery when provoked. Both have black and white striped heads, but I think the British brock is the more handsome of the two. Wisconsinites proudly call their home the 'Badger State,' although the nickname owes more to history than any special affection for the animal. Lead miners were called 'badgers' in the old days because they lived in caves cut out of the hillsides. It wasn't a compliment, but a badger was depicted with a pile of pig lead when the shield of the state's Great Seal was designed.

Badgers have rarely fared well when they encountered our species, but are better off in America than Europe where people have bothered these retiring, harmless creatures forever. Badger baiting has been banned in England since 1835, and the species now has the rare distinction of its own law. The *Protection of Badgers Act*, 1992, prescribes a maximum prison term of six months for interfering with them. They are even hunted for food, which sounds surprising for an animal belonging to a superfamily of polecats and skunks, but palatability aggravates their misfortunes because they are alleged to taste good. Badger hams were served in homes and restaurants in the West Country (even now, but covertly), and in some regions of France *blaireau au sang* is a *sett menu*.

Despite nocturnal habits, badgers are currently getting the limelight because they contract the bovine tubercle bacillus from which they suffer a chronic, respiratory illness. Many other wild mammals are vulnerable to the bacterium, but badgers are disproportionately blamed for outbreaks of tuberculosis in English cattle herds. The first infected badger was reported in 1971, probably after it foraged for earthworms in a pasture grazed by cows exhaling and voiding live bacilli. Since then, outbreaks are all too common and tragic because thousands of cows are slaughtered annually at tremendous economic cost. Fortunately for public health, the epidemic does not threat humans because livestock are tested for TB and milk is pasteurized.

Farmers hold badgers responsible for recycling the disease between cattle and a wildlife reservoir, and successfully lobbied the government to launch a culling program to break transmission. The first cull of thousands of badgers by gassing them in their setts with cyanide came under intense pressure from wildlife groups who marched with banners through villages and lobbied politicians. The policy was switched to shooting by marksmen, but this tactic was criticized because nocturnal animals shot in poor light might be wounded and left to a miserable death. Amateur naturalists organized patrols to rescue night casualties for the care of sympathetic veterinarians.

Public opinion polls reveal badgers are the first or second most popular native animal in Britain, and culling continues to rattle a nation of animal-lovers for whom the species has long been an icon for wildlife conservation. Many people claim the

162

program is an outrageous waste of taxpayer money, estimated to cost £10,000 ($13,000) for every badger killed, which should be redirected to a saner policy. Others point at evidence of only a 16% reduction in bovine TB for eliminating 70% of badgers over wide areas. While the theoretical potential for badger to cattle transmission is undeniable, the nature of the connection is still far from clear. The scale of the program is breathtaking since the government announced a target approaching 50,000 animals by the end of 2017, besides those known to die from road traffic accidents and illegal poisoning. Politicians plead their policy is guided by science as if hoping the authority of that word quashes all opposition. Animal welfare advocates offer their science too. But if controversy rages after huge investments in research on climate change, antibiotics in farming, and renewable energy, it is not surprising the relative poverty of badger research divides people.

Both sides claim science for their side, but politics trumps evidence. The government is accused of bending to the farming lobby, and one ecologist was so exasperated when policy was rolled out from a tiny survey he paraphrased the minister in charge: "It is not scientific, we cannot conclude anything, but it is sufficient for policy." When interviewed by the BBC, the minister deplored badgers for "moving the goalposts," but before John Cleese could rise to lampoon him the Prime Minister replaced the man. Badgers bother the highest in the land.

Although stupidity is no handicap in politics according to Napoleon, I have a few crumbs of sympathy for politicians pulled by farming interests on one side and wildlife activists on the other. The controversy started with Lord Zuckerman's report to the Ministry of Agriculture in 1980, which recommended a culling policy that has only grown more heated over the years. The complexity of a fragmented rural ecosystem combined with the impact of seasonal farming cycles makes the epidemiology of diseases carried by wildlife tough to study. Even when prima facie evidence points to a conclusion, a lack of adequate control data flaws the interpretation.

Consider some examples. In a pilot trial where a slight reduction in local badgers was hailed as the cause of fewer TB breakdowns, a closer inspection revealed the improvement came along too quickly for that explanation, and so unknown factors or whimsical statistics were responsible. In another study, cattle infection was lower at the center of a culling zone than at the periphery, again defending the case for culling. But when a sett falls vacant it is soon occupied by wandering animals that can bring disease to areas where it never existed or was eradicated. In a final example, badgers tracked with radio-collars hardly ever made close physical contact with cattle, which rules out airborne transmission, and since they are fastidious and strict users of 'toilets' they dig in the woods it is unlikely their feces spread disease. That leaves sputum and urine as potential vectors on turf, and this route needs more study.

We are then left with the question of biosecurity. Should pastures be quarantined where a herd outbreak has occurred, and slurry from farmyards and barns never moved to another farm? In districts of England and Wales where greater precautions are taken to protect livestock the infection rates are far lower, which supports the suspicion that avoiding transmission within and between cattle herds is more effective than wiping out the local wildlife. And, yet, culling goes forward relentlessly, and is expanding to more counties.

I admit a personal bias. If you perch in a tree for a fleeting sight of a black and white family gamboling below your heart is won by wild nature. This rare intimacy is more precious for an urban man, but those who never venture into dark woods can enjoy watching the adorable striped faces and shy ways on screen, and are grateful for their reputation for killing vermin.

If a single episode of culling was a proven remedy for removing TB from the island it might be stomached, but the annual massacre of a beloved and beneficial animal mostly free of disease and rarely meeting a cow will continue to inflame the public and drive contempt for officialdom to new depths. A large part of the problem is the divide between town and country which could be closed by farmers considering all the options and wildlife advocates listening to the strains of farm economics. If persnickety beefeaters surrendered their opposition to genetically-modified meat, the introduction of TB-resistant cattle herds from China could be good news for European badgers. But the best hope of ending the war is from investing in a vaccine to immunize cattle and wildlife against TB. A single large capital sum is less expensive than culling campaigns with no end in sight. It will satisfy both parties, and the police will be able to turn their attention from monitoring marches and marksmen to catching badger baiters. Then, as their friend Rat knew, badgers will return to a quiet life.

"Badger hates society, and invitations, and dinner, and all that sort of thing"
From *Wind in the Willows* by Kenneth Grahame

Some of my finest memories are intimate moments watching badgers. They taught me wilderness is any private space where you feel drawn to nature, whether in a wood with its secrets or on the shore with a mysterious ocean washing your feet. This must be experienced to be understood, and no words fully express them, but a late friend who introduced me to the badger world came close in his poem.

A BIOLOGIST IN PARADISE

I found them on a sunlit morning: excavations, deep, industrious.
Endless tunnels; spilling, yawning, all along the boundary hedge.
I must return to see the badgers; shy, nocturnal, so retiring.
Powerful, patient, non-enquiring lovers of obscurity.

Daylight fades and shadows lengthen as I breast the rising ground:
Careful how my footsteps fall; from now on I must make no sound.
All-important wind direction; bluebell-laden, blowing gently;
One place to avoid detection; lee-ward of the badger mounds.

Above, the first star glows, so soon to drown again as pastel moon,
Confident at tree-top height, paints the scene with borrowed light.
A tawny owl on silent wings, floating out from woodland's edge,
Content on smaller, furrier things, ignores me crouching in the hedge.

Deep in shadow, rhythmic murmurs; louder than the whispering trees.
Now the dusky silence shatters; senses reel - a badger sneeze!
Up into the silver clearing; fifteen feet away, no more,
Heavy bodies in procession; leading them, a kingly boar.

With sow and triplet cubs he stands; alert, prepared to bolt for home.
Striped heads weave the scented air; a masterpiece in monochrome.
All is well, the cubs are playing. Parents too, pretend to fight.
Grey mass swirling, bowling over. Joyous cries ring through the night.

Ever closer, tumbling badgers. What price now my hiding place?
Heartbeats pound my shrinking form; the boar and I are face to face!
A life-long second thus, we stare; man and beast, both minds aware
Of ancient memories laid bare to sunder night's enchanted air.

Then, wildly down the bracken slope; badgers fleeing, sore afraid.
Thudding footsteps, ever fainter, echo through the empty glade.
Trudging home through man-made world, no longer does my spirit
sing.
Nature's spell lets loose her hold. Perhaps I hadn't seen a thing.

PERCEPTIONS

From *Badger Watch* in *Various Verses by Gordon Burness*

SCAVENGERS

Scavengers get a bad rap everywhere, even from compassionate writers like Charles Dickens. Along the River Thames with the backdrop of a great modern city, you can see mudlarks searching the muddy foreshore for broken clay pipes and pottery shards or scanning with metal detectors for vintage treasure exposed by the low tide. For Gaffer Hexam and his daughter Lizzie in *Our Mutual Friend* the river made them a living by delivering corpses. The river still carries morbid freight at least once a week, but in Victorian times there was a flotilla of bodies among other garbage floating out of the city, the passage only slowing at the U-bend of the Isle of Dogs before the current flushed everything out to sea.

The bodies of drunks, murder victims, and people who could no longer bear life offered pickings for the Hexams to scavenge, except for paupers with empty pockets. Most of the stiffs were unidentifiable when they were given up to the authorities for burial, but when Gaffer rummaged a corpse one day he found papers that identified it as belonging to a notable man who had gone missing. The law hardly pretended to defend a man at the bottom of the social heap, and scavengers were particularly reviled for living in squalor among thieves and for their foul mouths. So, he immediately fell under suspicion when the body was thought to be a murder victim.

> Half savage as the man showed, with no covering on his matted head, with his brown arms bare to between the elbow on his shoulder, with the loose knot of a looser kerchief lying low on his bare breast in a wilderness of beard and whisker, with such dress as he wore seeming to be made out of the mud that begrimed his boat, still there was business-like usage in his steady gaze.
> A description of Gaffer Hexam in *Our Mutual Friend* by Charles Dickens

The word scavenger originated in Tudor England where a 'skawager' was a loathed customs collector, an occupation more honored today although giving travelers guilty feelings when they exit hastily under the green Nothing to Declare sign at Immigration. The dignity of the word crashed when it was transferred to street cleaners hired to remove waste and carrion dumped by the careless public in thoroughfares. This was an undervalued service until mid-Victorian times when scavengers were at last acknowledged for helping to safeguard public health from vermin and epidemic diseases that periodically swept through the capital.

Growing up in two London boroughs, I remember a scavenger leading an old horse and cart in our street. They were called 'totters' in other parts of the city, but all of them rang hand bells and had sing-song voices: "Rags and bones! Rags and bones!" While the man loaded his cart, we loved to stroke the horse stamping outside our home, its nose flaring a plume of steam and tail flicking flies away. If our wary parents saw us with the ragamuffin we were called indoors.

We had little household waste to offer in the 1950s because of post-war austerity and packaging was minimal. Most of our discards were reserved for the 'dustmen,' known as garbage collectors in America. But we saved choice items for the rag-and-bone man, including the carcass remaining from the Sunday roast joint which we heard could be rendered into soap. It made us wonder if Mom had filled her shopping basket at the International Store with something we had lately eaten. Even modern recycling technology struggles to compete with the miracle of changing kitchen waste into a bathroom product.

In the BBC TV sitcom *Steptoe and Son* which broadcasted weekly from 1962 to 1974, Harold and his irascible father Albert were partners in the trade, although not united in any other way. Harold aspired to be middle class and derided his Dad as "a dirty old man," but his pretensions of respectability always let him down, especially when he tried to impress girlfriends he brought home to the rag-and-bone yard. Albert never dreamed of a better life, and never understood his son's dissatisfaction with the one he had always known. The parody was hilarious, if cruel to the dwindling number of men in the trade, and the theme successfully crossed the Atlantic to become the series *Sanford and Son*. The Millennial Generation will find the episodes weird because scavenging for a living has disappeared after four centuries, and the last London collector went to his rest in 2007.

Animal scavengers have the same unenviable reputation as rag-and-bone men. Hyenas, raccoons, rats, flies, dung beetles, et cetera are all vermin, and, although avian scavengers are more generally loved, vultures are especially loathed.

When we see vultures riding the thermals, tipping to one side and then the other, dexterously using finger-like primaries extended from broad wings, they are greater masters of the air than any acrobatic stunt flier. We marvel how they catch the rising draft or slightest breeze even on a calm day. They look like aerial actors flying for the joy of pleasing an audience, even though we know the act is their way of life. To watch their largest relative hanging on a ten-foot wing-span over 5,000 feet of space above the Grand Canyon, is a memory to savor long after the vacation, no matter that the condor is the ugliest thing with feathers.

In eastern and southern states, kettles of black vultures are common sights. As they spiral in thermals, their sharp eyes scout the ground for carrion, while turkey vultures make solo patrols across the countryside using their acute sense of smell to catch the faintest whiff of a meal from hundreds of feet aloft. Where the turkey vulture dives, blackies soon follow. They are the more sociable of the two, but both are intelligent like the carrion-loving family of crows, and both are reviled. The sight of their naked heads bobbing in and out of the gore of a rotting carcass is so much more revolting than the look-alike heads of wild turkeys as they scour leaf litter for seeds and insects. Baldness is not a macho sign in birds, but it makes hygienic sense for these diners and helps to keep cool heads on hot days. Vultures look scuzzy after a meal and fly to a perch to preen because they are fussy about their toilet and their lives depend on a well-ordered and oiled plumage. But what looks and smells wholesome to them is odious to property-owners who have roosts near their homes.

Still known as 'buzzards' by non-birders, vultures are more abundant since they have been protected from unlicensed shooting by the *Migratory Bird Treaty Act* after 1918. They have spread north of the Mason-Dixon Line, even breeding in Canada. This drift is another portent of climate change, but their population growth is encouraged by a food source that hardly existed a century ago.

White-tailed deer in eastern states have boomed from about half a million in 1900 to 15-20 million today. Many of them browse in suburban gardens and public parks close to streets and highways, and roadside verges offer a tender crop of greens that is absent in shady woodland. When an eight-point buck recently visited our yard at dusk it skipped over a fence to dart across the highway followed by a line of seven antlerless deer, causing brake lights to flash on urgently and bring other traffic to a crawl. The Highway Traffic Administration records 1.5 million vehicular accidents involving deer every year, involving 150 human fatalities and 10,000 serious injuries, plus a billion dollars in property loss. The statistics came home when a car driven by two young family members was totally wrecked after hitting a deer at dusk when animals move to feeding areas. The memory of the bloody corpse continues to distress the pair.

By the time a highway maintenance crew comes to dispose of a deer carcass it is often nibbled to bare bones. Vultures are usually the first to arrive for a feast, boldly standing by their meal while cars whizz close by and seldom become road-kill themselves. Crows follow them, and when the birds retire for the night raccoons and opossums devour the remaining scraps of meat. Vultures and their allies are unwelcome visitors to landfills and dumpsters behind schoolyards and shopping centers, but remember their services are provided *gratis*.

While they have prospered under the protection of law, vultures are not faring well in India and Pakistan, and some species are endangered. Their populations and some of eagles have crashed by up to 98% from consuming carcasses of livestock treated with the anti-inflammatory drug diclofenac. It is banned for veterinary use in many countries, including India where people miss the scavengers and hope the big birds will bounce back.

173

Carrion makes an ideal culture medium for pathogenic bacteria normally destroyed in the gut of vultures, and when those scavengers are absent it is eaten by feral dogs and rats which become disease carriers and bugs surviving the passage to excretion spread rabies, anthrax, brucellosis, plague, and dangerous strains of *E. coli*. Animal bites have become more serious hazards for farm workers and children, and when carcasses are uneaten and left to rot they add to human misery by contaminating drinking water. For the Parsi descended from Persian Zoroastrians there is another reason to mourn because vultures have traditionally consumed the remains of deceased relatives on Towers of Silence at their cemeteries.

We might expect the foul habits of scavengers would disqualify them as symbols of a nation, but the American bald eagle prevailed despite a liking for road-kill, which they may share with vultures. Benjamin Franklin wrote his daughter Sally to express disappointment when the eagle was chosen for the Great Seal of the USA in case its lazy reputation compared to the loyal and courageous wild turkey tainted American character.

> For my own part I wish the bald eagle had not been chosen the representative of our country. He is a bird of bad moral character. He does not get his living honestly...too lazy to fish for himself... (but) the turkey is in comparison a much more respectable bird, and...though a little vain and silly, a bird of courage, and would not hesitate to attack a Grenadier of the British Guards who should presume to invade his farm yard with a red coat on.

If the behavior of the baldie makes them a dubious symbol for America, the British lion is another national embarrassment. Many top predators—lions, tigers, white sharks, and even piranhas—will eat carrion given an opportunity because it saves energy from hunting for fresh meat. Our prehistoric ancestors would have few qualms about carving left-overs from the prey of carnivores, and this writer is not embarrassed to admit enjoying the occasional ring-necked pheasant found still warm and intact in country lanes. It seems a pity to leave a corpse to other scavengers when it can be roasted with chestnut stuffing. This brings me back to our species, which is not only responsible for most carrion and waste but is trying to be a reformed character as a top recycler.

Junkyard Planet is a history of the recycling trade written by Adam Minter, the son of a Minneapolis scrap dealer. The humble rag-and-bone trade that died with Alf Masterton, the last professional scavenger in London, has evolved into a vast, billion-dollar industry through canny businessmen who know that one man's trash is another man's treasure. Minter celebrates the global trade in which the maw of modern technology reduces mountains of garbage and junk to saleable products, provides employment to many and makes millionaires of a few. It has dirty hands, but they sanitize a prodigal society.

In Dicken's novel, the corpse that Gaffer fished out of the murky Thames was not an ordinary catch of the day but the heir to a fortune made by his estranged father from collecting garbage on London's streets. The story circles back on itself, like the recycling industry it portrays, and it reminds me of an old saying that still rings in the north of England: 'Where there's muck there's brass.'[29]

CANDID ABOUT CATS

When a gray cat started prowling in our yard I assumed it was a new neighbor. I was wrong because she was a new resident.

I stumbled on her den by chance as it sheltered under shrubbery against the side of our house. After she scooted away from under my feet, I noticed the litter of three tiny kittens lying in a warm cup of fur and dry grass. I guessed from their opened eyes they were over ten days old, but not much more. The cutest kitty was tabby, another was black as soot, and the third was gray like her mother. She had chosen a safe place to nurse them, and didn't leave a trail in ground cover to attract the attention of our dogs.

I called a non-profit rescue service and a couple of hours later a lady parked her SUV in our driveway and got out to rummage in the back. She was lifting out a pet carrier and trap when I walked up. I greeted her with the smile I would give a heating engineer if my furnace broke down in a blizzard. She told me she had calls to rescue abandoned cats most days and at all hours of the day, so collecting the family in my yard was routine. There was something about her demeanor that showed a passion for this unpaid work, and I guessed none of her furry charges are treated as just routine.

The queen cat was away from her den when we checked, but the ball of kittens was still huddled inside and didn't object when we gently lifted them in the carrier. But how would we catch their mother? She was needed for at least another couple of weeks until they were weaned. We had to play on her instincts because she was too shy to be enticed back while we stood there, and was much too wild to catch in our arms.

I watched while the lady set the trap back-to-back with the carrier in which she lay the kittens, and then draped a cloth over both except for a small opening at the entrance. The hungry babies made whimpering cries that she would surely hear, and her maternal instinct would overcome any anxiety she had about the strange new circumstances. As soon as she stepped on a pedal inside the trap the door would harmlessly spring closed behind her. I waited indoors to listen intently beside an open window while the lady drove away for another charitable mission.

After three hours and a couple of beers, there was no sound and it was getting late. So, I stepped out in the gloaming and carefully peeled off the drape. I almost fell back at an explosion of snarls through the wire. The queen was a good mom and had returned quickly and too stealthily to be noticed. It was pitiful, though, to see her frustrated at the loss of freedom and unable to reach her kittens. I called the volunteer despite the late hour, hoping the family would soon be reunited in a large crate at the rescue center.

After we loaded the family in her car I asked what would happen next. The kittens would be offered for adoption after health checks and vaccination. Wouldn't they be too wild to live indoors? *No!* Despite a rude start in life they would turn into fine, domesticated pets and their feral origin would not leave a scar on their behavior.

What about their mother? Surely, no one would take her? She couldn't be tamed, and was in poor health after struggling to live outdoors. Would she be euthanized after weaning her litter, I asked in a faint voice? *Probably not!*

The lady watched my eyes narrow in the porch light as she explained the policy with a sigh.

A vet would check the cat over, give medication for any external or internal parasites, and test for rabies and feline leukemia virus. If either test came back positive she would be destroyed, but in the event of being clear of infection, which was more likely, she would be spayed and vaccinated. Then, the cat would be released where she came from.

"Oh no … not in my backyard!" I exclaimed silently to avoid offending the kind lady. I was horrified to think the feral cat would be lurking in my garden again, and imagined it stalking the wild birds I encourage to my feeder.

Many animal rescue organizations around the country have accepted the 'trap-neuter-return' policy. It eases our collective guilt for betraying creatures that were domesticated to serve our need for companionship, and are too often rejected or abandoned by their owners, and sometimes cruelly maltreated. You don't have to be an ailurophile to be moved by images of furry faces staring through the bars of a shelter with faint chances of adoption. Everyone should be appalled that millions of pet animals are euthanized for the lack of love and a safe home. Only a heartless person would carelessly dispatch them without trying to find a caring home, unless they have a serious disease or injury or are in pain at the end of their natural span.

Some people think it is unconscionable to kill any feral animal or its semi-wild litter if a shelter is available or it can be returned to a safe and familiar place—like my backyard. They should have better feelings for our beautiful native bobcat which trappers can legally take in Virginia up to a dozen every year for making pelts. Ironically, their best allies now are commercial forces because demand is depressed in Russian and Chinese markets where most of our furs go.

There are people on the other side of the argument who urge municipal authorities to cull every feral cat that is unclaimed, and exhort owners to keep their pets indoors. Animal control officers quickly mop up stray dogs from the street because the public dreads the risk of aggressive animals or rabies, and, besides, dogs don't thrive when they go solo. Cats receive little attention from these wardens because they are regarded more benignly, and for the much more important reason that many owners encourage cats to roam free. They return for food and shelter when they choose, and fend for themselves outside as long as they want.

One point of agreement between opposing camps is to encourage responsible ownership and sterilize all animals, except those that stay indoors or are selected for breeding. Otherwise, the differences between them are unresolved, and the number of feral and stray cats continues to rise.

I understand that to slaughter unwanted animals reared for our companionship looks treacherous. To be consistent, we ought to have farm animals on our conscience for they are sentient creatures too, if owning less intelligence (pigs excepted). The line drawn between species we choose to share our lives and those we like to eat is not sharp, and we prefer not to dwell on the difference, although sentimental feelings easily wander to feral and wild animals when they are cute or cuddly. Growing up on a literary diet of *Wind in the Willows* and *Watership Down* can leave faint echoes of animal sensibility later in life. When I found the feral family in our yard I was conflicted as a pet owner on the one hand and as a naturalist on the other. But the volunteer from the rescue squad never dithered about the right course of action, because she fervently believed life is always better than the alternative.

When I protested the cat would menace our wild birds, she replied: "For every 50 mice, voles, and baby bunnies brought home by my cats they only catch one bird."

Few people mourn the elimination of rodents, but bunnies? Had she read *Watership Down*? There are, of course, many reasons why she might believe her cats are more virtuous than others — they prefer fish to red meat, wear bells or are declawed, or the wild birds in her neighborhood have more cover to hide, et cetera. But there is no doubt about the national toll since a Smithsonian survey in the journal *Nature*. Outdoor cats kill 2.4 billion wild birds annually (billions!), including many of our most popular and beneficial species — cardinals, wrens, thrushes, bluebirds, and hummingbirds. In addition, they take 12.3 billion small mammals, which would be more commendable if rats, our Number 1 enemy, weren't taken mostly by birds of prey, snakes, and canids. Feral animals and strays were responsible for more than half of the kills, for they must hunt to eat, but domesticated cats that can't curb a hunting instinct even with a full belly took the rest. This stunning scale of slaughter is a major reason why common birds are declining across continents, and helps to account for the extinction of several dozen species. The impact of cats and other non-native predators on native marsupials and flightless birds in Australasia is even better documented.

The threat to so many native species is a powerful reason to keep pets indoors. Animal welfare is another matter for feral animals living in a shadow land between domestication and wild nature. Cats have evolved less than dogs from breeding selection, but their behavior is no longer well-adapted for life in the wild and far from their native range. When cats wander outdoors, they step toward jeopardy, whether it is an urban or rural district. The pitiful sight of a feline corpse lying by the highway is the most obvious reminder, and cats fitted with 'Kitty Cams[30]' in suburban Georgia reveal the breadth of hazards they face when roaming. The lives of semi-wild cats are even riskier, and much shorter. They are burdened with parasites, hunted by canids and some people, exposed to wild weather and the threat of starvation, and lack any humane care. Pictures of condemned animals in shelters pull at our heartstrings, but there are millions of others in our cities and woods that suffer and perish unseen.

It is hard to draw a mental boundary between feral animals visiting our yards and Fluffy on the couch because they look alike, have indistinguishable genomes, and, as my visitor assured me, even kittens born in the wild make wonderful pets. So, there was prejudice when I counted the life of the queen in my yard inferior and wanted her terminated. Call it catism. It awakes some uneasy thoughts and memories that take me back to childhood.

Like many curious kids, I wanted to know if animals have souls and asked if pets go to heaven. Neither a priest nor any grown-up offered a satisfactory answer, and now as an adult I never think of the question. Perhaps I should. We are most idealistic in early childhood when the world looks more black and white before knowledge and experience teach us otherwise. It was sentimental feelings about animals that prompted my question, and I pondered if they have a soul (even if I couldn't define it) because that premise would settle my vegetarian leaning and other uncertainties I was wrestling with at the time. I didn't plunge into Aristotle's *Ethics* at age 8, course, and perhaps I should because he admitted they have a soul, and who am I to challenge? He placed the animal soul on a second rank far below the rational human soul. His pupil Theophrastus vehemently disagreed, but failing to prevail in history the anthropocentric philosophy of Aristotle was passed to us via Thomas Aquinas. But as a child I remained confused.

In *The Problem of Pain*, C.S. Lewis argues that pets might be 'ensouled' through the believer's relationship to God. This theological speculation is not so wildly alien on second glance because science regards us as merely the latest model in organic evolution, or, in other words, part of a continuum of life. Where do we draw a line between animals and humans, and should it be on the evolutionary track of intelligence or sentience? For my part, I only own deeply speculative metaphysical inklings that admit relationships with animals will always be profoundly mysterious. I think scientists should admit this as humbly as the writer Henry Beston.

> We need another and a wiser and perhaps more mystical concept of animals ... man in civilization surveys the creature through the glass of his knowledge and sees thereby a feather magnified and the whole image in distortion.
>
> From *The Outermost House*

Lewis was more confident in his beliefs. He wrote, 'in so far as the tame animal has a real self or personality, it owes this almost entirely to its master. If a good sheepdog seems almost human, that is because a good shepherd has made it so.' I, too, wonder if the ineffable bond between owner and pet lends the animal a deeper sense of its own self than its cousins could ever have in the wild state. Until recently, most animal behaviorists denied that even apes have much self-awareness, much less sub-primates, but I think they must give way in the light of their research. I expect our estimation of animals will continue to rise.

To suggest our pets can become self-conscious is to skate on the thinnest ice, and puts me at risk of being called anthropomorphic, which is the cruelest epithet for a biologist. The ice may never support the weight of argument, or maybe it will grow thicker from research, but I will always wonder if our brainier companions have snippets of what people mysteriously mean by a 'soul.' If so, animals can experience some kinds of mental states and suffering that were often claimed to be our own, such as feelings of joy and grief. There is something inside us that wants to believe, no matter how apocryphal or contrary to reason, the stories passed to legend that attribute great feelings to animals, like Hachi who waited for nine years at a Japanese railway station for his dead master to return, and Bobby who guarded his master's grave at Greyfriar's Church in Edinburgh for longer. Cats are less obviously attached to their owners than dogs, although being more reserved by nature they would never admit they can mourn!

If some animals have any sense of self, if very shallow compared with ours, it is developed by domestication and enriched by experience. Without a herd or pack to shape behavior and reinforce ancient instincts, an intelligent pet focuses on its master and absorbs some of that character, for good or ill, and then acquires a new capacity for suffering physical and mental pain that is absent in wild relatives or those tamed after they have lost juvenile plasticity.

Some years ago, we adopted a young stray cat, calling her Thursday after the day she was found outdoors looking hungry, skinny, and bedraggled. She lived with us like a pampered princess for 14 years, and for half of her lifetime in a Fifth Avenue apartment in Manhattan with celebrity neighbors. It was my wife's compassion that brought her home, but Thursday never returned our affection or lost the aggressive streak that helped her to survive as a street cat. I had scratches to prove it. I don't think she ever had a soul! Unlike the kittens we rescued from our yard in Virginia, she was already too old to be imprinted by human kindness. Rescuing her from the street saved bird lives and stopped unbridled breeding, but it never made a civil cat out of her to deserve a place in feline heaven on our sofa where a more beloved puss, John Henry, used to reign. All cats are cats, but not all cats are equal.

When the animal rescuer called a few weeks later, we heard the gray queen had been difficult to manage and ferociously attacked her handlers. She was a good mother when we found her but was now ill-disposed to her kittens, and they had to be separated. Although a wild cat, she received the same treatment as others in the shelter, and her life was spared when viral tests reported negative. She was then spayed. We presume she was released in our yard, but were not given any warning when to expect her. I hope my wife does not sneak out with a bowl of milk to encourage her, because if I see that cat prowling around I will feel prejudicial.

THE DANCE OF THE LOBSTER

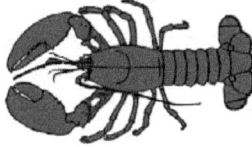

There was only one lobster left in the tank when I left the restaurant. I was sorry for the lonesome crustacean, but not as sad as I felt for its late companions. Their empty carapaces lay upside down on customer plates for the waitress to take away and unceremoniously scrape into a trash bin. I had no cause to look at them guiltily because I had steak on my plate and didn't have to look a cow in the eye on the way out, but somewhere in the depths of memory the tortured voice of a lobster was calling from 'Wonderland.'

"'Tis the voice of the Lobster", I heard him declare,
"You have baked me too brown, I must sugar my hair."
As a duck with its eyelids, so he with his nose
Trims his belt and his buttons, and turns out his toes.
When the sands are all dry, he is gay as a lark,
And will talk in contemptuous tones of the Shark.
But, when the tide rises and sharks are around,
His voice has a timid and tremulous sound.
From *Alice's Adventures in Wonderland* by Lewis Carroll

The Lobster in Alice was a spineless coward, but on a restaurant menu he can look like a monarch beside more plebian fare. The culinary emperor is Lobster Thermidor, a stately dish for special occasions that challenges a chef's skill and empties the customer's pocketbook. In the upside-down world of the Monty Python troupe it was served in a seedy café and crowned with enough spam to offend the most easy-going lobster:

> *Mr. Bun:* What have you got, then?
> *Waitress:* Well there's egg and bacon; egg, sausage and bacon; egg and spam … spam … spam… etc. … or lobster thermidor aux crevettes, with a mornay sauce garnished with truffle paté, brandy and a fried egg on top and spam.

The word thermidor was not coined for a hot dish but traces back to a day in 1894 when a Parisian restaurant served a special lobster dish to celebrate the opening of *Thermidor* by Victorien Sardou at the *Comédie Française*. The play was named after a summer month in the French Republican calendar when Robespierre was toppled, and the Reign of Terror was ended. For lobsters, however, the word still conveys high terror. For me, it summons an image of peering through steam over a cooking pot at an armored creature dancing in bubbling water with quivering antennae.

> There's a porpoise close behind us, and he's treading on my tail.
> See how eagerly the lobsters and the turtles all advance!
> They are waiting on the shingle – will you come and join the dance?
> Will you, won't you, will you, won't you, will you join the dance?
> From the Mock Turtle's Song from *Alice's Adventures in Wonderland* by Lewis Carroll

I wonder if it is cruel to cook crustaceans alive. It is a question that has hovered around boiling point for a long time, and the answer depends if we think animals can feel pain.

If Alice's Lobster said hot water hurt, would she be any wiser by comparing the sensation of plunging her own hand into a bowl of scalding water? Pain is a subjective experience that is not shared with other people like the five senses. The sensation of stroking a cat or watching the sunset or listening to a rock band or smelling the roses or tasting an apple can all be conveyed to another person with a fair degree of confidence they will understand. And if descriptive nouns and adjectives fail, there are similes to help. It might be explained to them, for instance, that the object was like the color of the sun, for an orange, or sounded like a trumpet, for a bugle.

Pain is a private experience for which we only have the crudest measures and no absolute standards. When a nurse asks patients to estimate surgical pain on a scale up to 10 everyone understands 0 is the absence of pain, but how can we know in any objective sense what intolerable pain at the top of the scale means to another person, or compare numbers in between? The scale is valuable for monitoring the degree of analgesia, but it has no absolute meaning. And, moreover, if a hot poker or traumatic injury hits the top of the scale is it experienced variably and, if so, do differences in perception or stoicism account for the gap?

Pain is pain, but it is not all the same. It can be acute or chronic, physical or psychogenic, nociceptive or neuropathic, somatic or visceral, localized or referred. There are gating mechanisms and subtleties in synaptic transmission that affect signal conduction up the spinal cord for processing and perception in the brain, and thus to consciousness of a noxious stimulus and its location in the body. My curiosity about modulating pain perception without drugs was stirred when I met an acupuncturist in Hong Kong and I volunteered to test if it worked. While he was needling my meridians, I was thinking how we rub a bruised knee to make it feel better after a fall. Do they both work by swinging neural gates open or shut: when I can comprehend a mechanism I accept claims more easily?

Pain is in the brain and not where it feels at the site of origin. We may say we share someone's pain, but we can only extend empathy and hope our care will make them feel a little better and less isolated in their misery. If it is such a puzzling subject to convey between people, how can we grasp pain in animals?

Pain is physiological as well as psychological, and verges on the philosophical. René Descartes regarded animals as mindless robots which, ipso facto, cannot experience pain. This view is neither humane nor enlightened, and has been used to justify animal cruelty, but a generation earlier the French philosopher Michel de Montaigne held animals in more humane regard:

> There is a certain respect, and a general duty of humanity, that attaches us not only to animals, who have life and feeling, but even to trees and plants. We owe justice to men, and mercy and kindness to other creatures that may be capable of receiving it. There is some relationship between them and us, and some mutual obligation.

There are opposing views of varying intensity about animal sentience down the centuries, but mostly little action to protect animal life. In a nation portrayed as animal lovers, British anti-vivisectionists campaigned for a law against animal cruelty as long ago as 1876. It mandated anesthesia for experimental surgery and protected animals in other ways. The benefits were only afforded to vertebrates, leaving lobsters, octopuses, and their tribes of armored crustaceans and smart mollusks to the whims of laboratory and kitchen practices. There were earlier bans on bear-baiting, badger-baiting, and cockfighting, but gin trapping of fur-bearing animals and hunting with hounds continued into the next century (and still are legal in parts of America).

As a physiologist I could be regarded as an apologist for animal experimentation, but in defense of my specialty I like to point out that biological discoveries have often leaned into greater care. The old dichotomy of 'them' versus 'us' began to fall away when we understood that apes are our cousins, and the gap has continued to shrink as we learn about animal physiology and behavior, and especially by differentiating intelligence in kind from intelligence in degree. Wolf behavior, eye and brain of octopuses, and brainpower of bears are some examples where research has acknowledged greater sophistication in nature than we used to admit. There ought to be more humbling respect for animal lives, pushing-back against careless or cruel treatment with stricter protection and compassion for suffering in more than our pets.

The science of life is still young. If thousands of researchers still wrestle over the nature of human consciousness, how can we expect to know what a lobster feels? More bluntly, will science ever interrogate the feelings of any animal? Are we sure lobsters can never be happy or feel pain, or will the debate be drawn to a truce in semantics? The lobster's 'brain' consisting of a string of ganglia has changed little and served it well since our common ancestor 500 million years ago while our lineage immensely elaborated the organ. The difference in scale and organization is beyond a concise description, but there is no basis for assuming a large cerebrum is required for feeling pain. All creatures down to microscopic sizes have behavioral repertoires for repulsion from harm. Pipet drops of acid near an amoeba and it moves away; cut a worm and it wriggles; immerse a lobster in hot water and it dances. Animals are wired to avoid new threats and evade familiar dangers, except for the occult perils of ionizing radiation. Whether we call them pain responses is a matter of definition although the behavior is obviously adaptive and beneficial. The rare condition of congenital analgesia puts patients in harm's way because pain stimuli don't provoke withdrawal reflexes to protect them from repeated injury. Pain is weighed according to circumstances: good when it helps survival, and bad if it causes suffering. The moral line for causing pain is drawn by sentience, not intelligence, and we struggle to rate it in lobsters.

The late Julia Child was a celebrity chef and a kindly-looking woman who merrily taught millions of TV viewers how to boil lobsters alive. I am sure she would be horrified if research revealed her recipe was torturing them. Doubtless she would then advise us to humanely dispatch them by jabbing a knife behind their eyes to the brain before cooking. It is a small concession that doesn't need the endorsement of science to change practices because red lobsters taste the same however they meet their fate.

The Australian philosopher Peter Singer who wrote the influential anti-vivisection treatise, *Animal Liberation*, challenges our complacent attitudes to the suffering of animals, including lobsters. He wrote, 'So even if there is some room for doubt about the capacity of these animals (crustaceans) to feel pain…they should receive the benefit of the doubt.' I don't agree with every pronouncement, but I salute his cautious attitude and ethical consistency. On the only occasion I was at dinner with him, I remember he ordered a vegetarian dish from the menu and there was no lobster tank in the restaurant he chose.

PART IV. VICTUALS

A GRAIN OF EXPERIENCE

S cience is giving refined carbohydrates a bad name, and after a half-century of condemnation it declares saturated fat is not so bad after all. Official dietary recommendations are moving targets for diners. I accept the general advice to cut down on carbs and fat, but still praise a loaf of bread.

The old dogma 'good carbs/bad fats' was turned upside down long before *The Big Fat Surprise* by Nina Teicholz. She argues carbs are not the virtuous fillers we were encouraged to replace the calories surrendered from fatty foods. It is hard, though, to resist a slice of crusty bread with a pat of butter which have accompanied meals for as long as I can remember, and, yet, there are plenty of people besides those with celiac disease who are giving up wheat bread. The last time I perused bookshelves at Barnes and Noble they were bowing under the weight of *Grain Brain*, *Grain-Free Gourmet*, *The Paleo Diet*, *No More Grains*, and other critiques of carb-laden foods and the staff of life.

No one knows when people started to eat wild cereals, although prehistoric tribes gathered them in forest clearings and grassy steppes long before they were cultivated for food. Acute intolerance to wheat antigens, usually meaning gluten, emerged no later than biblical times according to archeological evidence, and said to be a modern epidemic. The Mayo Clinic reports celiac disease is four times more prevalent than 60 years ago, an explosive increase that cannot be explained simply by undiagnosed cases in the past.

There is also a glutinous tide of non-celiac intolerance to wheat, although much of the evidence is anecdotal and controversial. The symptoms were easily dismissed as ambiguous or psychosomatic before laboratory tests were available, but the condition gains leverage as the medical profession becomes familiar with its presenting symptoms and more patients seek relief. It involves much larger numbers of people than celiac disease, and up to 6% in some population surveys. The symptoms resemble irritable bowel syndrome, which I leave to your imagination and rumor. New strains of wheat are blamed for celiac and non-celiac intolerance in much the same way as the modern environment is charged with the rise of asthma, hay fever, eczema, and other allergies. We are right to ask why they were less common in our grandparents' day, and science struggles to understand how our immune systems cope with change.

The genetics of wheat plants have dramatically altered since the first ears of wild ancestors were plucked by people. They have been hybridized, polyploidized, and cloned. Wheat and barley fields, still called 'cornfields' in Britain, even look different to when I roamed the countryside as a lad. The stalks are taller, the planting is denser, and hedges have been torn down to maximize crop acreage. There is an unnatural dearth of weeds, the red poppies that jollied the fields are gone, and I no longer hear partridges or see charms of goldfinches flitting over nodding ears of cereal. The changes started accelerating after my teen years when Norman Borlaug and other agronomists launched the

Green Revolution. Crop yields boomed from 'improved' plant genetics after selective breeding and, more recently, from GM technology while the chemical industry produced more potent fertilizers, weed-killers, and pesticides. GM glutens may have increased some allergies, but there have been so many shifts in the food industry between the fields and store shelves it is hard to unravel candidates for blame, and a mistake to assume one is the cause of all ills. We cannot turn the clock back to eat what our grandparents enjoyed, although some of us go against the grain with home experiments.

When I dust off my bread machine to make another loaf, I use 'strong' flour for the high protein needed to preserve a bubbly structure during baking. The experimenter in me wanted to test an old variety of wheat to see what kind of dough and loaf it made. I chose einkorn. It is an ancient grain, even older than spelt or emmer, and thought to be grain's great, great grandma. To make the experiment more authentic, I put the machine aside to knead the dough by hand. That may not make a better loaf, but the exercise was rewarding.

The name einkorn, meaning 'single grain,' suggests a native of Germany or Switzerland, but in fact it comes from the Levant, and, since it wasn't adulterated by cross-breeding with another plant, I call it a virginal grain. The first farmers prized it because cultivation saved time from harvesting wild cereals, but when higher yielding crops from other seed plants were adopted einkorn disappeared from the table. It is attracting attention again from curious cooks and bread-lovers looking for something new and agreeable to the gut. A grain uncontaminated by foreign genes is not necessarily more digestible because einkorn is not completely free of gluten, and celiac symptoms can recrudesce in people who eat it. It is a complicated story still being written.

Gluten is a family of proteins, not a single molecule, that 'glue' the structure of loaves to prevent collapse during cooking and cooling. Glutens vary between grains and, since the immune system respects specific molecules, one man's loaf can be another's 'poison.'

The Mount Carmel region of Israel was milder and less barren 15,000 years ago than it is today and offered a bounty of grass seeds, fruits, and nuts for nomads to gather back to their camps. According to one theory, a drying climate and dearth of wild food plants were responsible for the birth of agriculture to provide food security. The revolution transformed a former wandering life to a more settled existence with immense downstream implications for communities — management of livestock, more division of labor and wealth, and more robbery and violence. Traces of ancient wheat and rye grasses were discovered in caves and underground homes by the English archeologist Dorothy Garrod. She called the Stone Age people who dwelt there 'Natufian' after the Wadi an-Natuf locality where einkorn and a related species, *Triticum monococcum*, were cultivated. They still are grown elsewhere on a small scale.

Einkorn DNA has also been found from dredging a sunken 8,000-year-old Mesolithic site in the Solent, a shallow channel of water between Southampton and my birthplace on the Isle of Wight. The grain was shipped by European traders across a land bridge which persisted after the last Ice Age until rising sea levels cut the island off. The grain trade in those days shows how commerce marched ahead of farm technology; einkorn wheat wasn't grown in Britain for another two millennia.

It is a highly nutritious grain containing more protein and less starch than refined wheat. More granular and fluffier, the flour is rich in carotenoids that give a yellow tinge to the powder. Even before I plunged my fingers into the dough to begin kneading, I never expected the product to look anything like the bubbly *Wonderloaf* in grocery stores, and hoped it wouldn't. I counted on more flavor and better nutrition, and chose a recipe that was simplicity itself. There were only five ingredients in the mixture — flour, water, honey, salt, and dried yeast, plus a tad of Irish butter for good measure. I suspect there was less gluten in the flour because the dough was stickier and less elastic to knead than usual. It needed light handling to avoid overworking.

I wonder what the doyen of French bread-making Raymond Calvel (1913-2005) would think about my experiment. He is credited with restoring the popularity of artisan loaves in his home country and around the world. This is bread made the old-fashioned way that has returned as specialty loaves from small bakeries, and parallels the resurgence of craft beers from microbreweries. Calvel had no polite word for the fluffy stuff made in wholesale bakeries after World War II.

In a classic book that is in print again, *The Taste of Bread*, he called his bread-making technique 'autolyze.' That sounds like the familiar word 'autolysis,' a biological process of enzymic self-destruction of a tissue, but he meant a resting stage before kneading when particles of flour are rehydrated. I followed his recipe. Afterwards, I shaped and proofed the lump and finally dusted it with loose flour before baking for 35 minutes at 350°F. (about 180°C.).

I signaled the verdict with my thumbs-up. The loaf tasted different to any others I made or bought — it was nuttier, denser, crustier, and stored well. Still warm from the oven, I did something a loaf never forgives. I sliced it. When it was spread with a soft blue cheese that melted into the tiny pores it tasted delicious, and never provoked a 'wheaty' belly bloat.

The flour cost more than regular brands but no loaf is expensive, and it is worth an extra dollar if it makes you feel good and might be doing you good. No experiment can be claimed a success, however, until it is repeated. The next time I bake I will add another stage at the beginning. I will mill whole wheat berries to make einkorn flour to take me one more one step back to Natufian roots.

MAKE MEAT SPECIAL

Sometimes I feel carnivorous and occasionally vegetarian, but I am mostly between those poles. This cycle betrays unease with my food choices. I wonder if being even slightly carnivorous is healthy, how much it harms the environment, and if eating meat is 'natural' for us?

I cannot do justice to all those questions in a few pages, but they have been at the back of my mind since I was a child. I only courted vegetarianism briefly and half-heartedly, partly because it was hard for our mom to prepare separate meals for a lettuce-loafer. I felt guilty when there was steak on my plate for dinner, slightly more comfortable when fish was served, and blasé with mac-n'-cheese. There was an ethical pyramid of acceptable foods in my head and I continued to press grown-ups about the justice of killing animals for food, although they steadfastly returned blank looks. I still think they are good questions. If Aristotle's pupil Theophrastus was asked, the Father of Botany would declare it is immoral to eat meat, but a straight answer doesn't satisfy now. Aside from the morality, health considerations and spiritual discipline are paramount for people who choose vegetarianism, but I doubt it is right for everyone, and veganism is a stretch beyond the diet we evolved with.

The argument over meat-eating still hangs in my mind, but more on its impact on the environment and morality than about biology. After people exchanged a nomadic existence with tents for permanent shelters and then villages, new social orders emerged with creeping differentials. Meat was the luxury of rich and powerful families who owned herds of livestock and hunting preserves, and woe betide the peasant who poached venison or rabbit for his family. He subsisted on vegetables and his lucky days were supplemented with an egg or jug of milk. As a rule, the greater the quantity and variety of meat served the greater prestige for the host and the higher the status of his guests. The diarist Samuel Pepys wrote in his journal in April 1662:

> We had a fricassee of rabbits and chickens, a leg of mutton boiled, three carps in a dish, a great dish of a side of lamb, a dish or roasted pigeons, a dish of four lobsters, three tarts, a lamprey pie (a most rare pie), a dish of anchovies ... to my great content.

This was not a wedding banquet or an anniversary dinner. It was merely a feast shared with a few friends, but it took a massacre of farm animals and wildlife to impress them.

Meat is no longer the privilege of the few. Most people eat royally compared with their ancestors, although meat remains a great luxury for the abject poor subsisting on carb- and fiber-rich diets. The remaining bands of hunter-gatherers in the world break the connection between protein poverty and economic impoverishment, because they obtain a larger fraction of energy from animal protein and fat from collecting nutritious insects as well as hunting wild game. It doesn't follow from that example that a diet rich in meat is natural for us, any more than it is a birthright where it has become familiar and abundant. Flesh has become cheap and common fare where livestock are raised industrially and the fishing industry hooks and hoovers shoals of fish. Then animal protein becomes undervalued.

Surveys show Americans consume on average a half-pound of meat per capita every day, although I don't know anyone who eats that much. The statistic is a gross estimate based simply on dividing the population by our national production of meat, and a significant fraction goes to waste or feeds animals. Even after adjustment, the imposing number is a larger fraction for our body mass than compared with bears, badgers, and raccoons, all of them members of the Carnivora. We are far more carnivorous than most members of that order. The taxonomy of the Animal Kingdom is admittedly wonky because carnivores are defined by their butcher teeth, even for species subsisting mostly on vegetarian fare like the above examples. Other animals have been classified by the possession of a trunk, hoof, blow-hole, opposable thumb, et cetera. If molecules were classified in this cavalier way I doubt it would have helped the science of chemistry. We don't have the dentition of the Carnivora (Dracula excepted) but there is no order of Vegetaria or Omnivora to offer us a better fit, and anyway we are comfortably entrenched among the Primates which are defined by a handful of characteristics.

Although the typical diet of a species has little traction with taxonomy, you can tell if an animal is a true carnivore by examining its gut and looking inside its mouth for adaptations to its normal food. A true carnivore has:

a) long canines for grabbing prey and carnassial teeth for shearing meat,
b) a gaping mouth and large throat for swallowing food with little or no chewing,
c) a bulky stomach with very acidic gastric juice to sterilize raw meat,

d) a short small intestine in relation to body size,

e) a small colon.

At the other end of the spectrum, a strict herbivore has:

t) small, stumpy canines and flattened, tightly-packed molars for chewing fiber,

u) jaws that move sideways for grinding food,

v) an enzyme in saliva to start the digestion of starch,

w) a large stomach with one to four chambers,

x) less acidic gastric juice than carnivores,

y) a long small intestine,

z) a voluminous and baggy colon with a cecum for digesting cellulose.

The small intestine in carnivores is less than three times as long as their bodies (i.e., head plus trunk), whereas in herbivores it is ten times the length. The rationale is obvious. A short, simple tube is adequate for rapidly digesting protein and absorbing amino acids into the bloodstream, whereas cellulose fiber takes a long time to break down to its constituent sugar molecules. The rabbit family is a special case because its gut is not long enough to process the fiber in one pass, so it swallows the soft pellets after they are evacuated from the rectum for another round through the system.

The anatomy and physiology of the human gut are closer to herbivores, apart from ungulates which have a specialized rumen for fermentation. We call ourselves omnivores because we have always eaten a mixed diet since our hominid ancestors ate tropical fruits and berries with occasional animal protein, and some of our primate cousins still do. This kind of herbivory is more accurately rendered 'frugivory,' but if our ancestors were hunters as well as gatherers when and where did we start hunting and acquire an appetite for flesh?

The image of Fred Flintstone dining on dinoburgers not only misplaces him in evolutionary history but gives the false impression of carnivorous Stone Age Man. Bringing down large animals with spears, clubs, and chasing them over cliffs was inefficient and dangerous because hunters had to get close to their quarry until they invented bows and arrows somewhere around 60,000 years ago. They were tempted to scavenge carcasses as hyenas do after top predators are sated with their prey. Although hunting pressure combined with climate change are blamed for the extinction of Paleolithic megafauna, red meat was a rare meal until cooking was practiced because we are poorly equipped for chewing and digesting raw meat.

Early humans were locavores who harvested food within walking distance of camp. As they fanned across the world, they had to adapt to unfamiliar foods where different climates supported other fauna and flora. Before hunting big game became efficient, animal protein and fat mostly came from fish, shellfish, bird eggs, and insects to provide essential amino acids, fatty acids, and vitamin B12. Everything changed after herbivorous animals were domesticated some 400 generations ago. New occupations appeared, supply chains were created, and recipes and tastes altered. Moreover, even the composition of meat changed when livestock were confined instead of grazing freely like wild game.

Few species have undergone as rapid an evolution of diet as humans unless they drifted or were blown unintentionally across large bodies of water to foreign soil. It was advantageous for us as omnivorous migrants to be pre-adapted for a broad diet, and if we were strict carnivores or herbivores the human story would be different. But if forced to choose, it is smarter to incline toward herbivory, especially now with teeming numbers to feed. Herbivorous animals are more flexible than carnivores, for even strict grazers like cattle can digest animal protein when it is offered, as we remember from when it caused mad cow disease. Carnivores don't have the gut for plant fiber, except in the allegorical world of Isaiah where 'The lion shall eat straw like the ox.'

We have an adaptable physiology, but it nevertheless constrains us to consume food in modest amounts. For one thing, our stomachs cannot accommodate bulky lumps of meat, and for another they evolved for fruit and green leaves and don't secrete enough acid to kill Salmonella and other bugs in raw food. Moreover, a protein-rich diet puts us at risk of gout, especially individuals with a genetic deficiency in uricase that causes crystals to be deposited in painful joints. Possession of the gene avoids the problem in carnivores, so it was surprising when signs of gout were found in fossilized bones of a *T. rex* at the Cheyenne River Indian Reservation. The explanation may lie in the kidneys responsible for eliminating uric acid from the body because disease in those organs can cause gout in birds.

Meat-eating may have helped people to migrate and follow the retreating Ice Age. The supply of plant food dwindles in the cold north and winter, and nuts and vegetables hoarded in the fall can be spoiled by molds and vermin. Hunting wildlife the year round helped to satisfy appetite and stave off starvation. Native people in the Arctic still depend on meat and blubber from marine and terrestrial animals, and herding sheep, goats, and reindeer offered greater food security, although ushering in a new kind of crime — rustling.

Advocates of the so-called Paleo diet believe that to enjoy optimal health we need to bring our food choices in line with our dietary history and physiology, which they assume has changed little since the Paleolithic Era. But was there ever a standard caveman diet in the world? Like the remaining bands of hunter-gatherers in Africa and South America, they ate what they could catch, which depended on where they lived and the season of the year. Besides the bounds of availability, it is nigh impossible to define an ideal diet because nutrition is affected by age and lifestyle, health, and exercise, as well as the gut microbiome. Early humans lived strenuously to survive, and few reached what we now call middle age. What confidence, then, can we have in a Paleo diet for today's sixty-year-old couch potato, or indeed does anyone still observe the lifestyle of our ancestors? It is a fallacy to believe we could or should mimic the nutrition of a bygone era, but the most cogent reason for rejecting excessive carnivory is that it aggravates a stressed environment.

In a world of soaring population where a growing 30% of farmland is set aside directly or indirectly for raising livestock, the meat industry is on an unsustainable trajectory. Our appetite for red meat scours the land. It converts virgin rainforests to ranches, generates greenhouse gases, subsidizes monocultures of feed corn, consumes precious water, evolves pollution, moves animals from turf to corral, and abuses antibiotics. A perfect storm is gathering as forests are converted to grassland, corn to cow, and clean water to waste. White meat, which is preferred to red in Asia, is produced more efficiently than beef, as is protein from fish farming which, despite its drawbacks, relieves pressure on marine life.

Animal production for food cannot climb forever. The land has a finite carrying capacity and the Laws of Thermodynamics expose a profligate management of resources. As an illustration, imagine the ecosystem as a pyramid with energy transferred layer on layer from bottom to top by a thermodynamic 'hand-shake.' The kingdom of vegetable matter is the broad base energized by photosynthesis that feeds all the layers above. Herbivorous animals solely eating plants occupy the next level, and carnivores sitting at the apex dine on herbivores. Omnivores don't fit neatly in a layer because they have catholic tastes.

The total biomass diminishes steeply at each level because the efficiency of energy conversion is a mere 10%. That is why carnivorous animals are never abundant, and super-carnivores are rarest of all because <0.01% of the original energy remains at their level. Hence, we seldom eat top carnivores and, besides, we think big cats are unpalatable. There are always exceptions, of course, and on the top table we are fond of tuna, sharks, and other marine species that predate both carnivorous and herbivorous prey. Eating at that level carries more risks when eater and eaten are more closely related, and are never greater than when you eat your own kind. The Inuit who traditionally eat polar bear should cook the meat well to kill Trichinella and take care to avoid eating the liver which contains toxic amounts of vitamin A from concentration in the food chain, and 20-fold higher than in our livers.

Herbivores taste much better to us, and we eat plenty of them. There are currently around 1.5 billion cattle in the world, many of them raised for beef, along with countless other animals and birds farmed for meat. If we consumed our crops directly instead of channeling them through meat production, far more people would have a healthy ration of 2,000 Calories per day. The 10% rule-of-thumb predicts that for every 2,000 Calories of corn generated there is a net yield of only 200 Calories of cow. The lost energy could feed many more people, if not as much as tenfold that theory predicts. The meat industry counters that beef offers higher quality protein than corn, but no one ever suffered a nutritional deficiency from giving up meat, and the model for eating lower down the pyramid is unassailable for a wiser, farer, and kinder agricultural policy.

When U-boats blockaded food shipments to Britain in World War II, the island nation feared it would go hungry because it was not self-sufficient in food. The Government commissioned two Cambridge nutritionists to carry out a clinical trial to estimate the minimum food requirements compatible with good public health. The project sounds droll today because they drew up a list including Brussels sprouts and sausages (no Bratwurst, only patriotic British bangers), but then it was a matter of national survival. Homeowners tore up their lawns to make Victory Gardens, and backyards were brought into service for keeping a pig and chickens.

The scientists, Elsie Widdowson and Robert McCance, prescribed a ration to volunteers of 1 lb. of meat, 1 egg, and 4 oz. of fish per week, 5 fluid oz. of milk a day, and unlimited amounts of vegetables and wholemeal bread. It was a meager regime and a fraction of the meat we now consume, but was calculated to meet physiological needs for protein-energy, essential fatty acids, vitamins, and trace elements. When the subjects stayed healthy throughout the trial, the Government rolled out a ration policy for foods in short supply. It is often said that family health was never better: infant mortality fell to historic lows and, discounting deaths from hostilities, adult life expectancy rose. The downside was more British flatulence.

Since those days, the marketplace encourages Britons to eat ever more meat after the example of America, reflecting greater affordability and shifts in dining choices. Despite sound reasons for cutting back on red meat, policy-makers never offer more than bland health advisories, and have never levied a special tax on it. Of course, it cannot be condemned like tobacco because it is not toxic, but the farming lobby is powerful and won't voluntarily hurt its fiscal interests by switching from livestock to crop production. It remains, then, for individuals to decide where their interests lie for the sake of their pockets, their health, and the planet.

Cutting back is a step toward cutting out, but that first stride is often the hardest. It helps when we admit that red meat is special and costs the earth, and choose quality over quantity. If we are willing to open our pocketbooks for electronic gadgets and apps, why pass up grass-fed meat and pastured chicken and eggs instead of factory-reared products that cost a few dollars less? We ought to be more like discerning shoppers in a French village who fill their baskets with local vegetables, brown Marans eggs and a Bresse chicken. Anything more for a ragoût or salad is grown in their garden, for why else would a backyard exist in France? *Mangez bien!*

AN OIL CHANGE

Smoke evolving from oil heated in a wok is a signal to toss in the seasoned meat and vegetables for a stir-fry. Savory aromas carried by blue flurries are welcome appetizers, for what could be more innocent than smoke from cooked food or safer than working in a kitchen? That is what I used to think when smoke tranquillized the right side of my brain. My rationale left brain woke up one day when the clouds provoked a coughing fit, and I asked myself: "Is this healthy?" After dinner one day, I checked the chemistry literature to see if cooking was brewing toxins I inhale and eat.

This is not an original question. More chemists have asked it than you might imagine, but their advice is ignored in the kitchen. We turn to recipe books, TV programs, and the Internet for advice about healthy eating. There are nutrition experts and warriors who warn about kitchen smoke, but it was only when I looked at the science that I really engaged the matter. I knew, of course, that smoke and smoking are hazardous, but in the kitchen — that *sanus sanctuarium*?

Heating vegetable oil on a stove-top triggers a chain reaction causing an accelerating evolution of reactive aldehydes when the temperature rises above the 'smoke point.' The bevy of harmful molecules includes acrolein, 4-hydroxynonenal, and others with an affinity for DNA and make mutagenic adducts. I had not considered if I was cooking a cocktail of carcinogens, or that my choice of fats and oils makes a difference.

When saturated animal fats in lard and butter were condemned for causing heart disease, vegetable oils containing polyunsaturated fatty acids were recommended as healthy alternatives, but they are vulnerable to oxidation, more so than monounsaturated oils like olive oil of virginal reputation. This susceptibility is due to double bonds that react to make nasty products when heated. Saturated fats are so much more stable because, as their name suggests, they have no double bonds. After perusing these facts, it dawned on me that home cooking could make my kitchen more polluted than the street outside at rush hour, albeit with a different mix of toxins. My first reaction was to turn up the extractor fan to clear the air, but the second was more important because I changed cooking practices when I realized that vapors are not the only hazard. If cooking is prolonged at high heat or the oil is reused my meal bathes in a progressively stronger pool of poisons.

I thought of a neighbor who reuses oil in his backyard turkey fryer. The pot holds three gallons of a peanut-soy oil mixture that costs over $30 at Wallmart, so he is tempted to save money for the next cook-out. Would his family have a healthier meal if they ate out? They might. But how would they know if a fast food joint recycled cooking oil, or if it was past its use-by date? They wouldn't. Oxidation can be reduced by frying under a protective blanket of non-reactive nitrogen, but what restaurant will make that investment? Used oil can be chemically tested for safety, but when will a mass spectrometer sit on every kitchen countertop? Meanwhile, most people will continue to care more about ingredients in the cooking pan than the chemistry. We blindly trust time-honored recipes.

After the chemistry lesson, I watch for smoke and turn down the heat before the oil spoils. I sniff for the tell-tale acrid odor of acrolein, or even taste a drop of cooled oil on my tongue. The experimental impulse never died inside, so I tested several oils from the grocery store.

A few ounces were heated separately in a pan to 400° F. (204° C.) and then cooled for tasting. Canola and other refined oils never smoked, and stayed as tasteless as before. They are good for cooking at elevated temperatures. Extra virgin olive oil and walnut oil, on the other hand, began smoking long before that temperature was reached, and when they cooled their fruity notes were gone and replaced by a bitter taste. Those oils go off in storage. When I opened a bottle of olive oil found at the back of a pantry shelf with an expired date it smelled rancid, so I reluctantly threw it in the trash. Oxidation attacks unsaturated oils even in the cool and dark. This is a dilemma for kitchen scientists, but grandma never needed to worry because she cooked with butter and lard, which health experts scoffed at until recently.

If we look in history for a tipping-point we might choose 1955. That was a year when President Dwight D. Eisenhower at the age of 64 had a serious heart attack while playing golf in Denver. The stockmarket went into a spasm and his health became a lens through which the American public saw heart disease as a new epidemic. We could point a finger at his habit of smoking four packs a day, but that peril was not officially acknowledged yet. Instead, nutrition experts accused the diet of clogging arteries of both the President and population, and none led the charge against saturated animal fat and cholesterol more heartily than Ancel Keys. He was a celebrity campaigner, even appearing on the cover of *Time* magazine in 1961, and was followed by an omnibus of researchers, medical societies, and government officials. They confirmed his belief in the evil of saturated fat and the food industry galloped into the space left by retreating of old fats to transform grocery store shelves and the national diet to what we have today.

One of the arguments for cutting back on fatty meat, dairy products, and eggs was the unassailable rationale that fat makes us fat. Another 'proof' came from pathology which found abundant cholesterol in atheromatous plaques of heart attack victims that was presumed to be dumped from the bloodstream. On top of this circumstantial evidence, there were dietary surveys to add more weight to the argument and boost a wave of lipid paranoia. The flimsiness of the original data is now officially acknowledged, and strong advice to eat less fat is now repudiated by federal government guidelines: 'Cholesterol is not considered a nutrient of concern for overconsumption.' We can serve eggs on the table again without putting anxious hands on hearts.

When consumers started to turn their backs on saturated fat and embrace low-fat or fat-free alternatives, the food industry saw an opportunity for selling new products. But where to replace the missing calories and find a substitute for dairy fat and pig fat (lard) traditionally used as shortening for pastries, cookies, and cakes? The manufacturers chose vegetable oils rich in polyunsaturated fats which they converted from liquid to solid by chemical hydrogenation. They seemed safe bets because margarines like Crisco (crystallized cottonseed oil) were already on the market. These so-called trans-fats offered many advantages: they were solid at room temperature, tasted like butter, stable as lard or beef tallow for storage and deep-frying, and cheap to produce. As demand for vegetable oils boomed, farmers committed ever larger acreages to grow soybean and rapeseed for oil production. The safety profile of trans-fats was assumed and not intensively scrutinized. How times change.

Trans-fats are complex mixtures of unnatural lipid isomers now implicated in heart disease, cancer, stroke, and even type-2 diabetes. It is now their turn for condemnation. They still lurk in supermarket refrigerators for unwary customers who don't read labels, but are restricted in some countries and even banned from restaurants in New York City and other jurisdictions.

The food industry is understandably reluctant to turn the clock back to when animal fats ruled the marketplace because of the legacy of public anxiety left by Dr. Keys. Besides, the seal of official disapproval is not lifted. While the search for alternative fats continues, refined vegetable oils have been awarded a new role in deep frying. They are presented as a healthy choice because they don't raise the 'bad' type of cholesterol (LDL) in blood tests, although that is far from a perfect warning flag for heart disease in most people.

The public continues to be the subject of a vast dietary experiment that has failed to conquer cardiovascular disease, a national blight at the top of the CDC list of causes of mortality. Every stage in the history of dietary fat was hailed as a brilliant advance in public health until the story came apart. Moreover, dietary calories surrendered in the low-fat years were replaced by those in refined carbohydrates, which are now accused of contributing to the obesity and diabetes epidemics in adults and children. The scale of disease, disability, and death traceable to recommended diets over the past two generations is breathtaking and tragic.

This is one of several blows against public confidence in expert opinion and official prescriptions. To be fair, the relationship between food and health is very complicated, and it is hard to fund and execute lengthy clinical trials. Commercial vested interests in our food choices are hard to push back. There was a good reason why we called Grandma's pantry the 'larder,'[31] although her cooking was not such an unhealthy larded memory, and I doubt pastries, cakes, and cookies made with other fats taste any better today.

But despite my skepticism about the latest round of official advice, there are lessons to turn the tables on cooking practices, if not as far back as Grandma's kitchen. I banished margarine and polyunsaturated spreads and have returned a butter dish to the table, particularly Irish butter redolent of contented cows in fields of deep green turf and yellow buttercups. A slice of fresh bread with butter is hard to better. Butter also feels good rubbed with flour between fingers to make scones, to cream with powdered sugar for cakes, and even in the frying pan if it is first clarified to reduce the water in butterfat and skim off solids that would burn. Then there is coconut oil back with 60% saturated fat after a shameful reputation. Lard might seem a step too far, but it is tempting when there is something I fancy in Grandma's cookbook. All three have high smoke points along with seed oils, while olive oil and nut oils are reserved for salad dressings and other cool uses. The unprocessed kinds with the finest flavors are appetizing but come at the price of low smoke points and shorter shelf lives. Cookery has trade-offs.

I might have thought sooner and deeper about fats if my knowledge was not so divided between the mental compartments of kitchen and laboratory. In the 1950s, the chemist Denham Harman (1916-2014) was alarmed when Dr. Keys' program railroaded the nation into wholesale adoption of vegetable oils. He knew that unsaturated fats are unstable during heating and storage, and his research showed the degree of saturation affected the prevalence of cancer and lifespan of rats. I cited his free radical theory in one of my books, but the penny didn't drop in my brain all the years I was blithely cooking until the day my wok smoked.

A PINCH OF SALT

My high school class never forgot Basher, the retired boxer who became our chemistry teacher. He terrified us. The hulk sitting behind the front desk was infinitely old with jowls drooping like a Labrador retriever's, wispy hairs greased back for pathetic cover over his pate, a rare smile of broken gravestones, and a nose like a slug squished by a gloved fist long ago. Cowardly boys who fled the chemistry battlefield for Latin and Greek with more academic teachers wondered how the wreck could shepherd us through examinations, but we knew his secret. It was *FEAR*.

Most teachers had nicknames, but Basher was our best invention. He was a heavyweight boxer before the headmaster hired him out of desperation at a time of science teacher shortages in our borough. We imagined him shining at an interview as a natural showman, which he learned in the ring.

I shudder to recall the day he heated a beaker of benzene over a Bunsen burner. I don't remember the purpose of the experiment, but will never forget the sweet odor filling the room and now wonder why the fire department wasn't called and how many of my classmates are now in the care of an oncologist. On another occasion, he lifted a piece of silvery foil with a pair of tongs out of an oil jar.

"What's this Farrington?" he barked at a boy who dared to sit in the front row. We held our breath for the anticipated cocky reply.

"It's sodium, Sir."

In those days, teachers called us by our surnames, and we had to address them 'Sir,' even if they were female. Farrington was the class smart aleck, and afterwards in the school yard we kicked him in the shins for a correct answer.

Basher terrorized us like a U-boat captain pondering which defenseless merchant ship to sink. "Come on, boys. Tell me about sodium?" he baited us, pointing a stubby finger like a torpedo at a victim who bowed his head hoping he would be unnoticed.

"Please, Sir." Another boy in the front row raised a hand stretched out of a neatly-ironed cuff. "It's salt, Sir." The little crawler!

"WRONG!" he roared, and thumped his fist on the desk so a pen jumped. Glaring at the stupidity, he bawled, "It's a METAL."

He then did something the British Health and Safety Executive would condemn today. He held the foil so close to the Bunsen flame that it glowed like a firework, and so brightly we shielded our eyes.

"That's the element Na." He nodded at the Periodic Table of the Elements hanging on the wall. "Now boys, gather round."

We trooped forward to watch the magician. Chemistry experiments were infinitely more fun than Latin declensions, even at the risk of great peril. We never told our moms. We watched him drop the flaming metal in a tank of water where it raced around and fizzled on the surface until it was extinguished. Our curiosity grew by leaps and bounds when we learned the bubbles were explosive hydrogen gas. Another London schoolboy of an earlier generation, the neurologist and author Oliver Sacks, enjoyed the same experiment when he set sodium alight on a London pond. He wrote, 'It took fire instantly and sped around and around on the surface like a demented meteor, with a huge sheet of yellow flame above it' (*Uncle Tungsten: Memories of a Chemical Boyhood*).

Basher never tolerated wimps. What were a few controlled explosions in a classroom compared to the dangers that many of the staff had faced in the war? We guessed Basher led a squad of commandoes. Our fear was mixed with gratitude for lessons that were so much more practical than anything a boy could read in *The Dangerous Book for Boys*. One of the most useful lessons was the recipe he gave for making $NI_3.NH_3$ from innocent ingredients we could buy at the pharmacy. This contact explosive is completely safe provided it stays moist, but a dried smear goes off with a loud bang and puff of purple smoke from the slightest touch. It was the perfect revenge on a 'superior' pupil in the Latin class. We would huddle outside the school toilets during class breaks, listening for him to close a door and pull down his pants to contact the round seat ... We were not called 'Basherboys' for nothing.

I must resist telling other experiments and cycle back to the story of salt. This is not such an entertaining story because our teacher hustled past stable compounds, and the mischief we might have had with salt at cookery classes was beyond reach in the girls' school on the other side of an alarmed door. But as a novice biologist I soon learned that salt is important. Common salt, or sodium chloride, is a union of two highly-reactive ions forming the familiar white crystals. Unlike George and Martha in *Whose Afraid of Virginia Woolf,* two hot and opposite personalities

221

in chemistry never remain bachelor and spinster for long, but embrace in a stable bond.

As one of the commonest compounds in the earth's crust and highly soluble, sodium chloride is carried down rivers to oceans where it has been getting stronger over millions of years. If the first cells to appear on earth were in seawater, it was natural when multicellular bodies evolved to keep similar saline concentrations in body fluids and blood for bathing inside cells. As oceans became brinier, body fluids stayed the same to avoid salt degrading proteins, which could be lethal. Salted hams and saltfish are preserved because living cells are intolerant of concentrated salt. The problem of keeping excess salt outside the body in seawater and inside in freshwater, as well as eliminating excess intake with food, has been solved in clever ways by biology. Some animals have impermeable skins, some have salt pumps in gills and kidneys, and the albatross family and marine reptiles have special salt glands. The most remarkable adaptations are found in salmon and eels that face opposite salt stresses depending on the direction of migration. Fairy stories never accounted for how mermaids control their salt.

A sailor adrift on a raft in the ocean can survive no more than 10-11 days without drinking. The temptation to quench his thirst with seawater must be overwhelming, and especially if he watches seabirds skimming the waves with their beaks open, but to swallow it would drive him crazy with delirium. He would succumb if his kidneys were challenged beyond the limit of excreting salt from the blood. In the true story and movie *Unbroken* by Laura Hillenbrand, 'Louie' Zamperini survived by drinking rainwater while afloat for 47 days in the Pacific Ocean.

We have about 200 g of sodium chloride distributed throughout our body, or imagine a typical packet of salt in a grocery store which contains the equivalent of four human bodies. It would take about 50 packets to make a pillar the size of Lot's wife that was her punishment for looking back at wicked Sodom. We perish if we have too much or too little salt.

We need to consume 0.5 g a day (quarter teaspoon) to replace the salt lost naturally by excretion and sweating, but we consume much more. The American Heart Association has reduced its recommended lower limit to 2.3 g, or even 1.5 g for people at risk of high blood pressure and stroke. Few of us have any idea how much salt we eat or make any effort to reduce it. Many restaurants in France exclude a salt cellar on tables, and I hear it offends the chef to ask. Our salt intake is partly at the mercy of a food industry which spoons it into snacks and processed foods to make them tastier and saleable for longer. It is hard to cut back on it, like that other white stuff we love — sugar. Basher was talking as a chemist when he skipped sodium chloride, accusing it of being unreactive and boring, but I learned that to be a biologist I had to take that lesson with a grain of salt.

WHITE AND DEADLY

SUGAR

The only advice from Oscar Wilde I want to challenge is: "Everything in moderation, including moderation." I wonder if he would concede that sugar should be an exception. If he knew how much sweet stuff we consume he would surely agree it is an immoderate amount, but he would still insist that food and drink should be moderately sweetened to satisfy people like him with a sweet tooth. But if he read research reports he might even balk at that.

Some 20 years ago, I asked students at Edinburgh University to keep a food diary for their physiology class. Two weeks later I gave them a conversion table to calculate their average daily ration of protein, fat, carbs, and micronutrients. Except for their professor, everyone was amazed that the young men were consuming half their total carbs as sugar, equivalent to a 3-lb. bag (1.4 kg) of sugar every week in candies, cakes, sodas, juices, bread, processed foods, as well as beer in immoderate amounts. If they continued at the same rate for a lifespan, they would consume four tons of sugar as 20% or more of their total calories. The women consumed less of everything, but some were nonetheless so shocked by their data they announced urgent dietary changes. Sugar was first to go under the axe.

Scotland is sometimes called the land of bread and buns because the natives love carb-rich foods laced with sugar, like donuts and sticky buns. Greenock on the River Clyde became a sugaropolis because ships plying the Atlantic trade route from cane sugar plantations in the West Indies unloaded cargo in its docks. Early in the Victorian era, refined sugar emerged from former luxury status to become a sweetener everyone could afford, and then it was consumed to excess. It is now added to most foods—everything from bottles of apple juice to cans of zucchini—mostly unnecessarily, and often we are unaware how much until we read the label. Sweet-toothed folks in the British Isles were in the vanguard of sugaremia and consumption has boomed across the world with hardly a whimper of scorn until recently.

Why would anyone protest nature's sweet gift, whose name is even used metaphorically for love? Good and loving behavior has long been rewarded by sweetmeats, such as candies, chocolate, ice cream, candy cotton ('candy floss'), and deep-fried Mars bars with a whopping 1,000 sweet and sickly calories (originating in Scotland). My grandma gave me sugar lumps for 'energy,' as if a wee boy is not already hyperkinetic, yet no one accused her of causing harm. British dentists didn't advise us to cut back on candies, and were glad of the work offered by our cavities, laboring like road workers drilling holes with miniature jackhammers and caterpillar excavators. The reputation of British teeth may have started as long ago as Queen Bess's crumbling, black ruins that were diplomatically sealed behind pursed lips on canvas portraits of the monarch. Our dentists owed their livelihoods to our carelessness, but I mostly blame us for ignorance and not challenging the assumption that tooth decay is inevitable.

Apart from that black mark, 'sweetness' has resonated for centuries in the English language for everything wholesome and beautiful. We speak of a sweet girl or boy, sweet victory, sweet life, sweet friendship, and so much else. Gertrude used the word in her adieu to Hamlet: "Sweet to the sweet, farewell."

The words sweet and sugar are used synonymously and positively in every way. Sugar futures are sweet bets for investors because the commodity reaches three major markets that never flag—food, drink, and fuel. It was a sweet spot to serve on the International Sugar Council once the harrowing memories of slave labor in sugar plantations faded, and before the modern anxiety about the impacts of sugar cane and beet.

Our family doctor never cautioned us about eating too much candy, and I guess she never gave it a thought. But unknown to us and not far away, there was a maverick scientist fighting a single-handed battle against sugar interests. The man was John Yudkin (1910-1995), a London professor of physiology who published *Pure, White and Deadly* in 1972 (*Sweet and Dangerous* in America). We might be fooled by the title, thinking it is an imitation of an Agatha Christie novel, although in accusing sugar of being a slow poison he was writing an arsenic plot. The book brought his name to wider attention, though it didn't endear him to his profession, and especially not to the industry. Sugar barons and advertisers barred him from guest lectureships or serving on expert panels. A courteous man, he once wrote with that British understatement I find endearing, '... relations with one or two friends in industry have occasionally become rather strained.'

He had the rare distinction of being the author of a book that was condemned even before it was published, which places him in a pantheon including Christian martyrs burned at the stake for publishing the gospel. A reviewer for the World Sugar Research Organization declared '(this book) is science fiction ... and for your dustbin.' The criticism must have wounded him because one of my colleagues remembered him as a "jolly man" who always thought the best of others. It has recently come to light that the sugar industry doesn't have a clean conscience[32] any more than Big Tobacco. Among the studies it secretly sponsored since the 1960s, animal research showed sucrose increased the level of blood triglycerides, an indicator of cardiovascular risk. It pulled the funding plug, and still denies sugar does any harm to human health apart from having a caloric impact.

If World Sugar represented his bitterest enemy in industry, Ancel Keys at the University of Minnesota was his bête noire in academia. As I mention in another essay, Dr. Keys led a national campaign against saturated dietary fat, avowing that only when blood cholesterol levels were lower would the epidemic of heart disease be conquered in America. Sugar was not in his gunsights and Yudkin's big idea was an unwelcome distraction from the target.

Yudkin stood up to criticize Keys' famous *Seven Countries Study*, as well as much else that propped up the case against animal fat. He argued that the choice of countries was arbitrary and could bias conclusions, and he artfully pointed out the data showed a slightly closer association between sugar and heart disease or obesity than with fat. He looked for evidence from obscure corners around the globe. Canadian Inuit and African Masai hardly ever developed heart disease while subsisting for untold centuries on high fat diets of meat, blood, blubber, and milk, or at least they didn't until they switched to Western diets. It was a similar story after Sephardic Jews migrated to Israel compared to the low rates of disease in those who stayed behind in Yemen. And, lastly, he cheekily pointed out that although

Greek and Italian diets in two of the seven countries in the acclaimed study are low in 'bad' fats and rich in 'good' ones, the Mediterranean diet contains very little sugar.

Was the low-fat bandwagon propelled by vested interests? Was it based on the familiar but elementary error that correlation is not causation? To rub salt in the wound of Keys' theory, Yudkin showed a better correlation between heart disease and TV ownership than with fat. That is not as crazy as it might seem because TV was then a hallmark of affluence, and associated with a sedentary lifestyle, obesity, smoking, fatty diet, and sugary food. He was honest to admit the connection between diet and health is complicated.

He never met the wagon leader of the opposition, which was merciful otherwise they might have come to more than verbal blows. The bitterness was deeper than esoteric tiffs between academics, because there was a lot at stake for Keys who had convinced his government to recommend low-fat diets and brought most of the medical profession and the food industry to his side. If his theory was wrong, there was blood on his hands. Bad dietary advice would fail to turn back the tide of heart disease, and we are still waiting after more than 50 years.

Few prophets are honored in their time. While his profession and the authorities turned their backs on him, Yudkin staunchly held his ground and singled out sugar as a major cause of the triad of heart disease, obesity, and adult diabetes. He also laid a mixed bag of other ailments at its door, including gout, diverticulitis, dermatitis, duodenal ulcers, vision problems, and cancer. It seems unlikely that sugar is the bogeyman of everything, and exaggeration gave his opponents ammunition. If he had not demonized sugar so zealously he might have been taken more seriously and earned the credit awarded to others who grasped the baton after he died.

The fat theory started to melt down after a *New York Times* magazine article by Gary Taubes in 2002. He asked an elementary question: "What if fat doesn't make you fat?" Like Yudkin before him, Taubes suspected that heart disease and the rest of the triad were caused by hormones rather than globs of cholesterol on artery walls. The candidate he most had in mind was insulin.

When carbohydrates are digested, sugars are absorbed from the small intestine into blood and soon reach the pancreas where they stimulate insulin secretion. This hormone plays a vital role for keeping blood glucose in check by a 'molecular handshake' with a receptor on cells to open a gate for glucose to enter. Glucose enters a biochemical pathway to generate energy, and the surplus is stored as fat. The fruit sugar fructose follows a different pathway outlined in the next essay.

Clinical studies suggest a metabolic imbalance involving insulin is the root of troubles between sugar and some age-related diseases. More evidence came from an unexpected source. At the University of California, Cynthia Kenyon noticed that if the tiny worm *C. elegans* favored by geneticists is fed a sugary diet its insulin-like genes are switched on and it has a shorter lifespan. The discovery won greater relevance when she confirmed the finding in mice, and so convinced was she of the implications for human health that she changed to a low glycemic diet for herself.

I can now look back on Mom's rule for mealtimes as a healthier regime than we thought and wiser than she knew. Along with my brothers, the savory course was regarded as something to struggle through to earn the reward of a sweet dessert. She never allowed the order of courses to be reversed, and candy was forbidden between meals. If we had a physiology textbook at home, we would have learned that proteins and fats lying heavy in our stomach after a savory meal delay gastric emptying, so when sugar comes down the chute afterwards its progression and absorption in the small intestine as chyme is delayed. Thus, glucose does not make a sharp spike in blood, and the consequent damping of the insulin response is likely to be beneficial. The sweet course in a meal is better coming second.

Like many people, Yudkin struggled with a sweet tooth and an expanding waistline in mid-life. He switched to a low-carb diet to control his weight long before anyone heard of the Atkins Diet, but he was not the originator. That distinction belongs to a coffin-maker in Victorian London. William Banting (1796-1878) was a carpenter who knew something about corpulence, and had an innate curiosity that led him to self-experiment with a low-carb diet to lose weight. It worked! He broadcast his discovery in a book that sold widely, if not in medical circles that snubbed the amateur. Banting's formula was close to the modern Paleo diet and, by an odd twist of history, one of his descendants won the 1923 Nobel Prize for the discovery of insulin.

If we could ask Yudkin he might chuckle to hear sugar is now receiving a lot of blame for the epidemic of obesity and adult diabetes, and Big Sugar is accused of encouraging a kind of addiction, like Big Tobacco before it. You know the climate has changed when Dr. Oz warns about the ills of a nation craving for sugar.

It is surely troubling to read so many experts have been wrong for long. Science is the most objective path to knowledge we own, but it is a human endeavor and, hence, fallible. When a complex case is heard in the court of science, judgments are based not only on hard forensic evidence but on the balance of arguments and the rhetoric of the prosecutor and defending attorney. Ancel Keys would have made a persuasive trial lawyer, and nutritional science creates tough cases for juries offered contradictory data and flawed clinical surveys.

Nutrition is mocked as 'kitchen science,' and it certainly is one of the softer sciences of life. It looks like pure chemistry and physiology at first sight but, like a white meringue with a firm crust, it is soft and gooey inside. Food is a mixture of organic and inorganic chemistry whose complexity is compounded by the environment in which it is grown, processed, and stored, and its nutritional value is affected by the genetics and lifestyle of the people who consume it. No two people have identical metabolism. Food research has huge challenges and none of the advantages of pharmacology which tests every new drug in turn compared to placebo controls. Randomized, prospective clinical trials are not only too costly but impractical in food science: to compare diets vast numbers of subjects must be monitored for years to detect small disparities in health. Retrospective studies are mostly cheap and dirty. It is not surprising that debate rages over health foods, fad diets, and sugar.

If I had to choose a philosophy for nutrition I would pick the commonsense advice of Michael Pollan, author of *In Defense of Food: An Eater's Manifesto.* He urges us to 'Eat food, not too much, and mostly vegetables,' and applauds food that is fresh, minimally processed, and grown with environmental integrity. He recommends a diet low in raw sugar and glycemic carbohydrates to avoid spiking blood sugar and insulin. Oscar Wilde might have shunned his prescription of moderation because he loved sweetmeats, as would his father, Dr. Sir William Wilde, who made a fortune in the sugar industry.

WHO KNOWS ABOUT FRUCTOSE?

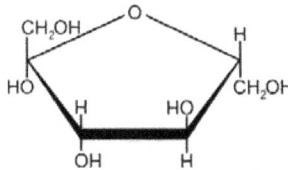

People down the ages have pondered if the apple Eve gave to Adam was a tempting metaphor of sweetness in the fruit of her body. Sweet apples are appetizing and, pound for pound, contain far less sugar than honey, although a larger fraction of it is the sweeter kind. Apples have more fructose, a sugar twice as sweet as glucose and sweeter than pantry sugar, properly called sucrose.

Aside from the Creation story, there is a theory that some plants evolved an advantage over others by natural selection of a biochemistry to generate super-sweet fructose in ripening fruit. Fructose is a sweet temptation Biological Eve offers to browsers who, in turn, help the plant to disperse its seeds to places where they can thrive and generate more of their kind.

Even the word fructose conveys a healthy ring coming from the Latin root for fruit, and we are encouraged to eat more. Everyone knows the old story that an apple a day keeps the doctor away, and in a modern spin fructose is recommended for people with diabetes because of its low glycemic index, meaning that consuming it will make a more blunted spike in blood. Fructose may not, however, be as good a prescription as we are told, and it has lost some of its salubrious cachet since high fructose corn syrup elbowed into the market 40 years ago. But even if fructose is getting a tarnished reputation, glucose still glitters.

At first, differentiation of these closely-related molecules looks odd. They have the same number of carbon, hydrogen, and oxygen atoms, although the possession of identical chemical formulas does not make them the same any more than genetically identical twins are the same person. Glucose and fructose are monosaccharides that form in equal amounts when an oxygen bridge in their parent sucrose is split by the enzyme sucrase. The daughter sugars so created have different shapes and metabolism with the same number of calories, although not all calories are created equal.

The shape of molecules affects the biochemical path they take, and even if they are exact mirror images they may not be able to take the same route. Consider sugar-loving yeast cells. When wine is made, yeast prefers to feed on the glucose in unfermented grape 'must,' but as the alcohol gains strength and glucose becomes less concentrated the fraction of undigested fructose climbs to preserve a residual sweetness, which vintners want to control. They choose strains of yeast carefully, sometimes favoring those with a greater affinity for fructose to make a drier product. Not all yeasts are equal.

Of the sweet twins, only glucose is essential for life. We don't need either in our diet because they are created from digestion of more complex carbohydrates or fats, and we manage perfectly well without any fructose. Sperm are nourished in semen by fructose from the seminal vesicles, an odd finding, but they can satisfy their energy needs with glucose alone in a culture medium for in vitro fertilization and other fertility treatments.

I am still amazed, though, that two sugars so similar in chemistry are handled quite differently in biology. Glucose is rapidly absorbed from the small intestine via a molecular gateway called GLUT4 to race in the bloodstream past the liver for delivery to every corner of the body. Glucose levels in blood are precisely controlled by the hormone insulin as it is the common fuel for metabolism and growth, and surplus is stored as glycogen in muscle and fat in adipose tissue.

On the other hand, fructose is absorbed more slowly than glucose, and so sluggishly in infants that too much in the diet causes diarrhea. The hepatic portal vein transports fructose from the gut to the liver where, instead of passing straight through like glucose, it is taken up into cells of this organ via another gate that does not depend on insulin (GLUT5). It is then processed differently to form glycerol, the molecular backbone of triglycerides. That may not be such good news.

A diet rich in fructose lower HDL, the 'good' carrier of cholesterol in the story of heart disease. Even more ominously, it raises a harmful fraction of LDL-cholesterol along with the triglycerides. In this unhealthy portrait, lipidinous fructose is a potential contributor to metabolic syndrome and, hence, to obesity and adult diabetes. There are suggestions, too, that it plays a role in non-alcoholic fatty liver disease, gout, and some inflammatory conditions. Eve was wise to offer Adam only one apple and not a basket of them!

When something is cheap and ubiquitous, we tend to equate abundance with beneficence. The longest aisles in supermarkets are stacked from head to toe with sweetened sodas and sports drinks. In other long rows there are bottles of fruit juices and cocktails containing a whopping 100 g or more of fructose per liter from the fruit and supplementary sugar. Among the most visited aisles in the store, they are stationed near the check-outs where we stand in line with time to look at a final tempting display of candy.

Consumers are starting to push back against these pressures and manufacturers are offering more unsweetened foods and sodas with artificial sweeteners, but it is often hard to figure from food labels exactly how much sugar we consume. Statements about 'serving sizes' confuse me because they don't correspond to amounts I choose for my plate or cup. Is concealment behind the switch from labeling tins and jars in ounces or grams, which I understand and used to be standard practice? We are more in the dark because labels record the amount added and not the fraction already in the product. This is either a tirade or a polemic and I will close with the observation that when we buy processed food instead of raw ingredients we are locked into choices made by manufacturers to tempt our palates and prolong shelf-life. We ought to pay more attention to what we are consuming, but feel swamped by so many distractions in modern life.

The sweetness of fructose is so cunning it makes cutting back hard. There is a devilish physiology working against our best interests, because the more fructose we eat the faster it is absorbed into our bodies. Moreover, in contrast to glucose the fruit sugar does not suppress the hunger hormone ghrelin, so we get hooked on fructose without feeling satisfied and continue to devour it.

When we were introduced to tea as children, our mom rationed us to a measly half-teaspoon of sugar to make it more palatable, but she weaned us off as soon as beverages became our daily habit. When I sipped from our Dad's cup in error one day the sweetness so spoiled the taste I thought it was a different drink. It took years of badgering him before he was persuaded to give up a lifetime of sweet tea because tastes acquired when we are young are hard to surrender. It was easy for us to stay 'tea-total' as we grew into adults, although I stayed addicted to chocolate.

Cutting down on sugar and worrying about fructose is now regarded as progressive instead of ascetic. Dr. Robert Lustig's attack on fructose in *Sugar: The Bitter Truth* has been viewed over six million times on You Tube[33]. And a former First Lady has criticized the food industry for hooking kids for unhealthy preferences: "Our kids don't choose to make food products with tons of sugar and sodium in supersized portions, and then to have those products marketed to them everywhere they turn."

Obesity is a heavy price for society's sugaremia. It was a much lighter problem in my schooldays when we mercilessly mocked fat boys because they were rare exceptions. We were not ashamed to call them gluttons, and eagerly waited for a corpulent anti-hero to appear in the next episode of the BBC TV series *Billy Bunter of Greyfriar's School*. That kind of prejudice has fallen back because overweight is the new normal and obesity is common, and so long as the guardians of our national health fail to regulate food responsible for the sweet tide waistlines will continue to expand.

Fructose is only a minor part of that story. We unconsciously consumed it for eons, albeit in small quantities, but it is now on the list of dietary demons. High fructose corn syrup is partly responsible for damning its reputation as a chaste fruit sugar. HFCS manufactured from hydrolyzed corn starch has become ubiquitous in staple foods and beverages, displacing cane and beet sugar because farm subsidies have made corn cheaper. But is HFCS so fiendish? As a natural 50:50 chemical combination of fructose and glucose, pantry sugar is equivalent to $HFCS_{50}$, not much different to the most abundant grades of syrup sold on the market ($HFCS_{42}$ – $HFCS_{55}$), so the impact on our health is likely to be similar, although environmental health is another matter.

Since clinical studies are too fraught to contemplate, researchers returned to the rat room to study fructose where they gave animals a supermarket menu of sweet treats with their normal diet. The studies did not find evidence of harm from fructose, perhaps because rats are too smart to binge on sugar or the research was ended too soon. It is always a question of amount, and even the most life-sustaining medium—water—is harmful if drunk to excess. The 16th Century father of toxicology, Paracelsus, wrote a great deal of nonsense but was wise when he said, "the poison is in the dose."

LOVE IT OR LOATHE IT

I am on the minority side of a debate over *Marmite*, which creates a wide aisle between people like congressional politics. People love it or loathe it, and very few cross those passionate poles.

In case you have not tried *Marmite*, or have only seen the little black jars with yellow caps on a grocery store shelf, I ought to explain it is something Brits spread on buttered toast. It has the pungency of rotted compost and the color and texture of molten tar. Aussies have their own culinary icon called *Vegemite*, which tastes slightly less raw than our formula, but is equally salty and savory. People who test these products for the first time should be cautious to spread no more than a unimolecular layer on a slice of toast, and even veteran gourmets take great risks chomping on a thick coating. I remember recommending a jar to a *Marmite* virgin who scooped it out greedily as he would peanut butter, assuming the more the better. *Ugh!* I raised my hands in horror, but too late before the morsel disappeared and I had to stand back waiting for a returning blast of crumbs and saliva. The expression of pain was awful to behold, and that was the last time he accepted my hospitality.

I have heard *Marmite* compared to odious gunks and goops, and more often to engine oil that has not been changed for 20,000 miles. Sometimes, it is confused with another British favorite, *Bovril* (bovine extract), but it is 100% vegetable in origin and its history makes an interesting tale.

More than a century ago, a Mr. Gilmour of Burton-on-Trent in the English Midlands had a brainwave. He noticed the Bass Brewery in his town carted away the sediment of dead yeast cells (lees) for scattering in farm fields as fertilizer. He mused that something profitable might be extracted from the sludge, and the entrepreneur soon succeeded. He salted and cooked the cells by a secret process to make a tarry paste. It didn't look appetizing, but when he used his family as guinea-pigs they declared it was delicious and asked for more. Thus fortified, he opened a factory in the town to manufacture *Marmite*, a name taken from a French word for an earthenware pot, which is depicted on the label to this day.

The new product became familiar throughout the British Empire. During the Great War, it was promoted as a health supplement in the rations of British troops on the Western Front. In World War II, it was fed with allegedly kind intentions to German prisoners-of-war by their British captors, who risked the accusation of serving them cruel and unusual punishment.

Marmite can be deviously introduced to unwary eaters disguised in stews and gravies. I confess I have not always owned up to guests. It conveys a wonderful savory flavor and pretends to be meaty.

There is no doubt that to become a *Marmite*-lover you must be introduced when you are very young, because I never saw addiction when a naïve adult tried it. It was a tempting treat mom served to my younger brothers on toasted fingers of bread she called *Marmite* soldiers, but I was a *Marmite* soldier at birth because she exposed me in the womb to her craving.

I fervently believe in eating a diet that leans toward a scientific balance of nutrients and micronutrients, and don't show much enthusiasm for so-called health foods. They are fads that come and go when research first extols and then repudiates them. *Marmite* is in a superior category because it is perennially popular with devotees who understand its virtues. It is second to none as a source of B vitamins. The manufacturer even fortifies it with extra B12 for good measure, although the belief that more is better backfired when the Danish Government banned this ambrosia from Albion. Maybe the Danes didn't know that *Marmite* must be consumed in tiny servings, although they had a point because tyramine is so concentrated it can provoke a bad reaction in people taking monoamine oxidase inhibitors.

One of the things I love most about *Marmite* is that it lives forever. It never goes off at room temperature, and must not be kept in a refrigerator or freezer which would turn it to a brick. The salt is too concentrated for microbes to survive, the same benefit that raw honey provides from sugars and peroxides preventing bacterial and fungal growth. Honey has long held a prized place in wound dressings that *Marmite* could replace, but that can never happen in our home because if I spread it on a scraped knee my dog would lick it off. She is a marmaholic too.

This subject reminds me about the story of an intrepid young woman from a middle-class English family earlier in the last century. Lucy Wills (1888-1964) was one of the first woman graduates in medicine and left London in 1928 to work in

Bombay. She noticed a high mortality rate among poor textile workers who were pregnant. Deaths were most prevalent in seasonal shortages of fruit and vegetables, which gave a clue to the cause of the disease manifesting as macrocytic anemia.

She ruled out all the infections she knew, and arsenic, which was a panacea for many ailments in the past, was not curative. After many trials and much speculation, she wondered if the women were suffering a nutritional deficiency, which would account for high-caste women staying healthy the year round since they could afford a mixed diet. When liver extracts containing vitamin B12 failed to help, she tried yeast supplements. Yeast reversed similar symptoms she observed in rats on a vitamin restricted diet, and when given to patients they improved quickly and dramatically. The active factor in yeast was a mystery for a long time, and dubbed the 'Wills factor' as a tribute to her breakthrough. Many lives were saved by feeding women *Marmite* as a cheap source of concentrated yeast. Later, the factor was identified as folic acid (vitamin B9), and when it was chemically synthesized it was made into pills for people who were revolted by the tar in the little black jar.

It pains me to end this essay with a tortured story of Marmageddon. On my first visit to New Zealand in 2011, the country was reeling from the shock of a recent earthquake whose epicenter was only six miles from downtown Christchurch. Nearly 200 people died in the tragedy, and the region has slowly recovered from catastrophic damage to homes, businesses, and public buildings, including a cathedral of great heritage value.

Destruction of the *Marmite* factory was one of the most heart-rending losses for Kiwis growing up with it. Stocks were quickly whisked from store shelves by anxious shoppers, and I imagine late-comers begging neighbors pitifully, "Kia Ora. Got *Marmite*, mate?" In every tragedy, however, there are winners as well as losers. Hoarders found buyers prepared to pay ten times the normal market price. Even if it tasted loathsome to investors, they rubbed their hands at the prospects for *Marmite* Futures as shipments of the precious cargo arrived from England to nourish an anxious nation.

PART V. SEASONS

MY GROUNDHOG DAY

My Groundhog Day will come round when our garden raider squats in my cross-hairs, but I will probably stop swearing to liquidate him when I see his goofy face buried in a riot of hair, pleading, "It wasn't me!" I know he is phony, but he melts my vengeful heart.

Last summer, I suspect the varmint grazed to the ground the stalks, leaves, and ripe fruit in my strawberry patch, which were quickly replaced by a riot of weeds. He is a canny creature who emerges under cover of darkness from his den. I doubt he would be convicted in a court of law because evidence of his guilt is circumstantial and blatant prejudice disqualifies me as a witness.

A neighbor leaned over the fence to casually inform me that while rocking on his deck with a beer he often saw a large 'hog' padding toward our property at dusk. "Whoa, he's a monster!" said the story-teller, stretching arms like a fisherman but offering nothing more than testimony and never explaining why his time at the firing range was not put to practical use. He might if he was a gardener. I am losing faith in the hunting instincts of this country because there was a time when Virginians savored *gigot de groundhog farci en croute* followed by strawberries and cream for dessert. Groundhogs (woodchucks) are meaty squirrels, larger than guinea-pigs and smaller than beavers, but the closest I have gotten to this traditional dish is ground hog from the supermarket (i.e., sausage).

Groundhogs don't hibernate here in Tidewater Virginia. *Tant pis.* After a heavy snowfall, I see pad marks across the yard with four front and five back toes mingling with the spoor of rabbit and deer visitors from the night before. Our raider is abroad the year round, whereas his northern cousins curl up in their burrows to grant gardeners and farmers some respite. There is, however, one member of his tribe that makes a welcome appearance in midwinter, and has made his home town of Punxsutawney, PA, world famous. Only a nation that loves tradition as much as hunting would celebrate the life of a hairy varmint.

Phil is a celebrity 'hog.' He boasts more honorific titles than the British Royal Family, and earned them through psychic powers beyond the comprehension of non-rodents. Scientists use complicated apparatus and algorithms to forecast the weather, and country gaffers note the abundance of berries and nuts or the timing of bird migration as portents of winter's reign, but Phil's predictions are the most anticipated. They are broadcast on media networks around the nation, and are the only reports from a rodent. He is the Nostradamus of the animal world.

On the second day of February named after him, he is coaxed out of his burrow and presented on a stage at Gobbler's Knob to his fans and TV crews. Everyone wants to know the forecast for the next six weeks before spring officially begins. Farmers need to know the last frost date and anticipate rising ground temperatures for sowing seeds, skiers want to know how long the slopes will stay open, travelers worry if a nor'easter will close airports, and school-kids hope for more snow days. A reverent hush falls on the assembly while the rodent summons his occult powers. He turns to whisper in the ear of his handler who stands at the center of a semi-circle of grim-faced men in black frock coats and top hats.

If Phil sees his shadow we can be sure that winter weather will continue, but if there is no shadow spring will come early. The crowd holds its breath.

This tradition started with German farmers who used badgers as their seers in Europe. That may account for Kenneth Grahame choosing Mr. Badger as the wisest animal in *The Wind in the Willows*. According to an old tale, if badgers crept out of their holes on Candlemas Day to find fresh snow on the ground they would walk around looking for a snack, but if the sun was shining and casting shadows they drew back into their underground setts.

The descendants of farmers who emigrated to the USA could not find the handsome beast with a striped face anywhere in the Atlantic states, and so they adopted Punxsutawney Phil as a substitute.

Groundhog Day falls between Martin Luther King Day and Presidents Day, and happens to be mid-way between the winter solstice and spring equinox. It coincides with the time when fertility was celebrated in the pagan calendar and later by Christians as the feast of Candlemas when candles were blessed in church like a festival of light to welcome the coming spring.

If Candlemas Day be fair and bright
Winter will have another fight.
If Candlemas Day brings cloud and rain,
Winter won't come again.
From traditional English verse

Phil forecasts hard winter weather when he shivers in his shadow. He withdraws to his parlor like a sagacious hobbit when the air is calm, clear, and cold on a sunny winter day. Those are conditions when an anticyclone is parked over the continent for days or even weeks on end. Phil's reputation takes a knock from false predictions, although true believers say he is inerrant and excuse him. The American continent is vast with so many climatic zones that a forecast found wrong in one place is likely to be correct in another. A handler can cause error, too, if he doesn't tell bleary-eyed Phil rousing from deep sleep that he is outside cloudy Pittsburgh and not in sunny Portland he was dreaming about. Some hardened sceptics are dismissive of the old 'hog,' so I checked his record for a five-year period for a weather station close to his burrow. As an ardent Steelers fan, he would approve my choice.

The average temperatures near Pittsburgh in February and March from 2009 to 2011 and again in 2013 were all colder than average, although Phil only saw his shadow in two of the four years. He saw it again in 2012, but the following two months were 10°F. warmer than normal. Wrong again! Looking further back, he seems to have been right about half the time, which is what you expect for a statistically astute groundhog given a binary choice.

Like traditional weathermen and farmers' almanacs, Phil's reputation depends on a much longer history of record-keeping than a few years. He announced the first forecast in the long winter of 1887-88, and has never missed one since. Besides holding the record as a weather-hog, he is also the most venerable groundhog in the world. Other members of his tribe live no longer than 6-8 years in the wild (hopefully less in my yard).

His longevity is attributed to an elixir served at summer garden parties while relaxing with friends for a strawberry tea. Every time he sips the potion it rolls his age back a year. The formula is kept secret by confidantes who obviously never tried it for themselves. But here's another enigma. You would not expect an animal whose youthful vigor is said to be recharged annually to reverse suddenly from the steady progression we notice in his brown and sleek pelt to gray and grisly, but this is exactly what happens from time to time. He appears dark and shiny again. I would call this casting back in time a leap year if the expression wasn't already in the calendar. Phil has been rejuvenated more times than Doctor Who in the interminable British sci-fi series.

Soon after the dawn broke last February, Phil reappeared for his big day on CBS News, blinking at the light in a blast of damp air. Followers gathered around in heavy coats had already forgotten the Patriot's win at the Super Bowl in their eagerness to hear more important news. Soon enough, we were told by a Victorian-looking gentleman that Phil had seen his shadow, so there would be six more weeks of winter.

As the first drops of rain fell and above the roar of wind through the microphone, the groans of the crowd were audible as they turned to shuffle off with bowed heads and furl black umbrellas like sprouting mushrooms. Afterwards, I read tweets from boorish sceptics who asked how a shadow can be seen on a rainy morning with cloud cover down to 400 feet, but the old rodent wasn't offended. He was curled up his burrow for another six weeks until springtime.

SEVENTEEN YEAR ITCH

It seems a long time since 1996 when Bill Clinton was in his first term in the Oval Office, Diana was still alive and separated from Charles, the Unabomber was apprehended, and Ella Fitzgerald passed away. I was living in Yorkshire with no thought of moving permanently to North America, and wondering if I had eaten bits of a mad cow. So much history has flowed through the presses since that year when Brood II cicadas emerged in the Atlantic states of America to urgently search for mates before they were annihilated. In the following seventeen years, their progeny stayed underground sucking on tree roots until the calendar flipped over to 2013.

I encountered the new brood in June of that year when I pulled over to a rest area on Interstate-64 west of Richmond. When I stepped out of the car, I was puzzled by a racket coming from all directions, loud enough to drown the din of highway traffic nearby. I had heard chirping cicadas before in 2011 when a 13-year brood emerged in my neighborhood, but in 2013 it was the turn of the 17-year ensemble to crawl out of their burrows to sing (*sic*).

Residents then have sleepless nights unless double-glazed windows provide a modicum of tranquility. The volume can reach 90 decibels, which I read is a dangerous level if it persists over eight hours. No respecters of government regulations or social courtesies, male cicadas chirp at full volume round the clock, as they must. Although they were idle for so long, time is not on their side after they emerge for their final act.

The nymphs had opened their tunnels in the compacted dirt of the parking lot to make about ten holes to the square yard, slightly larger than earthworms make. After casting off their brown shells, they expanded their wings and flew to a new life stage so completely different to when they were troglodytes. The cicadas were spectacles I was moved to think I may never live to see and hear again.

I watched them waddle unsteadily up tree trunks and down walls on six skinny legs, never bothering to avoid the many perils surrounding them. Some launched into the air like lumbering flying boats, but they rarely made much distance or headed in a purposeful direction. They mostly crashed into branches or to the ground where robins waited to pounce, their ochre breasts bobbing up and down as they stabbed live meals. Cicadas are hamburger-sized meals for birds, and equally nutritious, so the diners were soon sated and flew up to a branch to preen and watch food marching below.

It is not only an extraordinary life cycle that makes cicadas a marvel of the living world, but the mystery of how they synchronize a mass emergence. The timing of periodic cicadas is so precise that people can plan to take a vacation out of town in 2030 to avoid the next pulse. As soon as the ground temperature climbs above 64 °F. (18 °C.), nymphs detach themselves from roots and burrow to the surface. Like forgotten nuts buried by squirrels, they grow out of darkness to the light above.

They first break ground at the southern edge of their range in North Carolina, and then a wave of emergence progresses with the season toward Connecticut. Soon there are gatherings of over a million per acre, and countless billions across a state. But in the intervening years we are unlikely to see any, or if we do a closer look reveals a similar species that keeps an annual clock.

At 1½ inches long, they are the largest insects of their kind, and among the weirdest. They look like bugs in zoot suits with bulging red eyes and a black cigar-shaped body under transparent wings traced with orange veins. Their scientific name, *Magicicada septendecim*, celebrates a fantastic creature.

For most of their range, the distribution of 17-year and 13-year broods don't overlap, although they evolved from a common stock a few million years ago. Fifteen broods have been recorded across the country, twelve with 17-year cycles and three with 13-year cycles. Of 3,000 species of cicadas worldwide, only seven have periodic behavior.

When I stopped at the rest area I was on my way to the Blue Ridge to watch wildlife, but the cicadas were the most memorable sights of the day. Their appearance did not always inspire such joy and wonder. Some early American colonists regarded them superstitiously, confusing them with the biblical locusts that plagued the Egyptians in the Old Testament, or as fearful omens in the *Book of Revelation*: 'Then from the smoke came locusts on the earth …' I imagine every thirteenth or seventeenth anniversary year there were fiery sermons about Armageddon and trumpet warnings of an insect plague from a bottomless pit for tormenting sinners. Preachers could whip pious congregations to abstinence from drinking and fornicating, at least until the last invasion event was a faded memory.

For all their scary appearance, cicadas are some of nature's innocents: they neither bite nor sting, and because they can't eat they don't spoil crops. They 'flag' tree canopies to make leafy nests but this causes only minor damage from which trees quickly recover. After hatching, larvae fall out of their nests to the ground and quickly scrape a burrow to find a juicy tree root to suck on, but even this does not wound their host. They are beneficial dead and alive by providing a protein-rich feast for animals and fertilizing the soil after their bodies decompose.

The deepest secret is the enigma of how these hermits in non-communicating tunnels manage to synchronize emergence above ground. Each nymph lives in an independent cell, like a hermit in the desert. If they have internal clocks as accurate as ours, what kinds of molecules can count time? Do special proteins behave like sand in an hourglass, lowering a molecular vault to some threshold that rings a bell inside to trigger emergent behavior? Or is the answer more humdrum? Does the first to mature send a seismic message from its cell to wake up neighbors who then pass on the message, like drum telegraphy. If so, we haven't detected it.

Mass emergence seems a perverse strategy because it draws attention from predators, but there are parallels in some animal and plant communities where there is safety in numbers.

The year before Brood II appeared above ground was a mast year for oak trees. There were so many acorns strewn around parks and gardens that every footstep crunched like walking on cornflakes, while white-tailed deer gorged on the harvest and gray squirrels made hoards for winter. Mast years are unpredictable and rarely consecutive whereas cicada years can be forecasted in almanacs for decades to come. A strategy that seems prodigal can succeed for venerable trees and insects just fine if an abrupt superabundance of food so overwhelms the appetites of eaters that some are bound to survive.

That sounds like a pat answer, and we usually need to dig deep to understand nature. A simple explanation is more always appealing and memorable than a complicated theory, but sometimes a well-kept secret is more marvelous than a deeply understood fact, and that is another reason to celebrate *Magicicada*.

A SCYTHE FOR ALL SEASONS

O ld Cyrus thought he made the scythe redundant when he was awarded a patent in 1834 for a mechanical reaper. Scythes have mown hay for fodder and harvested grain for bread since Antiquity, and their smaller cousin, the sickle, was a familiar tool in the reign of Cyrus the Great and during the dynasties of Ancient Egyptians. No one lamented its passing, least of all Cyrus McCormick, the inventor in the Shenandoah Valley of Virginia who made his fortune and put blacksmiths who made traditional scythes out of business. I doubt if any farmer who hung up his scythe after buying a mechanical reaper and twine binder looked back fondly on back-breaking labor in the fields. And neither could he have foreseen suburban man take it down again, except to offer it to a museum or play the Grim Reaper on a theater stage.

I bought a scythe from an old man for $20. He had no use for it after moving to an apartment. It was an heirloom from his family farm, and I wonder if he thought it was a bad omen at his age. I expect he thought me a fool to pay for an obsolete tool with a rusty blade and an oak snath riddled with woodworm, but I was delighted to have something with more history than the new tools I buy at the Home Depot. A few strokes of a file restored its keen edge, and a lick of varnish on the sanded snath made the handle smooth again. It looked and felt good. I was ready to beat weeds in my yard, cast them to hell, and enjoy the physical and spiritual rewards of exercise.

Tolstoy understood this feeling long before psychotherapy. He mowed beside servants on his estate to embrace a social philosophy of entering into their labor and bridging the social gulf, even if they thought him a queer fish. He invented the nobleman Konstantin Levin as an illustration.

> The more Levin mowed, the more and more often he felt minutes of oblivion, in which it was not his arms which swung the scythe, but the scythe mowed of itself, a body full of life and conscious of itself, and as though by magic … These were the most blessed minutes.
> From *Anna Karenina*, Part III, Chapter V

The psychologist Edith Weisskopf-Joelson believed the spirit can be fed by combining physical and mental engagement to achieve a goal. She was inspired by the logotherapy[34] of Viktor Frankl, who wrote: 'the notion that experiencing can be as valuable as achieving is therapeutic because it compensates for our one-sided emphasis on the external world of achievement at the expense of the internal world of experience.'

I admit when I scythe weeds I never think of the activity as therapy or an antidote to existential nihilism, but I might muse how old Cyrus helped to start an accelerating revolution that is flipping us from the raw power of our bodies that was always understood to helpless dependence on external energy and technology which gets ever more inscrutable and makes us sedentary. His invention was timely for without mechanization how would farms in the Valley and prairies have grown enough crops for a rapidly expanding population in the 19th Century?

The reaper was an early invention forfeiting field labor and liberating workers for other occupations, some more agreeable and less laborious, some just as humdrum, and forcing many from the countryside to factories and sweat shops. Whither the future as we spin another industrial cycle that is automating production lines and white-collar offices?

And, yet, a cycle is turning as scythes make a come-back, though not this time primarily as farm tools. Swelling numbers of fans mow by hand for fun (*sic*) as free outdoor exercise, and an alternative to pulling levers and lifting weights in fancy gyms and expensive sports clubs. Most of this new cohort own gardens or small farms where they want to breathe fresh air while they work and listen to sounds of nature without drowning out by tractor-mowers and weed-whackers. The farmers of yore sang as they worked in peaceful fields, swaying with the rhythm of scythes for six days and rocking to hymns in the pews of little white churches on the Sabbath. They would be amazed to see the new piety of suburban man rolling with his scythe over devilish weeds. The old mowing song that runs for as many stanzas as there are yards in a meadow is heard again.

> One man went to mow
> Went to mow a meadow;
> One man and his dog Spot,
> Went to mow a meadow.
> Two men went to mow ...
> From traditional English verse

I love casting my tool back and forth over swaths of crabgrass and Japanese stiltgrass until I am tired and thirsty for a cold beer. When I look back at the fallen enemy, I know how Aragorn gloated after slaying orcs and goblins. Bunches of grass lie around in swatches, but it is heavy work made more laborious by a bend in the snath that forces me to stoop, for which I pay with my back the next day. The scythe I bought was too small for me, a better fit for Gimli, or I am not cut out to be an old farmer. I hung the tool in a corner of the shed and forgot about it.

Sometime later, I bought a superior scythe which is custom-made for my height and arm length and really sustains patience and labor. The Austrian scythe has become my favorite tool, making mowing a breeze, even a pleasure working across a field or weedy garden border. Cut half-an-acre a day with a ditch blade? No bother. Slash woody stems with the bush blade or mow the lawn with the sleek grass blade? Piece of cake. Men love new tools. In my zeal for expanding my lexicon I learned the name of every part from nib to toe. Words like peening, snath, tang, and chine are almost obsolete, but used to be familiar to country people for a tool that harvested their daily bread.

I advertise this scythe as a cool tool to my friends and neighbors. They want the demonstration wearing the correct gear of Lederhosen breeches and suspenders with a feather in a felt Alpine hat, but my knobby knees refuse the humiliation of exposure. I like to show them how much lighter it is compared to the clunky Anglo-American scythe. Women can swing it too. The blade is razor-sharp, but not as dangerous as a sickle which, like its sister machete, can accidentally clip a passer-by or even harm yourself in a weeding frenzy. The blade stays safely close to the ground like a keel breaking through water. Scythes are friendly tools that were never used as weapons in war and are too ungainly to be threatening.

The new scythe costs ten times more than my antique American, but a tool that has been hand-forged by a craftsman who served an apprenticeship in a European foundry will never come cheap. I like the sweep of its straight snath, and the work never tires me or strains my back. It is never dull work because I regularly take a break to hone the blade with a whetstone carried in a holster. Eventually, the edge must be drawn out on a peening jig between my knees as I sit on a stool in the yard hammering away like an old-timer minus a long white beard. I never use a grindstone to assault an object a craftsman took pride in making. Better than the heirloom and more efficient, it is an object of beauty.

Scything is becoming a cult in parts of North America and Europe where devotees organize contests and associations. Don't imagine this is the pedestrian equivalent of a quaint steam tractor chugging into a field at a state agricultural fair. A fit man swinging a customized scythe can keep pace with a motorized weed-whacker, and no amount of rain will dampen his progress or spirits. I foresee athletic mowers competing for cash prizes one day and becoming celebrities at the Olympic Games. Old Cyrus would shake his head.

DAYS TO REMEMBER

When Veteran's Day comes around it reminds me of a boy standing in the drizzle beside a war memorial in suburban London on the equivalent day in Britain, called Remembrance Day. Over there, it is observed on the Sunday closest to November 11, the anniversary of the signing of the Armistice that ended World War I. I have sepia memories from the early 1960s when I paraded with the 1st Farnborough Boy Scouts to the parish church to mark Remembrance Day, which is popularly known as Poppy Day.

We marched from the car park at the *George & Dragon*, a pub on the site of a former inn that served as a watering hole for horse-drawn coaches on the London to Hastings turnpike. We passed old cottages and flinty walls to the churchyard of *Saint Giles the Abbot*, and one proud year I was asked to carry the colors. Silent lines of people watched from the sidewalk as we followed the veterans, uniformed ambulance drivers and firefighters, and a group of men wearing the red sash of the *Ancient Order of Foresters*, who were always a mystery to me.

The church still looks as it did over 50 years ago, and has not changed much since medieval times when it was erected on an ancient place of worship. It has stout walls over three feet thick made of rough knapped stones collected from surrounding fields to last the ages. It is the epitome of an English village church with a western tower, buttresses, and red tile roof.

We assembled in serried ranks in the churchyard beside the girl guides ('girl scouts') and faced the stone memorial and cross with our backs to a yew tree that is possibly older than the church itself. In those days, the scout uniform meant a clean pair of short pants, a short-sleeved khaki shirt emblazoned with badges, and a green beret pulled over our right ear. No jackets or coats were allowed. Elemental forces reserved their strength all week to pelt us with freezing rain, so Remembrance Day had a double *entendre*. We were cold, wet, and unnaturally cowed for young teenagers. But we dare not complain and had to show a stiff upper lip because our parents stood alongside other elders who remembered sacrifices that made our present discomfort trifling.

The veterans of two World Wars gathered at the memorial to stand stiffly to attention, some leaning on canes and a blind man helped by a guide. Many of them wore dark gabardine mackintoshes on which they pinned a row of shiny medals from colored ribbons. Dad stood aside from them in the crowd with Mom wearing medals he polished that morning. We were united in wearing a felt poppy in our left buttonholes, and representatives of the British Legion and other organizations lay wreaths of poppies at the foot of the cross.

It is a complete coincidence I have just realized I typed the first draft of this essay on July 1, 2016, the centenary of the first day of the Battle of the Somme. On my last visit to the churchyard, I remember noticing under the cross the engraved names of several local men who died in that battle, mostly junior officers who were expected to lead their men 'over the top' as examples of valor. When we were boys we never bothered to read the names, perhaps because we had no family representation on the memorial and the sacrifices seemed almost mythical to me. We played war games blithely with friends. I didn't even think about pressing my father, "What did you do in the war, Dad?" until it was too late to ask. But despite the absence of visible compassion, we knew the ropes for good behavior during the solemn rite from practicing it every year. We waited for the roll call of about 50 names, then a baritone voice recited the *Ode to Remembrance*, and we joined in by repeating the last line of the stanza.

> They shall grow not old, as we that are left grow old:
> Age shall not weary them, nor the years condemn.
> At the going down of the sun and in the morning,
> We will remember them.

With almost uncanny timing, like the cock that crowed for Peter, the church bell started chiming eleven times. The last sober note was followed by the two longest minutes in the year that were so silent we could hear a breeze rustling the yew until broken by a bugle at the memorial where a uniformed young man blew the *Last Post* (equivalent to *Taps* in America). Soon afterwards, we filed through the narthex to seats assigned for scouts in the back pews where we could whisper at last. There was a tired joke that our cushions were removed before the service every year to keep us awake on the hard boards, so we had to rock from cheek to cheek the next hour to stop our buttocks going numb.

The church was an alien place for most of our troop who had a jaded view of the clergy I didn't share. The Rev. Aidan Chapman made daily visits to Mum for weeks when she was desperately ill at home, an oxygen tank beside her bed and expecting another baby. Home care for the seriously sick and home delivery were still common then in Britain, and our mother needed both. I never heard what comfort he offered, but I remember it was gratefully received. It was only when I was woken in the night by the cries of a new brother emerging into the world red, white, and blue and after she got through a serious bout of pneumonia that I realized our family had narrowly avoided a tragedy. Hence, when I saw the vicar in his black cassock and white surplice climbing into his nest in the pulpit to preach on Remembrance Day, I felt a sympathy for his cares. Would he find words to bring more solace than reminders of grief? Could he offer consolation for the loss and waste of lives? I never knew, of course.

I guess many people there were recalling faces and voices from little over a decade before, but how could a boy share the emotion for people he never knew, any more than strangers could feel for my mother's ordeal? The best he could do was stay awake, look attentive, and resist the temptation to pull the girl's pony tail dangling over the back of her pew. It is easier for today's American youth to have fuller hearts for their veterans than we did, because they are more likely to know people who have been in combat and lost friends. A personal connection lends flesh to the statistics of conflict.

That lesson came home one day when I almost bumped into a brawny young man in the aisle of a Virginia supermarket wearing a green sweatshirt labeled USMC. He was propped in a wheelchair without his legs. I felt embarrassed to hail him because that would mark him out as different to other shoppers. Aren't we supposed to avoid patronizing people with disabilities? And if our eyes met what could I say that wouldn't sound clumsy or embarrassing? Of course, it was shameful to worry about bruising my feelings, but would it be rude to ask, "Was it an IED?" How long a leash should curiosity be allowed, and when must it be reined in? I thought I ought to acknowledge him, saying, "Thank you for serving." He never knew he put a human face on the sacrifice of war that day, or made a difference the next November when I saw a fresh bunch of stars and stripes fluttering beside gravestones and mailboxes.

When I revisited the church in Farnborough, I found a new bench to sit on sheltering under the yew tree where we used to stand on parade. The imagination can flare on a quiet day in an ancient churchyard. The tree might have been treated as totemic by pagans cultivating a secret grove for votive offerings. Evergreen yews were favored symbols of fertility and longevity, and their branches were brought indoors for mid-winter festivals long before Christmas trees became fashionable.

As I sat under the boughs gazing at the scene, my eyes kept drawing back to the stone memorial as its designers intended. When I screwed them up the cross seemed transmogrified to a tree with outstretched branches, and back again. In Genesis, the Tree of Knowledge is never properly explained, and some bible translations call the Cross a 'tree.' There is something about trees that set me musing about our affinity with them, from when our hominid ancestors lived in their branches to the Celtic passion for forestland and, finally, to our late realization of dependence on them even as we destroy great swathes of forestland.

The British war artist Paul Nash painted *We are Making a New World* from a scene at the Western Front recalled from serving in World War I. You must see it otherwise you won't understand the title. The mud that swallowed human corpses is churned like gravestones around the boles of trees that turned to carbonized silhouettes on a fiery orange background. More than any other picture depicting the horror of war, I think the picture expresses a shared fate and a warning for a future braided with trees as some of the greatest representatives of the living world.

Trees have their own day of remembrance falling in April when they are at their finest and sprouting blossoms and greenery. The National Arbor Day[35] was created to remind us to be stewards of woods and forests and to plant trees to replace those lost from logging, disease, wildfires, and war. If ever a lyric poem was fitted to celebrate their beauty and bounty it was one composed by Joyce Kilmer in 1913.

> I think that I shall never see
> A poem lovely as a tree...
> From *Trees*

You don't need to be an artist, naturalist, or tree-hugger to be joyful at the sight of a fine specimen, but it is not only their size and age that captures awe. Their biology, genetics, and ecology are marvels that have supported us forever. I doubt if loggers who clear-cut our great forests efficiently like machine-gunners mowed down Tommies in 1916 ever stood back to wonder what friends they were destroying.

> The wrongs done to trees, wrongs of every sort, are done in the darkness of ignorance and unbelief... Any fool can destroy trees...
> From the *Sierra Club Bulletin* (1920) by John Muir

I like the legend of the 7th Century forest-dweller and patron of our old parish church of Saint Giles because he was held to be a guardian of the creation. In his time and for untold centuries before him, forests provided food, medicinal plants, and material for building and heating, cooking, tool- and furniture-making. We are far less connected with forests than when those generations revered trees and the spirits that guarded them—the 'green men' in England and equivalent wardens in other folklore traditions around the world. It was understood that preserving the sylvan landscape was vital for posterity to prosper, but when people moved to towns and cities those cares faded and timber became just another way of making a living or another table. It was like the forgetfulness of men and women who served in foreign wars.

If we say we cherish trees, our actions speak otherwise. They have a value more than utility. They are still preserve and embellish the land, and are emblematic of everything grand and worth preserving in nature. But it is hard for an urban man to remember.

Only tiny tracts of virgin hardwoods survive in Appalachia, but in western North Carolina there is a cove of enormous and ancient biodiversity with giant poplars that has been protected since 1936. It is called the Joyce Kilmer Memorial Forest, and a fitting monument to remember the soldier-poet who died on the Marne battlefield along with his beloved trees.

ANIMAL FEAST

A n ancient feast day is held every time October 4th comes around. I don't mean a feast of animals, like a medieval banquet bloated with meaty dishes of animals slaughtered on a lord's estate, but an ecclesiastical feast offered *for* animals. It blesses them and expresses good will toward them. The day commemorates a saint of the medieval church who is most associated with the love and welfare of animals. That's Francis of Assisi, of course, for who better fits the description? Ah, there's a man that even people outsider his denomination, like me, would canonize. The writer and Francis biographer G.K. Chesterton described him this way:

> There was something in his story ... most hidden and human: the secret softness of heart ... the love of landscape and of animals.

Although the official saint's day can fall on any day of the week, most congregations celebrate it the previous Sunday. Customs vary, but it is like no other service in the year for churches that encourage children to bring their pets, both great and small.

In one parish I know, the smaller animals are paraded to a station for blessing by the clergy. Johnnie brings his hamster in a box, Mary cradles her goldfish in a bowl, and a priest prays under his breath there will be no dog fights or 'accidents' in the aisle. There is a serious intent amid some droll scenes and I doubt Francis would have cared if protocol was upset so long as the spirit of the occasion was tender and generous. Whatever a person's religious convictions and observances, or if there are none, a ritual to meditate about our biological kin is worth keeping. The services animals render us are vast, and we should never forget the ineffable bounty of nature in which they are an ascendant part that inspired Francis.

> Praised be You, my Lord, with all your creatures,
> Especially Sir Brother Sun ...
> From *The Canticle of the Creatures* (or *Sun*)

The parade of animals is as much for children as it is about them. Children have more open hearts toward them, and our attitudes tend to harden as we grow up with new cares and responsibilities. Sometimes, it is not until our lonelier and graying years that we reach out for an animal companion again, but when we are kids we want pets to play with and for pouring affection on them. Our parents may object to creatures as demanding as dogs or cats and suggest more acceptable species, but whatever the choice we learn life lessons from animals when we draw closer. I absorbed two great lessons from them in childhood.

The first was to leave wild animals be and own a duty of care to those in my life. In a home without dogs or cats, I had to fill the gap with critters. Almost any would do. I had a tiny zoo in our shed to shelter rodents, reptiles, amphibians, and beetles collected from local woods and fields. I was especially fond of a slow worm I found around gravestones when the verger was not looking, and kidded my friends the legless lizard was a venomous viper. I had to let it go when it refused food, dead or alive.

My collection was much smaller and far less exotic than Gerald Durrell's menagerie on Corfu (*My Family and Other Animals*), but we share one tragedy. Our first animal to die was a tortoise ('turtle' in America). When I buried Terrence in the pet graveyard at the bottom of our garden I felt guilty for shortening a life taken from the wild where he might have lived much longer. My only comfort in hindsight is that the animal was sacrificial for others, because I never kept another wild vertebrate again. As for the rest, I released them before we went on family vacation when I could not feed or water them. That was a diktat from parents and the end of my zoo.

The second lesson from animals, as far as early memory can be trusted, was not one I was taught at home or school. It wasn't sex, although I witnessed behavior that put questions in my naïve brain. It was the bigger mystery of mortality. It takes time for a child to make a rationale connection between the public news of new babies in the neighborhood and the private loss of lives at the other pole of the lifespan. The second is a necessary corollary of the first, unless the population will explode, and is close to a law of nature for a sustainable future. I didn't have enough life experience to have any sense of how wide the gap is between poles and, besides, young minds have a peculiar sense of time, their years rolling forward slowly and death a remote, almost unimaginable, calamity at the end of time itself. Of course, I heard of people dying, but they were other folks and my grandparents were permanent and unchanging fixtures in my universe for a long time, and had existed from the remotest dot of time. The shorter lives of animals gave me a better perspective.

I guess the loss Grandma's dog, Lassie, started me thinking. I was heart-broken because we were born the same year and grew up together, but she raced ahead in age to die when we were 11 years old. My white mice had shorter lifespans and, although I didn't mourn them, they helped to steer a growing sense of scale and realization that everything has its season and expiration date.

The mystery of time and aging became so absorbing I later poured it into research and published a book on the subject.[36] By the time Grandma passed I was grown up, and knew that lives like hers full of years are the acceptable way of nature, and not a reason to 'rage, rage against the dying of the light.' That was something else I learned from animals I might call a third lesson. Tragedy is always a loss, but the opposite is not necessarily true. There can be loss without tragedy. Lassie was a loss and Terrence a tragedy. Francis passed around 44 years of age. We call that mid-life nowadays and premature death, but it was a riper age for a medieval friar and he had already achieved his mission. From the little we know, the man who was close to nature submitted peacefully to go gently into that good night.

THANKSGIVING

Christmas is the sound of carols, July the Fourth the sight of fireworks, and Thanksgiving the aroma of roast turkey. An umami breeze from the kitchen is the essence of Thanksgiving Day, but how turkey came to be associated with the holiday is something of a mystery. Turkeys crowning role at that season is a compensation, though a fatal one, for a species that lost the race against bald eagles to be America's national bird.

Wild turkeys were abundant when the first colonists arrived here in the early 1600s, but that does not necessarily mean they were on the menu at the very first Thanksgiving Dinner. We don't know for sure, and even the date and place of that celebration is contested. According to a tale often told and frequently disputed, it was inaugurated soon after the English Puritans arrived in God's own land of Massachusetts to celebrate their first harvest with friendly native people. It is a sweet story to chime with a proud history that parents like to tell children, but resented by Virginians who insist on precedence.

They trace their claim to a 1619 voyage of 36 men on the good ship *Margaret* out of Bristol, England. It was a tub only 35 feet long, less than double the length of my office, and yet it sailed across the ocean for ten weeks to the Chesapeake Bay. After weathering the last storm, the mariners steered their vessel into the King James River to anchor off the appointed land, which became known as the Berkeley Hundred and is today the Berkeley Plantation.

The ship's master, John Woodlief, was a returnee from England after surviving the 'Starving Times' nine years earlier at Jamestown Fort, some 25 miles downstream. It says something about the man that he left home comforts to return to Virginia, but he was wiser than on the 1607 voyage when he conveyed an assortment of idle gentlemen and press-ganged paupers, none of whom were prepared for the rigors of life on the edge of a wilderness. He brought skilled craftsmen this time to build the fragile colony as well as others needed to service a functioning community. He filled the ship to the gunwales with clothes, kitchen utensils, tools, weapons, bibles, and beads for trading with Indians. Among the goods were 8,000 biscuits and loaves, 160 lb. of butter, 127 lb. of bacon and horsemeat, 60 bushels of peas, 20 bushels of wheat, 6 tons of cider and 5½ tons of beer, which was safer to drink than well-water.

The London sponsors of the colony instructed the captain to perform a solemn service of thanksgiving soon after they arrived, and gave him this formula to read:

> Wee ordaine that the day of our ships arrival at the place assigned for plantation in the land of Virginia shall be yearly and perpetually kept holy as a day of thanksgiving to Almighty God.
> Attributed to a charter of the Virginia Company of London

There is a plaque at the Berkeley Plantation commemorating the service held in December 1619, a full year before the Pilgrims stepped off the Mayflower. A manuscript recording the voyage and first thanksgiving was lost until Dr. Lyon Tyler of the College of William & Mary rediscovered it three centuries later in an archive at the New York Public Library[37]. Virginians claim not only primacy but that their Thanksgiving was instituted as an annual religious observance, and not a one-off feast like the famous celebration at Plymouth. Despite the theological tone of the proclamation, the Berkeley bunch was composed of rugged pioneers who were more devoted to profit than piety. A legend tells of an entrepreneurial priest who used Indian corn to distill the first bourbon whiskey in 1621. Virginians like to be first in all good things, but this claim attracts a spirited rebuff from patriotic Kentuckians whose ancestors also sought southern comfort in pioneer times.

Unfortunately for Virginians, their rite was abandoned after an Indian raid at Berkeley in 1622 when families were evacuated to the relative safety of Jamestown Fort. Not until 1958 was it reinstated by the owners of the old plantation. The long gap enabled northern upstarts to boast they had launched the nation's most honored meal, and this became the received story when Southern culture was humiliated after the Civil War.

We attended the Berkeley Thanksgiving on Sunday November 6, 2016, a full fortnight before the national holiday. Crowds enjoyed the celebration under a blue sky as an Indian summer delayed the progress of fall. In a meadow that rolls down to the waterside from a ridge where the old plantation house still stands, families played games and visited food and craft stalls. There was a replica encampment and a corn maze, candle-dipping and doll-making, parading and dancing, music and magic. We watched a re-enactment of Captain Woodlief with his men landing from a replica of the good ship to give thanks after a safe ocean passage. Nearby, a small band of Indians stomped a

279

Friendship Dance to the rhythm of drum-beats, although I suspect their ancestors would be horrified to see them merry as Englishmen stepped on their turf. The crowd recited the Pledge of Allegiance (hand on heart), sang the National Anthem and, finally, the current owner of Berkeley appeared with one of Woodlief's descendants to retell the stirring history.

Most families postponed turkey dinners that day to the official Thanksgiving over two weeks later. If we could raise old colonists from their graves they would tell us that modern turkeys are pale, vast, and grotesque shadows of the birds they remembered fattening on fall mast in the forest. Wild turkeys were familiar fare, much as salmon and rabbit were for the relatives of colonists in England and France, and I imagine children groaning when it was served for the umpteenth time. It requires rarity and high market value to call something a delicacy.

In colonial days, turkeys were taken to Europe where they were selected to be meatier and less flighty by careful breeding. When some were returned they were crossed with wild turkeys to produce a bronze variety that was superior in size and vigor and tamer than wild birds. Continuing selection for these characteristics produced the carcass we know today. Thanksgiving turkeys had a complicated history involving trans-Atlantic journeys and intense genetic selection to create the familiar Broad-Breasted White whose legs and keel are now so short they cannot mate and need artificial insemination to breed. The original Bronze is now a rarity, although a nucleus of the stock that survived as a remnant in England recently made the journey home to a new free-range poultry farm in Virginia. Americans are great travelers.

The number of wild turkeys in the woods has fluctuated wildly too. By 1900, they were extirpated in most counties from over-hunting, but not to the extent of the passenger pigeon which was the most common species of bird (even in the world) and became extinct in 1914. Conservation efforts, reintroduction programs, and enforced hunting seasons have led to a triumphant return of a bird that is a common sight again in many of its old haunts.

We see the big birds rustling through leaf litter in our woods, gleaning fields, waddling along roadsides, and bobbing their heads for morsels to eat. Don't imagine their appetite distracts them for even a moment from potential danger; they see us from afar and rapidly get airborne with a racket of whirring feathers, carrying a 20-lb. carcass at an amazing velocity. Their sharp eyes have acute responsibility for guarding the payload of breast meat, and they gather in groups of adults and jakes after the breeding season for greater security. They may seem wise although when the fall hunting season opened before Thanksgiving last year there were 13 in our woods, but they weren't smart enough to know it is an unlucky number.

CHRISTMAS BIRDS

Friends and neighbors turned up early for hand-outs on Christmas Eve after overnight snow laid a thin white cover over our yard. They looked cozy perched on the picket fence and on branches in fluffy, multicolored jackets with caps pulled down to their beaks or turned up to make a crest. They were cardinals, chickadees, nuthatches, titmice, wrens, and an assortment of woodpeckers. The crow-sized pileated woodpecker stayed aloof in the back forty.

Most of the fall harvest of seeds and berries was already gone, and insects and grubs that were abundant had died off or were hibernating. Our visitors came early after an overnight fast and their hunger overcame shyness. They came for suet, black oil seeds, peanuts, and dried meal-worms in the feeder which I strategically stationed in front of my window.

They were not all polite visitors waiting to feed. Some weighed their chances with shock tactics to displace a bird at the feeder, but justice was soon served when it was their turn to be ejected by another bird dashing up. There was none of the table etiquette taught to children (or was before TV dinners), but at least there was some community spirit. The sight of a prowling cat or *kee-yeeear* sound of a hawk triggered a ripple of chirps to warn others. They plunged into dense cover before a red-shouldered hawk arrived in the yard looking for red meat as it patrolled close to the feeder on broad wings like a toy glider thrown by a child. I marked the hawk with a √ on my check-list. Birders are compulsive tickers.

I was watching through a window with binoculars from my armchair and within reach of a cup of coffee and a muffin. This was luxurious birding compared to crouching in a home-made blind (or 'hide') when I was a boy with fingers too numb to trigger a camera shutter.

I am one of thousands of amateurs up and down the USA and Canada who record birds for a citizen scientist program run by the Cornell Lab for Ornithology[38] in Ithaca, NY. The myriad of data submitted to Cornell generates an impression of the distribution and abundance of birds across the continent and for monitoring populations at a time of dramatic changes in climate and land use. Even people who hated school science can become this kind of scientist and enjoy the satisfaction of contributing to an important goal that demands little effort. Birding does not have to be sitting in the cold or plodding through snowy woods in wellies, and can be embraced by young and old, able-bodied and disabled people.

Mid-winter records are particularly valuable because bird populations are more stable between migratory seasons. The birds I see here are common garden residents, but unless I notice a leg band or a peculiar mark I have no idea if I am seeing the same individual later. I didn't hear the melancholy cooing of mourning doves as they peck under the feeder for seeds dropped by other birds or a mischievous squirrel. Nor did I see perky dark-eyed juncos. They are called snowbirds, an odd nickname for a bird whose plumage is shades of gray, but it was coined because they stay here when other species move south ahead of a polar front. Not far away I can record other birds that winter with us, like the snow geese, but the day I tell Cornell a snowy owl visited my yard a member of staff will call to ask how much eggnog I drank that morning.

White is the best camouflage in snowy places, but it has a downside by absorbing less heat from the sun. Just as we are sometimes forced into hard choices, nature abounds with trade-offs. Casting back to Physics 101 classes, I remember white-painted surfaces reflect 80% of solar radiation compared to only 5% for black, and when reflectivity and emissivity are combined the solar reflectance index of white versus black is theoretically 100 to 0. Some difference! It reminds me how soot powdered across a snowy path helps it to melt, and why Alpine glaciers are retreating from black carbon fallout from surrounding industrialization as well as from climate change. Imagine if colors were turned upside down and snow was black. Our world would be warmer, sea levels would be higher, fauna and flora would be different, and we wouldn't have snowmen on Christmas cards. So, let snow be white.

> My mistress' eyes are nothing like the sun;
> Coral is far more red than her lips' red;
> If snow be white, why then her breasts are dun
> If hairs be wires, black wires grow on her head.
> From *Sonnet 130* by William Shakespeare

The Christmas season offers temptations to stay indoors, but there is one long-honored activity that pulls birders out of their armchairs, come wind or snow, rain, or shine. The Audubon Society's Christmas Bird Count[39] originated at the beginning of the 20th Century. The conservation movement had a few visionaries in those days, notably John Muir and John Burroughs who saw plain evidence of environmental degradation and were alarmed by dwindling numbers of formerly common animals and birds. A custom carried over to the new century at that time of year was a 'Side Hunt' in which hunters were divided into parties to compete for the largest heap of fur and feather. Frank Chapman and a couple of dozen other naturalists mostly from the north-east started an alternative Christmas program for counting *live* birds. It has grown into an international effort with thousands of volunteers, including over a hundred around Williamsburg.

Across the Pond in a nation of bird-lovers, the British Trust for Ornithology sponsors population surveys too, but it chooses a gentler season to dispatch recorders. No bird is better loved over there or more closely associated with Christmas than the plump little robin with a scarlet breast that was known for centuries as the 'redbreast.' It is a cousin of the stout American robin only in name, being more a flycatcher than a thrush. Popularity is not, however, the reason why so many British Christmas cards depict the redbreast near a postbox in a snowy scene. The explanation is that postmen were nicknamed 'Robins' from the scarlet skirted frock coats and black top hats introduced by the British Postal Service in 1855.

Doves are also linked with the Christmas tradition. You might think they would be afforded special protection, especially here on the edge of the Bible Belt because one returned to Noah with an olive branch as a symbol of peace. They offer the slightest morsels, but hunters blast them out of the sky by the thousands after the season opens at the end of December, up to a bag limit of fifteen a day.

Peace to our gentle doves.

On the second day of Christmas
my true love sent to me:
Two Turtle Doves
and a Partridge in a Pear Tree.
From a traditional English carol[40]

PART VI. IN MEMORIAM

APPALACHIAN SPRING

The title of Aaron Copland's musical suite captures the essence of my feelings about Appalachia when nature wakes from a long winter sleep.

Springtime arrives late in the Allegheny Mountains, growing slowly like the music until a major arpeggio bursts out of an allegro storm. The gods thunder around our home, which squats timidly in a hollow between dark mountains, and I occasionally see a flashing spear of light thrown from a low cloud to burn some innocent tree with limbs outstretched in surrender. Branches rattle as a breeze chases along the valley, warning of an approaching gray curtain of rain I can hear over a mile away; the moaning of trees grows louder until there is urgent drumming on my tin roof. What a primitive wonder to watch a passing storm and listen to its symphony from the safety of the deck where I sit in my rocker bent over my journal.

The wild elements hurry to the next valley where they continue to vent their rage, leaving behind brighter clouds that gently rise above the mountain ridges. I sniff air washed of dank forest odors, and listen for distant violins and a piccolo playing tender phrases. Apart from the mossy-green relief of hemlock crowns, the oak, hickory, and beech trees stand in ranks of gray and umber stripes painted on Middle Mountain in the melancholy months, but of all the promises in life none is more faithful than the slopes will soon be covered again in a green mantle. I love it.

I have an image of Mr. Copland coming here to seek his muse because his suite always summons pictures of our mountains, and so I was disappointed when I read it is a musical sketch of a spring wedding in Pennsylvania, but I got over it. I know it doesn't really matter if an abstraction is inspired by something completely different, provided it means something to you. Perhaps the music has transported you to a beloved place, and feels just as special as it does for me.

I made a road trip through four states that straddle the mountain spine. It was May and daffodils still nodded in the banks and yellow coltsfoot sprouted beside roads where tires did not compress the gravel. The flowering at higher elevations was a full three weeks behind the coastal plain of Virginia where the season was already marching toward summer. The forests still looked like a host of carbon skeletons, although when I pulled branches down I saw hopeful buds swelling from the rising sap. It was past time to cut logs for next winter, and tree tappers had already carted away buckets of maple juice to their sugar shacks. It was the best time of year with the glory of summer still ahead.

Winter still clung to the high ridges. Ragged lines of trees silhouetted against a Payne's gray sky offered shade on sunny days for drifts of old snow to blanket roots. Melt water tumbled down the slopes everywhere, plunging over bare rocks, seeping through leaf litter and moss until it merged into little torrents to refresh streams that run dry in summer. The hasty rush of water eases to a graceful flow in the bottomlands. The watershed draining into streams gathers to rivers that follow country roads winding through valleys and crossing plains all the way to the Gulf or the Chesapeake Bay on the other side of the Divide.

There are few homes or homesteads in the high country and traffic is light, apart from an occasional logging truck. If I see a pickup parked on a grassy verge beside the forest in the fall I know there is a hunter about. A loud blast echoing around the hills reports he is bagging a squirrel or a wild turkey for the crockpot, and I might see him kneeling to field-dress a deer carcass.

But in springtime the forest is almost silent, although never empty. This is the season when local folks gather ramps from the first green carpet over dead leaves. Popular demand for the pungent wild leek now threatens its former abundance because I hear it is the new arugula for diners at hot restaurants in New York. The old man who fills his bag with bulbs on our land worries commercial harvesters will strip the hillsides. Ramps are his rite of spring. His wife parboils and fries them with eggs in bacon grease to serve with beans, potatoes, and cornbread. Mountaineers celebrate rampfests in community rooms and church halls, dining on folded tables to a background of traditional tunes played by neighbors on fiddles, guitars, and banjos. Richwood is an apt name for the heart of the festival in West Virginia.

Ramps are not the only fruits of the forest for those who know where to look. There are blackberries, nuts, and morels in the proper season, and secret places where ginseng still holds out. A local lady told me her mother taught her every edible wild plant and mushroom, so she could live off the land if she ever fell on tough times. There are few people like Ernestine to pass down traditional knowledge, and fewer in the younger generation who care to receive it.

When I drive past an abandoned homestead and see a gate open to a fallow field I am tempted to stop if it is safe on a narrow lane, or at least gaze in the rear mirror to imagine a past, if only for a fleeting moment. Old homes have stories I will never know about residents I will never meet, yet they feed a curious mind. How thankful the young farmer felt when his first calf was delivered, how proud the man who carried his bride into the home his uncle built, how jolly their children and grandchildren as they checked the chicken coop and stroked the milk cow. But there was another story of hardships endured. It could be bitterly cold working outdoors in winter, discouraging when the corn was raided by deer or blight spoiled the potato crop, and sorrowful when the eldest son left for the mines in McDowell County and a younger brother was drafted overseas. They never wrote down their stories, and even their names and dates are faded on the wind-scoured crosses in Mingo Flats.

Owning a small farm was never for the weak-hearted, and the Great Recession from 2008 is still causing pain in the mountains. Jobs vanished, property values wilted, and children who grew up in the hollows make their way more easily in the cities, trading a better standard of living for rustic beauty. They left without glancing back and will forget the family home with its broken sale board that Grandpa Jim wanted them to inherit. The home will be gone in a few years, along with the memories.

To a tidy mind, an abandoned house ought to be cleared instead of left to blot the landscape until the earth reaches up to embrace it. When a wooden home is deserted it slides into the belly of decomposers that change timber to dirt in one of nature's greatest feasts. Paint peels from sidings like bark from a birch tree, broken windows welcome roosting birds and bats, and creepers invade the walls with a tangle of vines that turn ruby in the autumn. After the weather proofing afforded by a roof is broken and indoors becomes outdoors, there is a swarm of worms, beetles, and molds waiting to attack the damp fabric. When a house is given over to nature's undertakers nothing can resurrect the ghost.

After the collapse, the gap opens to a vista of gray woods and a blue mountain. Only a brick chimney stands as an enduring memorial over a hearth that once warmed feet and cooked meals.

In some future era, I imagine a young couple hiking up the steep slopes of our mountain. They will pause on a grassy knoll to stare across the valley to the round peak of Elk Mountain and enjoy the forest greening in May. They will look down at the ruin they passed on the way up. It had robust cedar sidings and a green metal roof, but all matter obeys a grinding cycle, and nothing lasts forever. After the last owners abandoned the house and the weather took its toll, the frame rotted out and the roof collapsed in a summer storm to make a jumbled heap of wood and steel beside an overgrown path.

The woman asks, "Who do you think lived there?"

He shrugs his shoulders as he points a camera at her. "This one's for our grandkids." He frames her standing in front of a twisted hemlock even older than the house. *Click.*

Soon they will be gone. They haul themselves on low branches, clamber over mossy boulders, and balance on logs over streams until they reach the top. It is rough going until they reach the ridge.

Before the ascent, they picked over the junk around the ruin, hoping to find a souvenir like an antique penny or an old rifle cartridge, but the rusted scythe was too heavy to carry home.

They didn't find the jar I buried in the dirt near the front door. It was my time capsule. They never dreamt the first owner would leave something for them, for why would he bother and how would he know they would come? But if they had found it they could have learned who lived and loved there, about the local man who built the home, the dog that watched for wild turkeys, and the Old-Time band that played at a small party to celebrate the opening.

They might then imagine him rocking on the deck and deep in thought as a storm passes over the mountain. His mind was often captive to that music, which cast back to people who came before — a Shawnee hunting party, a pioneer farmer looking for a level patch, and a weary pair of loggers carrying a saw. Their lives were but breezes that passed unnoticed through the forest, but someone will come there one day to make a new home and find my story before it crumbles in the jar.

JUST BOB

Have you missed a memorial service for someone you loved, admired and who you owe your career to, or all three? If so, you will understand how I felt when I could not attend a service for my mentor, Robert Edwards (1925-2013) at Bourn Hall, a Jacobean manor house in a village outside Cambridge, England, thousands of miles from home in Virginia. That was where Bob and the gynecologist Patrick Steptoe (1913-1988) founded the world's first in vitro fertilization (IVF) clinic in 1980.

I imagined hinges on the heavy oak door creaking as people trooped inside under the lintel bearing the ancient motto *Jour de ma Vie* (Day of my Life). More than a hundred-people attended the thanksgiving party for his life. Bob never belonged to a faith community, and once told me he didn't like 'churchy music,' but there was something spiritual in his heart, and I am sure he would have loved the lyrics sung that day

Deep peace of the quiet earth to you ...
From *A Gaelic Blessing* by John Rutter

He left an extraordinary legacy in science and a medical revolution pioneered with Patrick and his assistant Jean Purdy that helps people to realize a dream of building a family. To date, the number of IVF babies has passed a quarter million in the UK, and above seven million have been born across five continents.

We miss him terribly. It seems incredible that someone with that much vitality is gone forever. Although the gap has started to heal, we still have fanciful thoughts of him showing up abruptly on our doorstep after heaven expelled him for disturbing the angelic peace. Deep into his eighties, Bob was still driven by an infectious enthusiasm for life and work. After retiring from Cambridge University and Bourn Hall, he was busy founding journals, writing and editing, lecturing and teaching, and collecting honors and awards around the globe. In the remaining time he cared for his family and his trees. But time eventually caught up with him.

He needed a gritty Yorkshireness seasoned with a sense of humor to negotiate a stormy passage to a controversial harbor. People who remember the early days wonder how Bob endured so much professional antagonism and personal animosity. The uproar from his research in the 1970s is now a fading memory that would puzzle the current generation growing up with IVF as a conventional medical therapy. Most people know a family that has benefited from treatment, and have seen it featured in TV documentaries and drama.

He told us it was the appeals and heart-rending stories of childless couples that drove him against a tide of opprobrium. In those days, gynecologists had little to offer patients and, too proud to admit defeat, were tempted to ignore that private suffering. Who could have guessed that a lad who grew up in a northern mill town and never trained as a medical doctor would become their champion and one of Britain's greatest scientists, any more than we expected a grocer's daughter from Lincolnshire to become the first woman Prime Minister and the Iron Lady? That Bob, a resolute socialist, admired Margaret is an example of his paradoxical nature.

He earned a Ph.D. at Edinburgh University in the early 1950s, where he collaborated with his future wife Ruth Fowler (1930-2013). His career was entirely in Britain after a fellowship at Caltech and short visits to Baltimore and Chapel Hill. His first job in London was research on contraceptive vaccines, and he had to find spare time after hours for eggs and embryos, his first love. He started to dream about developing human IVF to study the causes of birth defects, which seemed an absurd ambition at the time because IVF was only successful in rabbits, and not until he met Patrick did he realize the technique could be a gift for treating infertility. To ensure he would not hurt the reputation of his institute the director banned research on human ovaries.

He escaped to Cambridge for greater freedom in the laboratory of Sir Alan Parkes, a crusty old-school type, and the foremost reproductive biologist of his day in the UK. Most of the Cambridge dons came from well-to-do homes and famous public schools[41], and their privilege rankled with his socialist principles, but Bob found his feet and flourished to steadily ascend the academic ladder. But he knew he couldn't 'butter his parsnips' in that ivory tower; to develop IVF he needed cooperation from medical doctors as gatekeepers to patients for a steady supply of human eggs for research.

Every doctor in the country apart from Molly Rose at the Edgware Hospital kept the maverick at arm's length until a famous encounter with the perfect collaborator at the Royal Society of Medicine in 1968. That was Patrick Steptoe, a senior gynecologist from the boondocks of northern England who was developing the still controversial laparoscope which they needed to collect eggs by keyhole surgery. Patrick had many patients with blocked Fallopian tubes who could be helped by IVF, and so began the first steps of a long trail. It took a special chemistry and rare partnership of scientist and doctor to navigate the controversial course of a fertility revolution. Bob and his student Richard Gardner showed how to genetically test embryos, and in the end IVF has had far more applications than anyone, even Bob, ever imagined. But everyone agreed he was barmy in those days.

Barely a year after they started, the pair made a major advance which they published in the venerable science magazine *Nature* in 1969. It was the first authentic report of fertilization of human eggs in a Petri dish (erroneously called a 'test-tube'), and the breakthrough was helped by another student, Barry Bavister, who formulated a 'magic' culture medium. They struggled through a decade of obstacles, disappointments, and professional hostility until the birth of Louise Brown, when everything changed.

A less driven man would never stay the course. There were ghastly headlines demonizing him, accusing him of 'Playing God' as Dr. Frankenstein. But the more the label was seen the less offensive it became, and finally it was droll. Hardest to bear were attacks by fellow scientists and doctors, including a handful of Nobel prizewinners, but his senior colleague Bunny Austin was a tremendous source of encouragement. After the birth of Louise when *The Daily Express* ran the headline, *Baby of the Century*, there was far more celebration than condemnation. It would be a heartless person who said she should never have been born. She was a bonny baby, but it is sobering to think if by chance she had been unhealthy all progress would have stopped and left Bob and Patrick's reputation in tatters.

Bob was different to every other don I knew. He didn't come from a distinguished family or have a glittering undergraduate record and had to be a fighter to succeed with a controversial agenda in a competitive and sometimes backbiting profession. He gave us a wonderful example of egalitarianism and encouraged independent ideas that characterized his own career. He taught us to present and defend data, to criticize and contest theories, and often played the devil's advocate to tease us with playful arguments.

We were never remotely involved in the IVF program, which was mostly out of sight some 200 miles to the north near Manchester. I have been asked why Bob didn't draw more on the growing expertise in his team to accelerate progress. I think he kept us at arm's length from controversy which might have harmed us at tender stages of our careers. Today, he would be criticized for supervising students too lightly, but there was an unofficial sink or swim policy in the University which was tough but rewarded those with grit and an independent spirit. If we floundered there were other talented people in the group who generously came to our rescue. Never again did I know a happier or more productive workplace, and many of his protégés have gone forward to great distinction.

He was often absent in the north or abroad for meetings and lectures, and I admit we were often relieved to see the back of him! Absence made the heart grow stronger. You need to have known Bob to understand what I mean, how maddening our beloved professor could be. Ideas poured from him like print out of a newspaper press. He was hard to keep up with, and I never knew a more fertile scientific mind.

My first project was to test his brilliant theory about Down's syndrome in older mothers. I labored for several years, but was never able to prove it and grew more and more doubtful. His hunches weren't always correct, but he always had others up his sleeve. Long after I left the lab he ribbed me whenever we met:

"Haven't you proved my theory yet, Roger?" He was an endearing mixture of serious scientist and light-hearted friend.

My wife remembers when he visited Virginia where she was the embryologist for America's first IVF baby. When Bob asked for a tour of her lab, Lucinda took immense pains to make the place spotless, but he wasn't willing to be easily impressed. He reached to the top of a tall incubator to wipe an invisible film of dust on his fingertip to wave at her, then grinned like a Cheshire cat.

On another occasion when he stayed with us in Scotland, he took us out for dinner at a seaside restaurant. My two young sons turned up their noses at whitebait on the menu because the little fishes still had their heads and tails. He ordered a plate to bait them, devouring each one headfirst while staring at the horrified faces of my boys.

For many people, their fondest memories are when he sat on the lawn for anniversary garden parties at Bourn Hall in a crowd of IVF parents and their children, his crowning achievement. I wonder if he ever felt disappointment that his gift of fertility treatment is too expensive for many people. In the UK a patient's postcode address decides how much treatment the National Health Service will afford, and few states in the USA mandate insurance cover for IVF.

I last saw him in 2008 at his farm outside Cambridge. He was drifting through old memories and I thought he was stewing over something when he showed me his numerous awards and honors in a lighted wall cabinet. There were the Legion d'Honneur (France), CBE (UK), Fellow of the Royal Society (London), honorary degrees from Cambridge, York, Wales, Belgium, Greece, Romania, et cetera, the King Faisal Prize (Saudi Arabia), the Lasker Award (USA), and others I no longer remember. Who could ask for more tributes? But I sensed he was holding back some private regret.

We were disappointed when he was passed over for the 2007 Nobel Prize for stem cell research because he was the original pioneer in the early 1960s when hardly anyone was dreaming of regenerative medicine. It seemed unlikely he would receive the ultimate scientific accolade for IVF unless a call came quickly from Stockholm because Nobel Prizes are not awarded posthumously. Patrick was already out of the running and even missed his investiture at Buckingham Palace. We heard the Nobel Committee was under pressure to oppose a prize to IVF, so it was with enormous surprise and pride when we heard he was the sole awardee of the 2010 Nobel Prize for Physiology and Medicine. We savored it as a vindication of his struggles and stamp of international approval of a formerly controversial technology.

Poor health prevented him from attending the award ceremony. Martin Johnson, one of his first students and himself a Cambridge professor, gave a lecture on his behalf, and Ruth accepted the award from the King of Sweden. Her role in the story is much greater than told. Besides carrying the bulk of responsibility for raising their five daughters and managing their home and later a farm, she was a scientist in her own right and a steady and wise counsellor for his endeavors.

I attended a conference at his college, Churchill, a few weeks before he died. While peering in a cabinet displaying his papers and personal items in the college archives, I noticed Margaret Thatcher's legendry handbag in the next section. Was it a coincidence or a joke? Wags have told how the Iron Lady filled her bag with weights to swing at liberals and conservative 'wets.' I mused they were both strong characters who were born and died within days of each other. Both visionaries from opposite poles of the political spectrum, they attracted immense loyalty and opposition in about equal measure.

The juxtaposition of property seemed weird for a pair who would have been at loggerheads in an argument, but I recalled she had never openly criticized IVF, as a good many of her party had done, and, moreover, it was her government that awarded his first public honor. It would take the Nobel Prize twenty years later for one of her successors to recommend him for a higher honor, and came too late for him to enjoy. Knowing the man and his politics, I wonder if he would have owned the title 'Sir Robert,' or preferred to remain plain 'Bob,' the family man who helped people to have babies.[42]

DEAR JEAN

Dear Jean, I'm sorry I couldn't join the crowd to say farewell in Grantchester. Our friends told me it was one of those miserable days when gray clouds hang over the fens before the daffodils bloom on the Cambridge Backs. Scots would call it dreich which, pronounced correctly, sounds exactly as it means.

So much water has passed under the bridge since the last time I saw you. Then, I came down from Edinburgh to the *University Arms Hotel* from where you drove me to the mini-conference at Bourn Hall. I remember you looked pale and tired, but it seemed impolite to ask why.[43]

You would be amazed how many doctors and scientists at that meeting have gone on to glory, and sad to say some to Glory. You would never recognize our conferences in reproductive medicine today, some of them in huge convention centers accommodating thousands of people, and with so many lectures there are parallel sessions. You would hardly know anyone, most would not know your name, but it all started when Bob, Patrick and you got together.

I wonder what they would think if I told them about a day long ago when you showed me a living human blastocyst embryo. It was one of those moments for which a young scientist burns— the pride of being one of the first to see something astounding and obscure, even ineffable, that previous generations could not imagine, but has become a daily sight in IVF clinics around the world. A large clinic today manages over a hundred embryos belonging to a couple of dozen patients every day, and stores thousands more in its freezers. When fertility medicine was new every embryo was a breathtaking sight, and we wondered if the mite in the pink fluid at the bottom of the dish would become the baby a couple ached for after years of trying to build a family.

I remember asking you for help as I searched under the microscope for the tiny ball. You hovered behind me, worrying if a green student would spill the precious contents of the dish. Those were early days before Lesley Brown conceived and there were many trials and disappointments ahead. There must have been days when you wondered if IVF would ever help a patient, and I doubt you could imagine it would become routine and create millions of babies around the world.

I guess you never minded standing in Bob Edwards' shadow as his assistant. He often saluted you at the end of a lecture as the third pioneer along with Patrick Steptoe, but as the assistant to a famous scientist and a gynecologist (and being female) you didn't have much visibility or a published biography until recently[44]. The longer you are away, the deeper the mystery of your role in the program, and now that both men are gone there is no one left to tell the full story.

Why did you leave a career in nursing, and why switch to a lab job for which you were not trained? Of course, it wasn't any ordinary job. Bob's goal was no less than a medical revolution, and Patrick wanted to help patients who had been abandoned to infertility. It was never easy. Fertilizing eggs in vitro was called immoral and all of you were denounced from every corner of the Establishment. What did your friends say, or your family think, and how did you cope with it all?

I know how struggles are soon forgotten after reaching a goal, but you must have felt beaten down sometimes, because there was no light in the tunnel for a decade. You worked long, often unsociable hours and at weekends away from home, and had the immense challenge of nurturing embryos in an experimental medium with no outside experts to call for advice. I guess you managed by focusing on work and the struggle to glue two forceful personalities together, for if Bob and Patrick had parted nothing would have been achieved.

I recall you brushing off setbacks and never smirking when we asked for advice. You chuckled when a graduate student goofed, and had a self-effacing wit that was endearing. I think I grinned when you posted on the bulletin board an appeal for the correct spelling of the Philadelphia biologist Beatrice Mintz. 'Help! Is she Mince, Mints or Mintz?' Isn't it funny how trivial things stick in the mind while more important matters are buried in memory? Visitors remarked about your 'humor station' as they passed you before entering Bob's office, and I expect they noticed how earnestly you leaned into your work? When I was visiting Bob soon after Louise was born, I asked him how he found time to write the thousand-page *Conception in the Human Female* that reviewers called our bible. He cracked a cheeky smile and nodded in your direction.

I knew there was a stern spirit under your sunny exterior. One day during a national hullaballoo about banning a South African sports team I watched you go head-to-head with a foreign visitor defending Apartheid. You felt passionately for people you would never know, as you did for patients who depended on you, and

Bob hired you over better qualified candidates because he saw your mettle.

I wish I asked if you ever wanted to be famous, although I can guess your answer. Today, you would be queen of the realm, and still only 70 years old. You would have awards aplenty, laboratories named after you, dinner invitations to honor you, and guest lectureships galore. But you were always happy to be spared that kind of attention, preferring a quiet backroom to counsel patients or care for their embryos. You were content for Bob and Patrick to be the front men. Bob has gone down in history as a scientific pioneer, and Patrick won't be forgotten even though he died too soon for all the honors he earned. I hear that patients wander down the driveway at Bourn Hall to see Patrick's grave in the churchyard. He lies just 15 minutes away from you, but no one makes that journey.

I was asked about your story a few years ago. Knowing you were the first IVF embryologist in the world, a group of American nurses wanted to create the 'Jean Purdy Visionary Award' for the most outstanding practitioner of the year. I shared what I knew for the speech announcing the first award, and searched to fill my gaps. I scoured the Internet for your name, but the only Jean Purdy I found was working as a magician in London. You were the real thing! The award was a wonderful chance to stamp your name in the minds of professionals and patients who came after you, but it was never repeated. I was bitterly disappointed, but imagine you would put your arm over my shoulder, saying, "It doesn't really matter, Roger. Almost everyone is forgotten eventually."

> Far-called, our navies melt away;
> On dune and headland sinks the fire:
> Lo, all our pomp of yesterday

Is one with Nineveh and Tyre!
Judge of the Nations, spare us yet,
Lest we forget—lest we forget!
From *Recessional* by Rudyard Kipling

I wonder if you had qualms when you were studying fertilized eggs, or if you were terrified the embryos you and Bob passed to Patrick for patients might conceive an unhealthy baby. I heard you had a religious faith, so I guess you would be happy to know the big three monotheistic religions eventually embraced IVF, with the exceptions of Roman Catholicism and a few fundamentalist denominations. You won't be surprised that philosophers and theologians still argue about the moral status of embryos, although every country has now legitimized or turned a blind eye to IVF.

The blastocyst you showed me was like a portent of the next medical revolution. Bob was first with the idea of using embryonic stem cells to cure diseases and treat traumatic injury, and the cells may even help people suffering from the same condition that took your life. Was that idea already in your mind the day we looked through the microscope together? If you take nothing else from this message, I want you to know that progress never stopped.

I asked a friend to take me to Grantchester churchyard. It was my first visit to the village since I used to cycle there from college or punt against the slow river current for a drink at *The Green Man*. Sometimes, I would share a cream tea with friends at *The Orchard* tea garden, forever associated with the poet Rupert Brooke. The tragedy of his short life draws me to verses he composed in Grantchester and reminds me of you.

And laughs the immortal river still
Under the mill, under the mill?
Say, is there Beauty yet to find?
And Certainty? and Quiet kind?
Deep meadows yet, for to forget
The lies, and truths, and pain? . . . oh! yet
Stands the Church clock at ten to three?
And is there honey still for tea?
From *The Old Vicarage, Grantchester* by Rupert Brooke

I ask myself why it took me so long to write this, and why now? I wonder if it was Bob's passing or Louise's birthday that nudged me. Or was it the sight of your plain memorial that moved me on that bittersweet visit to the churchyard? You are lying in an inauspicious corner under a tree close to your mother and grandmother, and there is nothing to draw the eye of visitors who come searching for the names of the distinguished deceased on headstones. Wind and weather are starting to wear the letters on the gray slate, and someone left a bunch of plastic flowers. I would like a stonemason to make a more durable memorial and engrave a fitting tribute.

Here lies Jean Purdy who died in 1985 aged 39
The World's First IVF Nurse-Embryologist and Co-founder of
Bourn Hall Clinic[45]

If there is any consolation, it is that your story is more poignant because your name is not blazing in books, your life has not been told on screen, and you were not laid in a cathedral crypt. It resonates with the hidden life of George Eliot's heroine Dorothea, and if Rupert Brooke was still living at the Old Vicarage I would ask him to stroll over to compose an ode.

THE BARD OF BECKENHAM

Gordon was born in London in 1928, but when he died in the Beckenham suburb at the age of 86 he left no large footprint in history, although the few people close to him knew a remarkable life had passed.

He declared his school education was "virtually terminated" in 1939 by the outbreak of war. Two years later, he was evacuated to the Welsh countryside where he often got into trouble and was "punched to the ground by his headmaster for being the worst boy in school." Exiled to a remote hill farm from where he rode to school on horseback, he mostly absorbed country wisdom about birthing cows, slaughtering pigs, fishing, and shooting. He returned home in 1944 in time for the V-2 rocket bombardment of London, but the family home came through unscathed.

The first phase of life over, he enrolled as an apprentice toolmaker and worked in a factory for many years until it closed. The workforce was given a redundancy package of £200[46], but he had no qualifications for alternative employment. Eventually, he was offered a job as a security officer on a private property where he had once hunted illegally: the poacher turned gamekeeper.

Poaching was a temptation when meat was still rationed after the war. It could bring home a savory supper to share with his widowed mother, and a few quid from selling pheasants and rabbits to his buddies at the factory. He was almost caught one day, but managed to slide his .22 rifle inside a baggy trouser before a gamekeeper ran up to interrogate him. Gordon had honed a gift of the gab since schooldays, and the keeper was quickly satisfied he was a harmless stroller with a gammy leg.

On another occasion, a policeman stopped to check the legality of Gordon's car as he was about to drive away. He loved that car. The name *Reliant Robin* resonated with his optimistic outlook and fondness for birds. As a three-wheeler, like the motor bike and sidecar he was licensed to drive, he didn't need a driving test and never got around to buying a road tax disc as required by law (equivalent to license plate tags in America). I remember how the officer searched his windshield for the disc and was silently weighing what to do while Gordon chatted at him incessantly. I heard the man chuckle as he walked away.

When Gordon's poaching days were over, he traded his gun for a camera and launched a new phase as a wildlife photographer. He learned how to build blinds ('hides'), track animals, and mimic bird song, although, apart from a single trip to Scotland, he never traveled far and fervently believed in the virtues of knowing one's home turf intimately. He published lavishly-illustrated articles in magazines, and became known in naturalist circles after he published a book about an albino badger discovered in our local woods with two young brothers[47].

I met the trio in 1962 under inauspicious circumstances. I was a young teenager watching a badger sett one night when they surprised me by shining a flashlight in my eyes as I perched in a tree leaning over a badger path. We were both possessive about that sett, and Gordon expressed his feelings bluntly, but after a meeting the following day he accepted me as his third pupil and we remained friends for the rest of his life.

He had been angry because they were watching for the albino and didn't want interlopers to scare the shy animal away. We named it Snowball, but in public we codenamed it Popeye in case anyone overheard us chatting at the fish-and-chip shop where we rendezvoused after an evening in the woods. Gordon wanted to know if Snowball would mate and pass his genes for albinism to cubs, or if the closely-knit badger society would shun him as an alien. Years later in the New Guinea Highlands, the question came to me again when I met a blind albino man covered with burgundy lesions as he sat apart from his tribe under an equatorial sun. It was the worse place on earth to be albino, but Snowball was luckier as a nocturnal creature and he did sire offspring. Gordon's book was successful and led to a program about the badger on *Blue Peter*, a BBC TV children's show.

A fourth phase began when he took up oil painting after his last nocturnal visit to the woods. Completing 72 canvases over the next few years, he framed and mounted them on walls around his home where they slowly acquired a yellow glaze from cigarette smoke. He had an excellent brush technique considering he was untutored, and always painted to a background of classical music. So passionately did he love Wagner's music that he called the *Ring Cycle* "a thirteen-hour cerebral orgasm," and made a portrait of the composer.

Despite his vacuous schooling, he was a natural wordsmith and turned to poetry, his fifth phase, when he lost the inspiration to paint. He told me his compositions reflected "our frailties and his personal views," and I suppose it is true that the oeuvres of artists and poets are often mirrors of character. His fun-loving

313

mind could spend weeks poring over works created solely to amuse himself or the rare visitor. His jokes were creative and limericks droll, and he remained unfailingly cheerful even toward the end when he was almost blind and weak from ill-health.

Few visitors dared enter his home as he drifted into a hermit's existence. Besides dense clouds of toxic smoke, there was a risk of injury sitting in a broken chair or poisoning from a cup-of-tea brewed in the kitchen. There was a tacit understanding that no one sat in the sofa because that was where he slept. He had two bedrooms upstairs either side of the 'necessary,' but they were empty rooms and I only ventured there once because there were no climbing ropes or pitons. The exterior of the house was in dire need of repair and painting after a half century of neglect that made neighbors of proud little houses down the row lament the Luffwaffe bombs missed Number 58.

It was always a rewarding experience to see Gordon because he would regale you with stories and jokes, and when the conversation lulled the walls offered more entertainment. The first pictures to catch the eye as you entered his hall were skillful renderings of the Mona Lisa and Her Majesty Queen Elizabeth II, and the only ones you will ever see bare-breasted. Gordon had a large imagination. On the living room walls, he displayed other favorite works: *Ice Cream* (retitled from Edvard Munch's *The Scream*), *Ballistic Mistle* (a mistle-thrush exploding out of a shotgun barrel), *Gone Fishing* (a fisherman catching a plesiosaur), *Flight of the Swan* (with its beak bending against the picture frame), *Sea of Breasts* (image under this headline), and mysterious figures dancing or playing pipes in woods. His poetry was equally idiosyncratic, full of word-play and humor. He would be amazed that his anthology was published posthumously, from which I have extracted *Object of Desire* as an example.

The briefest glimpse across a crowded room;
Then lost behind a sea of smiling faces.
Desire wells up, dispelling gloom.
He leaves his bar stool; looks in vain for spaces.

His fight begins; elbows, tinkling glasses.
But, deaf to each "What ho", and "Hello darling",
His tortured soul retains a treasured image,
As he ploughs on manfully, unregarding.

Now, bursting through the surging, bobbing multitude,
Arms outstretched, half crouching with suspense,
He sees at last the object of his longing—
And plunges through the door marked 'Gents.'
From *Various Verses* by Gordon Burness[48]

Gordon loved the ladies and they returned the compliment because he was charming and funny. Although several fell in love with him he never married, which was a great kindness because he prized his privacy.

He cared for an ailing brother and afterwards for an elderly mother, but for two decades after they died he was a recluse in his living room, which is aptly-named for the cell he inhabited round the clock. It contained the only things that still mattered, and he only ventured to the kitchen when necessary or the bathroom when desperate, and never went out except for a medical emergency, and then most reluctantly. His retiring habits were badger-like. Josie, a good-hearted neighbor, mailed his letters and brought him shopping, including the vital cigarettes they both craved. He offered his home as a refuge for her habit because smoking was banned in her home, but it was only her non-smoking husband who succumbed to lung cancer, an irony that Gordon would have enjoyed if it was not tragic.

Gordon smoked continuously from boyhood. Over the years, his ceiling and walls turned from cream to banana yellow to deep orange, but it was a lost cause to persuade him to give up. "Fags help me think," he told me, which I have heard other writers say.

He had a deep interest in science and asked searching questions about astronomy and biology. He was ahead of me with news about the Hubble telescope, and had his own theories about the tapetum in nocturnal animals and how the pineal gland keeps time. He invented mechanical devices, but the two that were manufactured he forgot to take out patents.

I wonder what he might have achieved if he had started life in better times and with more advantages. But he never complained and asked for nothing more than a smoke, the latest test cricket score, and a chin-wag with friends. He said he was lucky because he had done everything he ever wanted. It is rare to know someone whose needs are so easily satisfied and had few wants.

A DEATH OBSERVED

We miss Virginia. Her life was sown, grown, and ripened in the state that gave her a name. She slipped away quietly one night, her passing unnoticed until she had gone, but it is often like that.

Our neighbor was one of over 150,000 people who passed that day, but the only one we knew and loved. Born into a farming family, she was married twice, widowed once, and bore some private tragedies and trials that everyone who lives to 90 must expect and endure. Her first marriage failed after an only child died in infancy, but she found happiness again when she met Mike. Alone in old age, she was 'befriended' over the phone by a man in Jamaica who defrauded her of half her life savings. In her last years, she endured a growing burden of illness and pain, and close to the end a hurricane almost snuffed out her life when a tree crashed through the roof as she lay asleep in bed.

Virginia lived the two lives described by Susan Sontag—a bright and healthy existence for many years followed by the other kind. Illness is the night side of life, and a more onerous citizenship. She bore it bravely before crossing the frontier to a shadowy territory so familiar in name yet so strange in nature. A priest told me in his experience people die as they have lived. It was true of her story because she left us peacefully. But, like other final farewells it left me wondering how she could have flown so abruptly beyond reach after being vividly with us.

> But who shall forecast the years
> And find in loss a gain to match?
> Or reach a hand thro' time to catch
> The far-off interest of tears?
> From *In Memoriam* by Alfred, Lord Tennyson

When I write about someone missing in my life it helps to cast back to happier memories when we were together, and the exercise makes people alive on paper by anchoring them in a history I can return to. It never empties the pail of grief, of course, and we must move on with the business of the living.

Can a biologist say anything meaningful about that strangest of journeys? Not much, I vouch, because ours is the science of life and it is not our job to flip the coin to read the other side. And those who, like me, specialized in the first chapters of life are least qualified. It is a happy bunch who study embryology because, although embryos must negotiate the perils of early development, there is hope they will emerge triumphant to a full span of life.

Since biology is the science of life, death looks like its defeat, but is the end a moment of departure or an eternity of arriving? If death is not locked in time it is outside the realm of science, beyond the reach of its method. Ask about 'thanascience' and I will tell you it is nonscience.

Thanatos, the dreaded leveler of mankind, was a Greek daemon, a sort of nature spirit or custodian of the departed who served the Gods with his brother Hypnos (Sleep). Achilles saw plenty of bloodshed on the battlefield and advised Odysseus that death is no respecter of person: "it comes alike to the idle man and to him that works much." Thus, Thanatos is an amoral character and no respecter of person. He bore away warriors from the battlefield and took Virginia's innocent boy Skippy after a medical error long before he came back to release her from pain and frailty.

There is an entry ramp on Interstate-64 outside Charlottesville where the traffic was slowing to crawl one day as we passed the scene of an accident. A state trooper in a khaki shirt and Smokey-the-Bear hat was talking to a man leaning against the patrol car with blue lights flashing urgently. A few feet away across the white line separating lanes a bulging yellow tarp was spread on the highway, and a motorbike lay on its side nearby. No one seemed to notice the empty shoe, but I could not avert my eyes from the object. *The shoe, the shoe ...* that's the thing I remember every time I pass that junction. Is it the poignancy of separation from a warm, familiar foot in one wrenching moment that I cannot forget?

It is so much harder to accept an untimely death than when time's arrow has traveled its full flight before coming to ground. What does that reveal about our attitude to aging?

Melancholy Jaques, a nobleman in *As You Like It*, catalogued seven stages of life, the last being "sans teeth ... sans everything." Then the fool declared "... from hour to hour, we rot and rot; and thereby hangs a tale."

Biologists protest Shakespeare's portrayal of old age. We don't believe healthy bodies "rot and rot" over the years, or that death has commerce with life by trading time for vitality. Yet, aging is a slippery subject, guarding its secrets jealously. There are many chronometers in our body, but a master timepiece marking

319

the passage of organic life to date, and how much longer there is to go, is elusive—if it exists at all.

To measure biological age, we fall back on insurance actuaries and government statisticians who annualize the risks of dying. The curve starts upwards after our teen years, rising at a compound rate of interest called the force of mortality. But even though the climb is inexorable, it doesn't mean we die day-by-day from the moment of birth, as Jaques would have it.

The chances of dying double every seven years, a prime number that was laden with mystical significance. An average person lives longer than in his day, sailing past the old prescription of three score years and ten (a multiple of 7), and, yet, the gift of extra years is taken for granted like a birthright. We are pushing toward a limit set by our biology and genetics, and I wonder when many people will beat the 122-year record of Madame Calment's lifespan. I read speculative theories this will happen for people alive today, but I doubt it and, moreover, I dread it. Dramatic extension of the human lifespan would be offered first to people who are already privileged, people like us who consume unfair shares of the world's wealth. It would also cause untold economic and social turmoil in a globe already crowded and ecologically stressed, so superlongevity should wait until world population stabilizes at a lower level. Dying on time is merciful for the generations below.

I am amazed how cellular vitality triumphs for so long before decomposition and heat-death in obedience to the Second Law of Thermodynamics. We continue to live despite the odds, but aging is neither the price for living nor is it ubiquitous. There are a few species of animals and plants with indeterminate lifespans insofar as they can thrive for decades or even centuries without aging, although none is immortal and sooner or later all succumb to accidents that insurance companies call Acts of God. Most animals have a lifespan that reaches a terminal phase of deterioration at a tipping point on a gradient when vitality can no longer be sustained, and a precipitous fall is imminent.

While Thanatos bides his time, there are kindly killers constantly pruning unwanted or harmful matter. Cell death is executed everywhere and continuously from embryonic stages to old age by a genetic program called apoptosis. The word meaning fall leaves was coined from the Greek by some of my former colleagues in Scotland.

Deciduous trees shed leaves in drought or after a killing frost and in preparation for winter when photosynthesis becomes unproductive. When a layer of cork forms at the base of petioles, like a tourniquet on an arm, the leaves change color, wither, and die. This is a beneficial death and hardly any loss to the plant because 70% of the precious nitrogen, sugars, and minerals are withdrawn for storage in the trunk or recycled in the leaf mold by decomposers for future reabsorption by tree roots. Life and death dance in a cycle.

Many cells in our bodies are continually being thrown on a sacrificial heap, particularly worn-out surface cells of skin and the intestinal lining that are shed to make way for new growth. Other cell types are removed in situ to make a more perfect form, like the molding of scar tissue or the snipping of cells between digits of club hands and feet in fetuses. Cells in the immune system that are redundant or potential agents of autoimmune reactions are tagged for elimination, like winding orange tape round a tree trunk for the attention of a tree surgeon. Tumor cells, those grim reapers, are also attacked, but often with too little gusto by natural killer cells. There are many kinds of death to celebrate.

But when a pretty bird is snatched from our feeder by a hawk or a swallowtail butterfly is caught by a praying mantis it grieves

321

us, even though we know predators and their progeny would starve on a grass diet without 'meat.' Thanatos works paradoxically, taking prey that is weak or careless so that others can thrive to keep the wheel of life turning through natural selection to drive biological progress. Yet, what seems wise in nature is cruel when it strikes at home.

> Are God and Nature then at strife,
> That Nature lends such evil dreams?
> So careful of the type she seems,
> So careless of the single life.
> From *In Memoriam* by Alfred, Lord Tennyson

The *Book of Revelation* forecasts there will be silence when the last Seal is opened in heaven. In scenes starkly rendered in black and white with bouts of agonizing existential silence, Ingmar Bergman's *The Seventh Seal* portrays the knight Antonius Block returning from the Crusades to a Swedish homeland ravaged by the Black Death. He meets the personification of Death dressed as a hooded monk who invites him to a game of chess on the beach. The knight wins the early moves, but hubris so weakens his judgment he makes bad choices that enable his opponent to take his pieces one-by-one. In desperation, he knocks the board over hoping they can start over again, but Thanatos remembers the place of every chessman. The game resumes to its inevitable conclusion. *Checkmate*.

When a subject is too hard to bear we laugh it off to lighten our mood. In Woody Allen's *Death Knocks*, a hilarious parody of Bergman's gloomy *Seal*, Nat Ackerman receives a surprise knock at the door of his New York apartment. The visitor looks strangely familiar, like an identical twin, but he wears a black cape and carries a broken scythe over a shoulder.

Nat: You look a bit like me.
Death: Who should I look like? I'm your death.

Nat protests that Death has come too soon. He is still in rude health and has plans for a life he can't imagine ever ending. He challenges Death to a game of gin rummy and wins a pyrrhic victory. You can imagine the rest of the story.

Death is depicted like his Greek namesake in *The Book Thief*, a story set in Nazi Germany by author Markus Zusak. Thanatos is not the master of the house, more like a janitor who performs his duties efficiently, solemnly, and without ever understanding or even asking the reason why.

Biology too, if only in this respect, is barren soil offering an endless dark night of the soul. Apart from religious belief, the humanities are the other spirits that struggle for meaning in the darkness. The wisest path is to circle back to start over again for a journey that never ends.

In T.S. Eliot's last major work, *Four Quartets*, the poet wrestles with the ineffable boundary of time and eternity. He travels from a mysterious revelation in the rose garden at Burnt Norton to East Coker where rustic villagers clomp nuptial dances. At last the narrator stands by a cornfield nourished by the mortal remains of his ancestors who fertilized the dirt.

People take what they may from literature and science, but to me these metaphors ring truer than the mysticism of William Blake for their organic-ness and earthy wisdom. At the center of a turning wheel of life, Eliot observes a stillness and the kind of peace and enlightenment that Dante and Hindu traditions observed.

Candles offer more light in churches and temples than just the power of their lumens, because although they can never illuminate a mystery they are its symbols through ritual. When we lighted candles to memorialize Virginia's life, my thoughts wandered back to biology and to when I was tramping near a marsh in the creeping dusk at the end of a day. I remember a dancing light, the will-o'-the-wisp emanating from the bog of decayed biological matter. The eerie flicker wasn't an alarming sight, and nothing like the faerie light of *Paradise Lost* drawing unwary travelers to their doom, because I knew it was a manifestation of the carbon cycle, the raw chemistry of new life. Like an Old Testament allegory, the burning bog gently drew a sense of standing on holy ground.

THE RED GODS CALL

When I fly out of JFK airport and look out the window I often gaze down at the empty expanse of marsh in Jamaica Bay instead of across to the Manhattan skyline. I then think about Robert Tuttle Morris. He was a surgeon and nature-lover who hunted ducks flying over the reeds and bobbing in rafts between the banks of inlets. The TSA would be alarmed if our flight captain reported a man leveling a twelve gauge below, but Bob left the marsh long ago.

The Jo Co Marsh was a favorite hunting ground after he arrived in New York City in the 1880s to study medicine. He started a career as an assistant to senior surgeons called to the homes of well-to-do New Yorkers. Operations were less risky at home than in hospitals where contagious diseases were rife and the poor and indigent were treated. He qualified as an attending surgeon at Bellevue Hospital in downtown New York, the oldest public hospital in the country. At the end of the day, he would collect his dog from a kennel in the hospital yard (it was different in those days) and run to Penn Station for a train. Thirty minutes later, he alighted at Rockaway, the closest dropping-off point for Jamaica Bay.

He kept his gun and ammo at the Atlantic Hotel owned by his friend Bill Dorman and, after a brief exchange of news, hurried off on foot to the marsh with his Labrador retriever at his heels. When ducks and geese were out of season, he took fishing gear to catch the plentiful striped bass, bluefish, porgies, flounders, and sheepsheads in the Broad Channel. Sometimes a friend helped him to set lobster pots, or catch soft shell crabs, or harvest all the oysters they could cart back to the hotel for a roast. They had sea appetites and marine treasure to satisfy them.

The bay still offered good hunting in the 1930s when Bob was in his seventies, although the metropolis was steadily encroaching from the east. But he now visited the marsh with a camera instead of a gun and was a patron of the Audubon Society. He hoped the Jo Co would become a bird sanctuary and its slow-flowing channels and tiny islands would be off-limits to hunters. Now that 90 airlines operate out of JFK and the marsh is closed to the public he has gotten his wish, if not his desires. No device invented for farms is as effective a bird-scarer as the roar of twin Rolls Royce engines low overhead.

When I fly the route from New York to Virginia I often muse about his life and times and how attitudes have changed. Flying alongside the East River I can see the gray stone edifice of the New York Presbyterian Hospital close to where Bob was a surgeon at the former Cornell Clinic and where my wife and I worked in recent years.

When we were on the faculty, I regularly attended Grand Rounds to keep up-to-date with advances in other specialties, and occasionally I was the lecturer. It is one of those old auditoriums where the audience looks down on the speaker from semi-circular rows of wooden benches steeply tiered above the broad bench where the speaker stands. The sessions were well-attended by staff and students, as well as a few curious people off the street.

Some men in the audience were obviously advanced in years because they struggled to their seat with a cane, and those hard of hearing stepped down to the front row. They were retired doctors in freshly-laundered white coats, and many of them were distinguished physicians and surgeons in their day. A generation earlier, I might have consulted one of them for a sick relative or my own operation, but now ...? One of them, a former departmental chairman, confessed: "It's pathetic. We can't give it up."

In an achievement-oriented society, it is hard to close the pages of a career, especially one as demanding as medicine which robs more recreational and family time than in Bob Morris's day. It is not just a matter of surrendering a salary at retirement, but giving up the dignity and prestige of a hard-earned position. We might wonder why Bob left an illustrious career while he was still vigorous, but he had the satisfaction of looking back at revolutionary changes he helped to forge in his profession. How much more can a septuagenarian contribute, apart from writing his autobiography[49]?

He began practicing in what he called the Second or Anatomic Era of medicine after graduating from the College of Physicians and Surgeons. The era of anesthesia had recently started, but infection was a mystery and Louis Pasteur was still at work. Bob recalled a patient's family would welcome the surgical team to their home dressed in black frock coats and top hats, as if they had come to a funeral wake or to take them to the opera. The proceedings were a good deal less hygienic than a night at the theater. Surgeons would wash their hands after an operation instead of before, and young turk like Bob who insisted on sterilizing the surgical instruments was considered a dangerous radical. Flies never bothered them because they went straight to the wound. And one of Bob's mentors used to clench a scalpel in his teeth while adjusting a tourniquet, and then give the blade a few quick strokes across his shoe leather to make the edge keen before amputating a leg. Fortunately, there is something called progress.

In science, we are less inclined to blindly follow our professors and are taught a theory is only as good as it can be defended with data, but for most of history medical training was more an apprenticeship under a master. Freedom of thought and experimentation were frowned on and clinical practices were fossilized by tradition and authority. Bob questioned conventional practices even before he visited Sir Joseph Lister and other European luminaries, and came home as an American pioneer of aseptic surgery. His conversion experience was greeted with sneers from a hidebound profession until his patients were seen to do better, which forced his peers to take a second look at his innovations for wound healing and smaller incisions. The turning of radical ideas into conservative habits is a story repeated in every walk of life.

On reaching a reflective age and knowing how fame fades he was comfortable, even eager, to stop striving for achievement. He left medicine to younger men and women and advanced to a new life stage. A passion for nature and country life was no longer suspended by a busy career, and could be fulfilled for as many years as he was fit. "I felt that I had been born for the woods, the rivers, the mountains, and the sea. Anyone who wanted New York might have it and all that was in it. My light heart was out of doors. Only my heavy feet remained in town."

He must go—go—go away from here!
On the other side the world he's overdue.
'Send your road is clear before you
Where the old Spring-fret comes o'er you,

328

IN MEMORIAM

And the Red Gods call for you!
From *The Feet of the Young Men* by Rudyard Kipling

To borrow an expression from his soul-mate Kipling, he heard the Red Gods calling. The poetic right side of his brain was at last getting the better of his professional left side.

By the late 1920s, Bob retired to an estate he purchased earlier after alerted to a sale by Ernest Seton Thompson, a neighbor who founded the Woodcraft Indians and Boy Scouts of America. It was 440 acres of unspoiled woodland and abundant wildlife between Stamford and Greenwich, CT, and only 18 miles from the New York City limits. It was called Merribrooke after the beautiful Mianus River that ran through the woods down to the sparkling Long Island Sound. While he could not protect Jamaica Bay from invasion by suburbia, at least he had some control over this property, and now he had time to pursue wildlife conservation and experimental horticulture, and to write books and poetry about everything he cared about.

This was one of the happiest times of his life, blessed by the arrival of a daughter in his graying years, and shared with friends and distinguished visitors. There was a burden, however, not so much the cost of managing the property as the responsibility of preserving a beautiful place for future generations. He fought battles and lawsuits with corporations and lawyers who wanted to develop the land and divert the river to a reservoir. On the margin of a manuscript for his autobiography, he wrote a note to his editor requesting its addition in print: 'If succeeding owners can keep Merribrooke as a wild park for centuries to come with residences only on road frontage, I shall ask these other people to be grateful to me for preserving a beauty spot intact near New York City at great personal effort and financial loss while 'improvement' ogres stood about with snuffers all ready for putting out Nature's light.' We don't know why he scrubbed over the words, and maybe he was doubtful that nature's gems can be preserved forever from human greed.

He sold off parcels of land when his health faltered in the decade before his death in 1945. A large tract went to the salacious torch singer and actress Libby Holman. I was amazed to learn that much of the original estate still survives as a public recreation area called the Mianus River Park offering woodland trails for walkers, hikers, and cyclists. It vindicates his devotion to its protection during his worthy retirement years.

The first time I visited I could not find any public information explaining how the park avoided being swallowed by developers, and never saw the name of the man responsible. If we asked him today, he would shrug his shoulders. He knew from a life in medicine that reputations are ephemeral, how progress rolls over past achievements, and people pay little heed to history. Even the greatest doctors and scientists, like Lister, Darwin, Pasteur, and Einstein, are dispensable because breakthroughs are inevitable, and progress is inexorable. In the long-run, knowledge doesn't depend on a special individual, although a singular genius accelerates its advance. On the other hand, the legacies of outstanding artists, writers, and musicians are more durable because their contributions to culture are unique. Others may copy their work, but their masterpieces would never exist if the originators never lived.

> ... nothing stays, all changes; but not words, not paint
> Lily Briscoe in *To the Lighthouse* by Virginia Woolf

Bob understood the distinction when he laid down his scalpel to pick up a pen for a second career as a writer and naturalist. Ask any young doctor today who was Dr. Robert Morris and I guarantee you will get a blank expression, but his books on nut growing, war, poetry, and other subjects survive in libraries and I still see them for sale.

Most people never hear the Red Gods calling, and many cannot afford to go, but for the rest I urge them *Go – Go – Go*. Leaving behind a vocation you love can be painful, but if you have served it long and well and now feel passionate for a fresh challenge or have something long postponed, the chance should be grasped before it slips away forever, whether it is a craving for nature, golf, painting, DIY, growing bonsai trees, or anything else for heart's ease. Women adjust more successfully than men, perhaps because many of them have balanced a mother's share of family life with employment. We men can learn from them.

I think Bob hung up his white coat because his father never had golden years in retirement, having died soon after a term as Governor of Connecticut. The call came urgently to me because my father too never had time to *Go*, and so I took a leaf out of Bob's book.

> Old age hath yet his honour and his toil;
> Death closes all: but something ere the end,
> Some work of noble note, may yet be done …
> From *Ulysses* by Alfred, Lord Tennyson

Index

Jamestowne Bookworks

Williamsburg, Virginia

The following titles have been published

A Surgeon's Story – the Autobiography of Robert T. Morris. Roger Gosden & Pam Walker (2013)

In Vitro Fertilization Comes to America – Memoir of a Medical Breakthrough. Howard W. Jones Jr. (2014)

Various Verses by Gordon Burness – Complete Works of the Bard of Beckenham. Roger Gosden (2015).

Howard & Georgeanna – Sixty Years of Marriage & Medicine. Howard W. Jones, Jr. (2015)

Walter Heape, F.R.S. John D. Biggers & Carol Kountz (2016)

Forthcoming

This Old House in Appalachia. Prose, Poetry & Pictures to Celebrate and Lament a Mountain Home. Roger Gosden (2017)

More from A Biologist in Paradise. Roger Gosden

Preview

Second volume of
A Biologist in Paradise

A second volume of over thirty essays and memoirs is in preparation with six or seven parts: Animalia, Bee Lines, Best of Friends, Garden Paradise, Genetics & Genealogy, On the Road, Wings & Skins.

PROVISIONAL TITLES

The Tale of an Axolotyl	We're Bananas
A Tree for Hugging	Nose to Proboscis
Beelines	Playing Possum
Beloved Bats	Redheads
Dragon Run	Room for a Womb
Gold in my Garden	Root for Evils
Hairy Bell-ringer	Snake Hole
Here be Dragons	Star Struck
Hunter's Heart	Tangier Island
Bad King Richard	Trust your Gut
Flight of the Dough Bird	Turtlemania
Mastodon in our Town	Two Beekeepers in the Bush
Milton's Mulberry	Who's Seen a Thylacine?
My Dog's Dinner	Wings

Other Books by Roger Gosden

Biology of Menopause: the causes and consequences of ovarian ageing. Academic Press, London. 1985 (ISBN 0.12-291850-9)

Ovarian and Testicular Tissue Transplantation (with Yves Aubard). Medical Intelligence Unit. R.G. Landes Co., Austin, Texas 1996 (ISBN 0-3-540-60894-X)

Cheating Time - Science, Sex and Ageing. Macmillan, London (1996) (0-333-62823-3). Published in North America by W.H. Freeman & Co., New York (ISBN 0-7167-3059-6) (1996, paperback edition 1999)

Designer Babies - The Brave New World of Reproductive Technology. Victor Gollancz, London (1999) (ISBN 0 575 06648 2). Published in North America as *Designing Babies* by W.H. Freeman & Co., New York (ISBN 0-7167-3299-8) (1999, paperback edition 2000)

Biology and Pathology of the Oocyte: Its Role in Fertility and Reproductive Medicine (with Alan Trounson, eds.). Cambridge University Press (2003) (ISBN0521799589)

Preservation of Fertility (with Togas Tulandi, eds.) CRC Press, Taylor & Francis Medical Publishing, London (2004)

Biology and Pathology of the Oocyte: Its Role in Fertility and Reproductive Medicine with Alan Trounson & Ursula Eichenlaub-Ritter, eds.). Cambridge University Press. (2013) (ISBN 978-1-107-02190-7)

ENDNOTES

[1] http://rogergosden.com/

[2] http://www.jamestownebookworks.com/

[3] http://www.literacyforlife.org/

[4] http://cmsimpact.org/code/code-best-practices-fair-use-scholarly-research-communication/

[5] https://openclipart.org/

[6] http://www.virginiamasternaturalist.org/

[7] In contrast to pantheism (*all-is-God*) in which the physical universe is equated with the Almighty, panentheism (*all-is-in-God*) is a belief that God is in everything, although superior to and not defined by it. Panentheism is held across a wide range of belief systems, from Neoplatonism to congregations within all the world's great religions.

[8] http://www.bbcearth.com/blueplanet2/

[9] https://www.aldoleopold.org/

[10] Helen Hamilton & Gus Hall. *Wildflowers & Grasses of Virginia's Coastal Plain*. Botanical Research Institute of Texas Press, 2013

[11] https://naturalresources.wales/days-out/places-to-visit/mid-wales/cors-caron-national-nature-reserve/?lang=en

[12] https://www.durrell.org/wildlife/visit/

[13] https://www.wildlifecenter.org/

[14] https://www.npr.org/sections/health-shots/2017/07/17/536676954/forest-bathing-a-retreat-to-nature-can-boost-immunity-and-mood

[15] The 37 genes in the mitochondrial genome are strictly inherited through maternal lineages all the way back to Mitochondrial Eve, who lived 200,000 years ago in Africa.

[16] https://www.23andme.com/

[17] http://www.cesarsway.com/

[18] http://positively.com/

[19] http://retractionwatch.com/

[20] https://islandpress.org/book/shifting-baselines

[21] https://www.nps.gov/olym/learn/education/upload/The-Grand-Banks-Collapse.pdf

[22] *American Chestnut: The Life, Death, and Rebirth of a Perfect Tree.* University of California Press, 2009

[23] https://www.acf.org/

[24] http://historicjamestowne.org/

[25] Cro-Magnon man is in the direct lineage of modern man

[26] http://www.gurche.com/main_frameset.htm

[27] Sheffield Wednesday is a soccer team in South Yorkshire

[28] Tyke is a local name for a Yorkshireman

[29] Northern English slang for money

[30] http://www.kittycams.uga.edu/research.html

[31] The word 'larder' originates from when a small room or cupboard was set aside for storing bacon

[32] The history and evolving story of sugar and human health http://journals.plos.org/plosbiology/article?id=10.1371/journal.pbio.2003460

[33] https://www.youtube.com/watch?v=bbh8SMsA7RI

[34] https://en.wikipedia.org/wiki/Man%27s_Search_for_Meaning

[35] https://www.arborday.org/celebrate/

[36] *Cheating Time: Science, Sex and Aging* by Roger Gosden. W.H. Freeman & Co., New York, 1996, 1999

[37] The Nibley Papers

[38] http://www.birds.cornell.edu/Page.aspx?pid=1478

[39] http://www.audubon.org/conservation/science/christmas-bird-count

[40] Partridges never perch in any kind of tree

[41] In Britain this means elite, private schools

[42] Roger Gosden is currently writing the authorized biography of Robert Edwards, provisionally entitled *Let There Be Life*

[43] Jean Purdy died of malignant melanoma in March 1985

[44] Roger Gosden (2017). Jean Marian Purdy remembered—the hidden life of an IVF pioneer. *Human Fertility* (accessed free online)

[45] A durable memorial acknowledging Jean's endeavors and achievement will be unveiled in Grantchester churchyard in 2018

[46] Equivalent to US$500 in those days

[47] *The White Badger*. Gordon Burness. George G. Harrap & Co., London, 1970

[48] *Various Verses by Gordon Burness*. Edited by Roger Gosden. Jamestowne Bookworks, Williamsburg VA, 2015

[49] *A Surgeon's Story. The Autobiography of Robert T. Morris*. Roger Gosden & Pam Walker. Jamestowne Bookworks, Williamsburg VA, 2013